United Nations Conference on Trade and Development

Sharing Asia's Dynamism:
Asian Direct Investment in the European Union

United Nations
New York and Geneva, 1996

UBN 1426824

Note

The UNCTAD Division on Investment, Technology and Enterprise Development serves as the focal point within the United Nations Secretariat for all matters related to foreign direct investment and transnational corporations. In the past, the Programme on Transnational Corporations was carried out by the United Nations Centre on Transnational Corporations (1975-1992) and the Transnational Corporations and Management Division of the United Nations Department of Economic and Social Development (1992-1993). In 1993, the Programme was transferred to the United Nations Conference on Trade and Development and eventually became the Division on Investment, Technology and Enterprise Development. The Division seeks to further the understanding of the nature of transnational corporations and their contribution to development and to create an enabling environment for international investment and enterprise development. The work of the Division is carried out through intergovernmental deliberations, policy analysis and research, technical assistance activities, seminars, workshops and conferences.

The term "country" as used in this study also refers, as appropriate, to territories or areas; the designations employed and the presentation of the material do not imply the expression of any opinion whatsoever on the part of the Secretariat of the United Nations concerning the legal status of any country, territory, city or area or of its authorities, or concerning the delimitation of its frontiers or boundaries. In addition, the designations of country groups are intended solely for statistical or analytical convenience and do not necessarily express a judgement about the stage of development reached by a particular country or area in the development process. The Asia-Europe Meeting (ASEM) countries include Brunei Darussalam, China, Indonesia, Japan, Republic of Korea, Malaysia, Philippines, Singapore, Thailand and Viet Nam in Asia and all European Union member states.

The following symbols have been used in the tables:

Two dots (..) indicate that data are not available or are not separately reported. Rows in tables have been omitted in those cases where no data are available for any of the elements in the row;

A dash (-) indicates that the item is equal to zero or its value is negligible;

A blank in a table indicates that the item is not applicable;

A slash (/) between dates representing years, e.g., 1994/95, indicates a financial year;

Use of a hyphen (-) between dates representing years, e.g., 1994-1995, signifies the full period involved, including the beginning and end years.

Reference to "dollars" ($) means United States dollars, unless otherwise indicated.

Annual rates of growth or change, unless otherwise stated, refer to annual compound rates.

Details and percentages in tables do not necessarily add to totals because of rounding.

The material contained in this study may be freely quoted with appropriate acknowledgement.

UN2
TD/UNCTAD/ITE/IIT/1

UNITED NATIONS PUBLICATION

Sales No. E.97.II.D.1

ISBN 92-1-112405-0

Copyright © United Nations, 1997
All rights reserved
Manufactured in Switzerland

Preface

The European Union is the largest host to foreign direct investment in the world, absorbing nearly two-fifths of global investment flows and stocks. Asian countries, for their part, have recently emerged not only as the largest host region in the developing world but also as a home to dynamic international investors. Indeed, flows from Asia have played a major role in the recovery of international capital flows from the foreign-direct-investment recession of 1991-1992, contributing about two-thirds of additional outflows during 1993-1994.

Asian investors have, however, paid relatively little attention to the European Union and other parts of the European continent. This is evident from the relatively small European shares in the investment outflows from such Asian economies as Hong Kong, the Republic of Korea, Malaysia, Singapore, Taiwan Province of China and Thailand.

The objectives of the present study are:

- To develop a clear picture of foreign direct investment from Asia -- including Japan, but focusing especially on developing Asian economies -- in the European Union (and Central and Eastern Europe). Detailed statistics on foreign-direct-investment stocks and flows, broken down by sector and host country, are not readily available. The study brings together data from various national and international sources and presents them in a form that depicts the present state of Asian foreign direct investment, particularly foreign direct investment from developing Asian economies in Europe, in as detailed a manner as possible.

- To explain this picture in terms of the constraints that Asian firms face, the advantages they have, and the potential benefits they obtain from investing in the European Union.

- To identify policy measures that can help to increase Asian investment in Europe, to the advantage of both partners.

Asian countries have demonstrated a strong propensity to save, and prospects of their continuing high growth of income are very good. Many of them are also building up strong technological and entrepreneurial capabilities. Thus, increasing volumes of Asian capital are expected to search for profitable overseas locations in the future. Europe, with its lower saving propensity, could benefit from Asian capital surpluses and its entrepreneurial dynamism. In exchange, Europe has accumulated a wealth of technological knowledge and know-how, and it has large absorptive markets -- both very much in demand by firms in Asian economies. An improved understanding of Asian foreign direct investment in Europe and exploring ways in which it could be encouraged is thus of mutual interest to both the European Union and Asia.

With this objective in mind, the study begins, in Part One, with an overview of global flows of foreign direct investment from Asia (chapter I), and proceeds to examine the extent, growth and composition of Asian investment in Europe (chapter II). In this context, Asian investments and their future prospects in Central and Eastern Europe are also considered (chapter III).

Some of the Central and Eastern European countries offer attractive locational advantages of low cost production and market access to the European Union through the Europe Agreements. Attention is focused largely on foreign direct investment from the newly industrializing economies of East and South-East Asia, since they are leading the internationalization process in Asia. (Japan has a longer tradition of investing in Europe. Its investments in Europe have already been examined on numerous occasions; it is, therefore, treated only in brief.)

Part Two examines why Asian investment in Europe is as low as it is, beginning with the recognition that, as Asian developing economies are just emerging as outward investors, this is not surprising. It analyses the constraints presented by legal and other impediments to outward investment in Asia and inward investment in the European Union (chapter IV). This is followed by a brief examination of the locational advantages that the European Union and some countries in Central and Eastern Europe have to offer to Asian transnational corporations (chapter V). Finally, the growing ownership advantages of Asian firms, including those that form the basis of their trade, are analyzed, in order to understand their relative importance and identify the competitive capabilities of Asian economies and firms (chapters VI-VIII).

Part Three, then, is concerned with policy implications, given that both Asia and the European Union are interested in raising flows of investments from Asia to Europe. It deals with actions that could be undertaken by Asian (chapter IX) and European (chapter X) countries independently from each other, as well as jointly (chapter XI), to encourage investment from Asia into Europe and to strengthen their partnership for mutual benefit.

The study was financed by the Ministry of Foreign Affairs of Thailand. It served, among other things, as an input into the ASEM Governments and Private Sector Working Group meeting, Bangkok, 7-8 July 1996.

Rubens Ricupero
Secretary-General of UNCTAD

Geneva, November 1996

Acknowledgement

This study was prepared by a team comprising Karl P. Sauvant, Masataka Fujita and Padma Mallampally of UNCTAD's Division on Investment, Technology and Enterprise Development, in cooperation with Jamuna Prasad Agarwal, Sanjaya Lall, Hafiz Mirza and Peter Nunnenkamp. Specific input was received from Victoria Aranda. The study benefited from comments received from Michael McDermott, Eric Ramstetter, Rana Singh, Stephen Young and James Zhan. The processing of the document was done by Teresita Sabico and Jenifer Tacardon, coordinated by Richard Bolwijn.

Contents

PART THREE
POLICY IMPLICATIONS: BUILDING ON THE
EXISTING PARTNERSHIPS

Boxes

Figures

Tables

Annex tables

OVERVIEW

The European Union constitutes the world's single largest market for goods and services, and the world's largest host region for foreign direct investment (FDI). It promises to become even larger in these respects when its membership extends to include several Central and Eastern European countries. Europe is also a storehouse of technological assets and capabilities.

The strategies of firms worldwide must therefore take into account the advantages of being present in Europe, both from the viewpoint of strengthening their competitiveness and from that of locational portfolio diversification.

Asian firms, and their home countries, are no exception: as their outward FDI capabilities increase, investing in the European Union becomes a matter of increasing importance. At the same time, Asian economies -- and, in particular, Japan and the developing economies of East and South-East Asia -- are rapidly expanding their economic strength through capital accumulation as well as technological progress. Asia has become home to dynamic enterprises seeking opportunities to expand their markets, to improve further their technological capabilities and, ultimately, to become globally competitive players. Attracting FDI from these enterprises is therefore becoming -- or will become -- of considerable interest to the European Union and its potential member-economies in Central and Eastern Europe.

Asian foreign direct investment in the European Union

Asia has emerged as a dynamic region with several rapidly growing and internationalizing economies. Japan occupies an important position as an outward investor, with large and growing stocks of investment in both developed and developing countries. Asian developing economies have also recently emerged as dynamic international investors, raising their share from 2 per cent of worldwide FDI outflows during 1980-1985 to more than 10 per cent during 1991-1995. At least three of the newly industrializing economies (Hong Kong, the Republic of Korea and Taiwan Province of China) are now net outward investors. China, as well as several South-East Asian economies, have joined the ranks of countries with sizeable outward FDI, albeit at levels lower than the inward investment they host. Much of the credit for the recovery of world FDI outflows from their 1991-1992 recession goes to Asian developing economies. For instance, investment flows from Hong Kong, the largest investor among Asian developing economies, have exceeded those from Japan in every year since 1993.

Investment from developing Asian economies has been growing in all major host regions. But, thus far, it is principally concentrated in East and South-East Asia, which has received nearly seven-tenth of outward FDI from the region. These inflows are, indeed, very important for the host economies involved: for nine major Asian developing economies, FDI inflows from other Asian developing economies are, with nearly 40 per cent, larger than inflows from either Europe, Japan or the United States. Outside the region, the largest share goes to North America. The European Union receives little -- a mere 5 per cent during 1990-1993.

The relatively low share of Asian developing economy FDI directed towards the European Union mirrors the relatively low proportion (around 3 per cent) of European Union FDI that goes to Asia. On the surface, this suggests that Asian TNCs neglect Europe as much as European TNCs neglect Asia. However, this picture of "mutual neglect" hides a basic asymmetry: European economies are highly industrialized, and their firms are experienced overseas investors. Asian developing economies are relative newcomers in the industrial and FDI fields, with a smaller, narrower base of advantages that they can exploit, and much less knowledge of what international production involves and what it means to operate abroad, let alone in more developed economies. Thus, while -- as far as FDI is concerned -- it may be appropriate to describe European firms as neglecting Asia, Asian firms are beginning to discover Europe. European firms have failed so far to build upon a long-standing base in Asia; Asian firms are just at the beginning of their entry into Europe.

In fact, a number of TNCs from Asian developing economies have already established an important presence in Europe. Most Asian FDI activities are concentrated in the United Kingdom, Germany and the Netherlands. The largest investor of non-Japanese origin in the European Union is Hong Kong, accounting for about one quarter of the European Union's inward FDI stock from Asian developing economies. Other Asian developing economies have also seized investment opportunities. In particular, the Republic of Korea, which already ranks as the second largest investor in the European Union from developing Asia, is expanding its investments in many countries in Europe.

Although data on the sectoral and industrial structure of Asian FDI in the European Union are fragmentary, those that exist suggest that, in general, manufacturing and services were of similar importance in the outward FDI of Asian newly industrializing economies (Hong Kong, the Republic of Korea, Singapore, Taiwan Province of China). For other Asian developing economies, a large share of their FDI is in services, much of it of a trade-supporting nature. Foreign direct investment in the manufacturing sector is heavily biased towards the electronics industry (accounting for three quarters of all manufacturing investments of the four newly industrializing economies in the European Union). The distribution of FDI in the services sector is much less concentrated than in manufacturing. Investment in trade figures prominently, but FDI in financial services industries is equally important. This reflects the fact that the internationalization of Asian firms proceeded first through exports, before turning to production.

In this respect, Central and Eastern Europe has become an interesting investment area as well. This is the case partly because that region represents an important market in and by itself, and partly because Central and Eastern Europe is a gateway to Western Europe, facilitated by the Europe Agreements. Korean TNCs, in particular -- which are perhaps the most globalized among the TNCs from Asian developing economies -- have pursued access to the European market through FDI in selected countries of Central and Eastern Europe. The most remarkable of these is the acquisition of car manufacturing plants in Romania, Poland and the Czech Republic by Daewoo, taking advantage of privatization programmes in these countries.

The contribution of Asian TNCs to total FDI inflows and stocks in the European Union is, as yet, small. However, Asian firms have emerged as dynamic global investors of equity capital. Their share in world outward FDI is increasing. Although, so far, non-Japanese Asian FDI is mostly of an intra-regional nature, there is a trend towards a greater geographical dispersion. Asia is a growth centre. It has played an important role in the recovery from the FDI recession. Europe is receiving more attention from Asian TNCs, and Europe needs investment. All this suggests that, what we have seen so far, is only the beginning of a process.

What drives Asian foreign direct investment in the European Union?

While TNCs from Asian developing economies have begun to invest in Europe, and the pace is quickening, building up these investments -- as, indeed, in developed countries in general -- is not easy. There are three sets of constraints:

- There are *competitive constraints* on the part of many Asian investors, reflecting that most Asian economies are less developed than most European ones. These constraints are particularly evident in complex manufacturing activities and advanced services like infrastructure, communications, merchant banking and media. They explain in part the pattern of Asian investment in Europe, although firms from the newly industrializing economies do invest in manufacturing and more advanced services, apart from trade promotion.

- Asian investors, being relative newcomers to international operations, are oriented towards neighbouring countries where *transaction costs* (including knowledge of local markets, culture and conditions) are lower. When they invest in developed countries, they are oriented more towards North America than to Europe, because of the evolution of their trade, political and educational relations in recent decades. Moreover, transaction costs in the unified market of the United States tend to be lower than in the fragmented and differentiated markets of Europe.

- There are constraints as far as the *regulatory framework* is concerned, but these are mostly home country constraints, not host country ones. Host countries, i.e., the European countries, have liberalized their FDI regimes to a large extent, even though there remain pockets of (mostly sectoral) restrictions. Most home countries, i.e., Asian economies, have only begun to liberalize their outward FDI regimes, although some have gone very far in this respect and have even begun to promote outward FDI through various measures. This applies not only to Japan, but also, and in particular, to the newly industrializing economies, and, increasingly, the ASEAN countries. The liberalization of outward FDI policies has been spurred by the realization that, in today's liberalizing and globalizing world economy, firms need a portfolio of locational assets as one source of their international competitiveness.

Why, however, should Asian firms invest in Europe?

There are many benefits of FDI in Europe which are increasingly recognized and accepted by Asian governments. These include access to a large, rich and discriminating market, which, to serve, may need a direct presence, especially as Asian firms move to more complex products; access to advanced technology and skills; locational advantages of producing in Europe and especially in Central and Eastern Europe (because of high skill levels, flexible labour markets, supplier networks and technology systems), and despite wages that are generally higher than in Asia; using affiliates in Europe as part of a globalization strategy; overcoming protectionist sentiments; winning infrastructure and government contracts; participating in European Union research-and-development programmes; forging closer relations with European firms; and diversifying the investment portfolio. In general, Europe offers a diversity of opportunities to firms from different Asian economies to invest according to their respective advantages.

The developing economies of Asia have so far reached European markets primarily by exporting rather than FDI. Their FDI in Europe has been largely supportive of their export activity. However, the competitive advantages that lead to successful exporting often also lead to direct investment in its own right, generally in ways that further complement trade. Investment tends to support the development of competitiveness by allowing resources to be spread over the most efficient sites, providing technological market feedbacks and allowing the upgrading of domestic operations. Japanese FDI and export growth in Europe have gone together, with service investments supporting manufacturing exports. Asian FDI in Europe is driven by trade -- but with each investment made, this is less and less the case as further investments draw on the underlying competitive strengths of the firms involved.

These competitive strengths are revealed in the export performance of Asian economies. The engine of Asian export growth to Europe have been manufactured products. But there are large differences between Asian economies. The newly industrializing economies, as well as China, are the main exporters of manufactures, with the ASEAN (4) (Indonesia, Malaysia, the Philippines and Thailand) closely behind. The technological basis of their comparative advantage varies also: the newly industrializing economies and Malaysia tend to have more technology-intensive exports than the others, while exports from China, Indonesia, Thailand and India are primarily in resource and labour-intensive activities. However, in terms of domestic technological capabilities to undertake overseas investment, firms from the Republic of Korea (followed by those from Taiwan Province of China) are well in the lead over the others; this reveals itself in recent industrial investments in Europe.

The principal basic ingredients on which firms build their ownership advantages include human capital and technological capacities. Not surprisingly, Asian developing economies differ considerably with respect to these ingredients, as indicated by their enrolment ratios at different stages of education, particularly tertiary education, and their research-and-development expenditures. In particular, the Republic of Korea, with enrolment ratios in tertiary/technical education comparable to those of many developed countries, has a significant lead. As a result, Korean TNCs are able to develop a strong technological base and differentiated products comparable to those of developed countries. This gives them a distinct edge over firms from other Asian developing economies in investing in Europe. The technological advantages of firms from other Asian developing economies are more suited to form the basis of FDI in other developing economies, although there will be technological niches that they could also exploit in Europe.

Policy implications: building on the existing partnership

Driven by growing exports, as well as independently from them, Asian FDI in Europe is on the rise. Still, it is incipient and needs to be nurtured, especially since most Asian firms have little or no experience with investing in Europe. Governments have a role to play.

As far as Asian home countries are concerned, there is a trend towards the liberalization of outward FDI (as part of a broader market-based outward oriented development strategy) -- an important momentum. Naturally, this process has to be gradual, and needs to take into account national development objectives as well as various constraints. Where these constraints are of a balance-of-payments nature, there are a number of ways to deal with them, including through approval procedures and the application of various criteria. Beyond liberalization, a number of Asian governments have begun to give a helping hand to their outward investors -- but more could be done in this respect. The principal areas here are education, training and orientation programmes; the provision of various information services; the promotion of partnerships and contacts; and the rendering of financial assistance. Asian governments could benefit from an exchange of national experiences in all of these areas.

Although the diversity of Asian economies means that it is difficult to have a uniform programme relating to FDI in Europe, it might nevertheless be useful to have an umbrella for the various activities described so far, e.g., in the form of a "Europe-Invest Programme". It could be established by interested countries, with offices in the participating countries. The brief of each national Europe-Invest office could differ, depending on circumstances and needs; and each could link back to national institutions, including export-import banks and other agencies involved in outward FDI.

But any action along these lines would, of course, not be a substitute for action by Asian firms: it is they that must spearhead any drive to increase FDI in Europe, based on a recognition that they, too, benefit from investing there.

There is also a role to play for the European Commission and the Union's individual governments, considering that European countries, as recipients, benefit from inward FDI as well. While the European Union's FDI framework is liberal, there are a number of areas in which liberalization could go further, especially as regards certain sectoral restrictions and certain operational impediments towards foreign investors (e.g., personnel restrictions, visa and residency requirements, performance requirements, and certain investment-related trade measures). Moreover, precisely because FDI and trade are inextricably intertwined and Asian

FDI in the European Union is to a considerable extent trade-led, maintaining and improving a liberal trade regime by the European Union is important to ensure that the mix of FDI and trade can be used by firms in the most efficient manner.

Governments of member countries and the European Commission can both furthermore assist prospective Asian investors actively in a number of ways to establish themselves in Europe and, once established, to prosper there. Europe's Investment Promotion Agencies (which, after all, seek to attract FDI) could play a useful role in this respect. They should make a special effort to target, attract and help Asian investors, including by establishing branches in Asia. The European Commission could also consider the possibility of extending some existing European schemes devoted to expanding FDI in Asia (e.g., the European Union Business Information Centres) in a manner that they can simultaneously promote Asian FDI in Europe.

Finally, considering that most laws, regulations and administrative procedures governing inward FDI are established by the Union's individual governments, the framework facing a foreign investor is quite complex and sometimes difficult to decipher. In spite of some progress in this area (e.g., on cross-border mergers), there is scope for further harmonization, including as regards a European company law. Perhaps a comprehensive European Union-wide treatment of FDI could be considered, e.g., in the form of a European Union FDI code and a European Commission FDI coordinating unit. From the viewpoint of Asian investors, such an approach would be beneficial because it would be comprehensive, increase transparency and reduce transaction costs.

And, of course, there is also scope for action by the private sector in Europe. Asian firms, including Japanese firms, are innovators in a number of areas. European firms can benefit from the experiences of Asian TNCs by establishing joint ventures and strategic alliances, or even merging. For example, local European knowledge and skills could be effectively married in Central and Eastern European infrastructure projects with Asian firms' recent successful experience in "building" Asia.

Last but not least, there are a number of areas in which Asian and European governments could benefit from joint action. Some of these areas require cooperation by their very nature, especially where the strengthening of the international framework for FDI is concerned (if, when and where that is deemed desirable); in other areas, practical cooperation would be to the benefit of all countries involved, and, therefore, should be considered.

The international framework for FDI consists of various agreements at the multilateral, inter-regional, regional, sub-regional and bilateral levels. At the bilateral level, the most important instruments are bilateral agreements on the promotion and protection of FDI (in regard to which one could perhaps build on their promotional part) and double-taxation treaties (which are of great importance for the conduct of international business); not all Asian economies have concluded such agreements. But there are also other areas in which agreements between governments can facilitate the operations of business; the mutual recognition of standards is of particular importance here.

This study has identified a number of actions that Asian and European Union governments could fruitfully take, each on its own, to increase FDI flows from Asia to Europe. A number of actions have also been proposed elsewhere for European Union and Asian governments to increase FDI flows from the European Union to Asia; the nucleus for these is the Asia-Invest Programme of the European Commission. In each case, the successful implementation of these actions would greatly benefit from -- if it does not require -- active and practical cooperation between institutions in Europe and Asia.

If a Europe-Invest Programme -- or any other mechanism of this sort -- were to be established to coordinate and mutually support Asian activities regarding FDI in Europe, the obvious question arises whether it would be appropriate to create a common roof for the Europe-Invest and the Asia-Invest Programmes, to coordinate the two Programmes, reduce duplication and enhance synergies. Such an approach could build on existing successful measures and instruments and apply them in either direction. Moreover, some of the objectives of the programmes could be better achieved because policy makers and business people from both areas would be working together in order to facilitate FDI in both directions. And, finally, by having a single programme working in both directions, Asian and European governments and business would have an equal stake in making the process work.

PART ONE

ASIAN FOREIGN DIRECT INVESTMENT
IN THE EUROPEAN UNION

ASIAN FOREIGN DIRECT INVESTMENT IN THE GLOBAL ECONOMY

The current trend towards globalized production and markets is largely driven by booming foreign direct investment (FDI) at a worldwide scale. Asian countries were among the first to benefit from globalization. Besides their major role with regard to international trade expansion, they have also become major players with respect to FDI. Japan established itself as one of the most important players in terms of outward FDI flows, whereas its role as a host country for FDI remained marginal. By contrast, Asian developing countries emerged as among the most attractive investment locations and absorbed rising proportions of worldwide FDI outflows. Asian developing countries are less well known for their engagement in establishing production and marketing bases through outward FDI, which has increased considerably since the 1980s.[1] The focus of this chapter is on this latter development. First, however, the pattern of outward FDI by Japan is being described briefly, and dealt with separately due to Japan's much more advanced level of economic development and its longer tradition as a foreign investor.

A. Foreign direct investment from Japan

Japan ranked third (behind the United States and the United Kingdom) in terms of outward FDI stocks in 1995, which amounted to $306 billion (table I.1). By contrast, seven countries[2] held higher FDI stocks abroad than Japan in 1980. Japanese stocks soared more than eighteenfold during this period. As a result, the share of Japanese stocks in worldwide FDI stocks tripled from 4 per cent in 1980 to 11 per cent in 1995.

In terms of FDI outflows, the picture is somewhat different (table I.1). Average annual FDI outflows from Japan increased nearly sevenfold from $5 billion to $32 billion, if the periods 1980-1985 and 1986-1990 are compared. Subsequently, however, outflows from Japan declined to an annual average of $24 billion during 1991-1995. This implies that Japan's share in worldwide FDI outflows during this period (10 per cent) was only half its share in 1986-1990 (19 per cent). The decline in Japan's share is mainly due to two recent developments: first, other developed countries experienced a much more modest reduction of FDI activity in the early 1990s (this refers to European Union countries), or even reported rising FDI flows (notably the United States). Second, various developing countries emerged as foreign investors. Most important among these are Asian developing economies. As a matter of fact, FDI outflows from the four Asian newly industrializing economies (NIEs) have exceeded Japanese outflows since 1993.

Table I.1. Outward FDI of Asian economies, 1980-1995

(Millions of dollars)

Region/economy	Outflows (annual average)			Outward stocks		
	1980-85	1986-90	1991-95	1980	1985	1995ᵃ
Asia	5 749	39 893	49 637	21 504	49 952	469 919
Japan	4 641	32 073	23 963	18 833	44 296	305 545
NIEs	700	6 714	20 827	1 039	4 395	134 421
Hong Kong ᵇ	455	2 252	14 797	148	2 345	85 156
Korea, Republic of	66	361	1 919	142	526	11 079
Singapore	128	684	1 820	652 ᶜ	1 320 ᶜ	13 842 ᶜ
Taiwan Province of China	51	3 417	2 291	97	204	24 344 ᵈ
ASEAN(4)	257	378	1 887	597	983	12 302
Indonesia ᵉ	9	3	16	-1	49	113
Malaysia	239	296	1 482	414	749	9 693 ᵈ
Philippines	8	2	2	171	171	167 ᵈ
Thailand	2	77	386	13	14	2 330 ᶠ
China	150	711	2 956	..	131	17 268 ᶠ
India ᵉ	3	2	6	4	19	94
Pakistan	-2	15	-6	31	127	251ᵈ
Memorandum:						
World	50 894	171 402	236 220	513 497	685 306	2 728 198
Developed countries	48 125	160 217	206 289	507 251	663 985	2 511 761
European Union	24 653	91 664	108 080	213 157	286 485	1 208 838
United States	12 351	21 218	56 790	220 178	251 034	706 958
Developing countries	2 762	11 163	29 694	6 167	21 222	215 060
Africa	998	1 012	638	500	6 581	15 271
Latin America	444	1 467	2 590	2 910	7 207	25 476
Central and Eastern	206	854	789	1 066	1 727	9 835
Europe	7	22	237	79	100	1 377

Source: UNCTAD, FDI database.

a   Estimates.
b   Estimated by using the country's inward FDI in the United States and China. Thus, the data are underestimated.
c   Cumulated outflows since 1970.
d   Estimated by adding outflows to 1988-stock data.
e   Estimated by using the country's inward FDI in the United States. Thus, the data are underestimated.
f   Estimated by adding outflows to 1989-stock data.

Japanese FDI is largely concentrated in North America, which absorbed about 44 per cent of Japan's FDI outflows in 1991-1995 and accounted for the same share in overall FDI stocks held by Japan in 1995 (table I.2). The regional distribution of Japan's outward FDI stocks shifted considerably towards North America since 1984. The same applied to Japanese FDI stocks in the European Union which, however, accounted for less than half the United States share in 1995. In terms of FDI outflows from Japan, the European Union ranked second (behind the United States, but ahead of Asian developing countries) as a recipient of such flows in 1991-1995. Japan's engagement in Central and Eastern Europe, including the prospective European Union members, remains marginal with regard to both flow and stock figures.

The shift of Japanese FDI stocks towards the United States and the European Union went along with declining shares accounted for by major developing country groups. In the case of Latin America and Africa, this decline can be attributed to economic problems these regions were facing in the 1980s, frequently characterised as the "lost decade" in Latin America and "economic marginalisation" of Africa. By contrast, the share of Japanese FDI stocks held in Asian developing countries declined by nearly 10 per centage points, although these countries became the economic powerhouse of the world economy. This suggests that Japanese investors considered their presence in neighbouring countries to be sufficiently strong, while they felt the need to strengthen their engagement in the Single European Market and in the United States.

Changes in the sectoral structure of Japan's FDI may further explain why developed countries accounted for a larger share of overall stocks in 1995 than in 1984. Foreign direct investment in the primary sector, which was largely located in developing countries, became less and less important. The manufacturing sector, too, lost slightly in importance in Japan's overall FDI stocks,[3] although the picture varies greatly between industries (table I.2). A major shift occurred towards the services sector. Other services (including real estate), in particular, as well as finance, insurance and business services, figured more prominently. This development (especially as concerns FDI in real estate) is a major factor underlying the increasing role of developed countries as a target of Japanese FDI.

Table I.2. The structure of outward FDI by Japan,[a] 1984-1995 [b]

(Percentage)

Region/industry	Flows 1991-1995 (annual average)	Stocks 1984	Stocks 1995
Total (Billion dollars)	40.3	72.0	512.2
By country/region			
European Union (12)	18.1	8.6	18.0
other European OECD countries	0.7	3.7	1.0
Central and Eastern Europe	0.2	0.3	0.1
North America	43.9	29.8	43.9
South and East Asian developing countries	20.1	25.1	17.2
Latin America	8.6	18.1	11.5
Africa	1.1	4.4	1.6
By sector/industry			
Primary	3.0	18.6	4.8
Secondary[c]	32.4	30.3	28.7
Textiles, leather, clothing	1.6	2.7	1.4
Chemicals	4.3	5.1	4.1
Transport equipment	4.0	3.9	3.7
Tlectric and electronic equipment	7.2	4.6	6.8
Tertiary	63.5	48.5	64.9
Trade	11.7	15.3	10.7
Transport	5.5	6.7	5.6
Finance, insurance, business services	13.7	9.8	18.1
Other [d]	32.6	15.6	30.5

Source: UNCTAD, FDI database.

[a]   Based on appovals/notifications. Thus, the data reported in this table are different from those in table I.1.
[b]   Fiscal year ending March in the following year.
[c]   Individual industries selected according to factor intensity (textiles, leather, clothing: labour intensive; chemicals; physical capital intensive; transport equipment; human capital intensive) and relative importance (notably electric and electronic equipment).
[d]   Including real estate.

B. Foreign direct investment from Asian developing countries

1. The rise of outward foreign direct investment

Asian developing countries have played a major role in the recovery of international equity capital flows from the FDI-recession of 1991-1992. Although the data situation is far from satisfactory (box I.1), indications are that, of the $27 billion rise in global FDI outflows between 1992 and 1994, about 60 per cent originated from these economies, particularly from Hong Kong (UNCTAD-DTCI, 1996a, annex table 2). As mentioned earlier, FDI outflows from the four Asian NIEs have surpassed Japanese outflows since the early 1990s. In addition, ASEAN countries[4] and China emerged as relevant foreign investors. Taken together, Asian developing economies contributed about 11 per cent to worldwide FDI outflows in 1991-1995 (table I.1). Their share increased by five times from 2.2 per cent in 1980-1985. The rather recent nature of considerable FDI outflows from Asian developing economies has as a consequence that their contribution to worldwide FDI stocks is still more modest: it increased from about 0.3 per cent in 1980 to 0.8 per cent in 1985, and subsequently soared to 6.0 per cent in 1995.

Box 1. Data shortcomings with regard to outward FDI by Asian developing economies

As compared with international trade data, the statistics on FDI are generally deficient, e.g., in terms of coverage and consistency, as well as with respect to the comparability of flows and stock data from different sources. Data problems clearly go beyond these well-known shortcomings when it comes to outward FDI of Asian developing economies. The most serious limitations include the following:[a]

First, data availability is constrained since detailed information on outward FDI is not reported by the public authorities of some Asian developing economies. Hong Kong provides a case in point. Moreover, the data that are available for Hong Kong (and, though to a lesser extent, for Singapore) are distorted by the fact that they include indirect investment which originates from other countries, but which is channeled through Hong Kong (and Singapore) to Asian developing economies, notably to China.[b]

Second, data deficiencies are particularly pronounced when it comes to the sectoral and industrial structure of Asian FDI in the European Union. Disaggregated information is largley lacking for South Asian economies, China, Indonesia and the Philippines. The data which are available for the four Asian NIEs, Malaysia and Thailand are frequently not comparable. Among NIEs, the Republic of Korea and Taiwan Province of China report fairly detailed statistics on the sectoral breakdown of FDI in European Union countries. By contrast, the data situation is unsatisfactory for Hong Kong, for which some data on specific manufacturing industries are only available for its outward FDI in all host countries as a whole. The latter also applies to Malaysia and Thailand. Aggregate figures on outward FDI may be misleading, particularly if FDI in real estate tends to be significant but cannot be separated from FDI in other services and in manufacturing.

Third, inconsistencies often exist between the data provided by Asian home countries of foreign investors and the data provided by the European host countries. In some instances, this is because home country data are based on FDI approvals, whereas host country data relate to realized FDI. Yet, there is sometimes little choice but to refer to FDI approvals, as reported by Asian home countries, since European host countries do not provide information on inward FDI stock or flows from individual Asian developing economies.

---

  a   For a detailed discussion of data problems with regard to Asian FDI in Europe, see Schultz (1995).
  b   For a more detailed discussion of some of this indirect investment and its underlying motivations, see Zhan (1995).

These trends are even more remarkable if compared to the development of FDI outflows from non-Asian developing countries. Africa's minor role with regard to outward FDI is not surprising given its relatively low level of economic development, but middle income Latin American countries could have been expected to keep up with Asian developing countries in terms of outward FDI. Foreign-direct-investment stocks held by Latin American countries in 1980 ($2.9 billion) indeed exceeded FDI stocks held by Asian developing countries by a factor of 1.8 (table I.1). In 1995, however, the FDI stock held by Asian developing countries was more than six times higher than the stock held by Latin America. Average annual FDI outflows from Latin America in 1991-1995 ($2.6 billion) were not only surpassed by FDI outflows from the four Asian NIEs ($21 billion), but also by FDI outflows from China alone ($3 billion). Among all developing regions, Asia clearly became the dominant player with regard to outward FDI. The region as a whole accounted for 86 per cent of FDI outflows from all developing countries in 1991-1995, and for 76 per cent of FDI stocks held by all developing countries in 1995.

Yet, the aggregate figures for all Asian developing countries tend to obscure highly diverse developments at the country level. (Boxes 2-8 contain brief profiles of the outward FDI activities of leading Asian developing countries.)   A few economies in this region clearly emerged as the leading foreign investors. This applies to Hong Kong in the first place, which contributed 58 per cent to FDI outflows from all Asian developing economies in 1991-1995, and 52 per cent to their FDI stocks in 1995 (table I.1).[5] It must be noted, however, that part of Hong Kong's outward FDI -- perhaps about 30 per cent of the total (Low, Ramstetter and

---

Box 2. Hong Kong

Hong Kong was in 1995 the fourth largest international direct investor in the world after the United States, the United Kingdom and Germany. Its FDI outflows (1995: estimated $25 billion, UNCTAD-DTCI, 1996a, annex table 2) exceeded those of Japan for the third consecutive year. About 52 per cent of all Asian developing countries' outward FDI in 1995 stemmed from Hong Kong (UNCTAD-DTCI, 1996, annex table 2). It should be recalled, however, that perhaps as much as 30 per cent of this investment is indirect FDI (Low, Ramstetter and Yeung, forthcoming).

China is the dominating destination of Hongkongs' direct investment abroad. More than half of its FDI is located in China. Recently, some Hong Kong firms there seem to face increasing problems of labour management and lengthy administrative procedures (Chen, 1996, p. 18). Only 3 per cent (1992) of Hong Kong's FDI is invested in the European Union. APEC hosts the lion's share of the rest (Chia, 1995).

Local Hong Kong firms, especially in manufacturing, have invested in China and other neighbouring countries to take advantage of their relatively lower wage costs. But some of the investors have also been motivated by risk diversification and to exploit export quotas of the host countries under the Multi-Fiber Arrangement. Larger Hong Kong TNCs are regionally more diversified, especially in selected services (banking, telecommunication, hotel and trade). The Single Market Programme induced many Hong Kong firms to open servicing affiliates, increase participation in trade fairs, and enter into joint-ventures with European firms.

Most of Hong Kong FDI in the European Union is in wholesale and retail trade. Dickson Concepts Ltd., for example, acquired in 1991 a London-based department store, Harvey Nichols and in 1992 an ailing shoe company, Charles Jordan Holding AG in France. The Industrial Equity Pacific Ltd. took minority ownership of three department stores in Paris in 1988 and two years later of Rover stores in the United Kingdom. Similarly, several other Hong Kong firms (Jardine Matheson Holdings Ltd., Jardine International Motor, Jardine Insurance Brokers, Goldlion Holdings Ltd., Asia Commercial, National Commercial, National Electronics and Stelux Holdings) have established bases in the European Union. Some of them are owned by foreigners from developed countries, especially the United Kingdom and Australia, but for all practical purposes they are operated from Hong Kong. The transfer of power to China in 1997 has motivated some of them to shift their head offices abroad, e.g., Jardine Matheson to the Bahamas, Hongkong and Shanghai Bank to London (Kögel and Gälli, 1994).

Yeung, forthcoming) -- actually originates from other economies. For instance, firms from Taiwan Province of China channelled their FDI flows to China through Hong Kong. Likewise, some investment is due to round tripping of Chinese funds, which return via Hong Kong to the mainland. Similarly, a part of Singapore's outward FDI -- perhaps as much as half of the total (Low, Ramstetter and Yeung, forthcoming) -- consists of indirect FDI.

These qualifications notwithstanding, the contrast between Hong Kong and Singapore as outward investors is particularly striking as far as the four NIEs are concerned. Although the per-capita income of Hong Kong and Singapore is similar (World Bank, 1995, p. 163), the latter country's FDI outflows in 1991-1995 (FDI stocks in 1995) amounted to only 12 (16) per cent of Hong Kong's FDI outflows (FDI stocks). Taiwan Province of China ranked second behind Hong Kong among Asian NIEs in terms of average annual FDI outflows in 1991-1995. It was the most important investor country during 1986-1990. Subsequently, FDI outflows from Taiwan Province of China lost momentum, but the economy maintained its second rank with regard to outward FDI stocks. In contrast to Taiwan Province of China, the Republic of Korea was a latecomer among major Asian investor countries; starting from a relatively low level in the 1980s, FDI outflows from the Republic of Korea recorded a fairly steady increase to an annual average of $ 1.9 billion in 1991-1995. In any event, Hong Kong, the Republic of Korea and Taiwan Province of China have become net outward investors in terms of FDI flows.

Not surprisingly, FDI outflows from lower income ASEAN countries remain modest by the standards of the leading NIEs. ASEAN(4) as a whole reported FDI outflows in 1991-1995 and FDI stocks in 1995 which were very close to the respective figures for the Republic of Korea. More interestingly, though, FDI activity is heavily skewed within ASEAN(4). Investment outflows from Indonesia were very low and stagnant. Malaysia is at the opposite extreme. Investment outflows from Malaysia have increased steeply since 1993, and exceeded the

---

Box 3. Taiwan Province of China

Taiwan Province of China is the second largest direct investor from developing Asia, holding nearly $24 billion of FDI stock in 1995 (UNCTAD-DTCI, 1996a, annex table 4). The European Union hosted $500 million of this in 1994. More than half of it is located in the United Kingdom. ASEAN (4) and the United States host about one third each. A sizeable portion of FDI has gone indirectly via Hong Kong to China. Taiwanese FDI is dominated by small and medium-sized firms which contribute the greatest part of domestic manufacturing value-added. In some cases in electrical equipment and chemicals industries in the developed countries, Taiwanese FDI originates mostly from large companies (UN-TCMD, 1993, p. 41). Most FDI, especially from small and medium-sized enterprises, is motivated by rising costs in the domestic economy, currency appreciation and risk diversification. Larger TNCs have gone global also to establish market positions, promote brand image, acquire technology and secure natural resources.

Unlike Hong Kong, more than one half of total Taiwanese FDI is in manufacturing (table I.3). The same holds for Taiwanese FDI in the European Union (table II.10). Tatung, the Taiwanese electric and electronic company, started production of electric fans and colour televisions in the United States in the 1970s and in the United Kingdom in the early 1980s (ibid., p. 42). Strong growth of Taiwanese FDI in the European Union during the late 1980s was induced by the Single Market Programme. Leading Taiwanese investors in the European Union are also electric and electronic firms, especially computer manufacturers such as Acer Computer, CMC Magnetics Co. and Kuman. Recently some of the public sector Taiwanese banks have established branches in Germany, the United Kingdom and the Netherlands to serve increased trade between Taiwan Province of China and the European Union.

Box 4. Republic of Korea

The Republic of Korea is the fourth largest Asian outward investor of equity capital. Its FDI stock reached $11.1 billion in 1995 (table I.1 and UNCTAD-DTCI, 1996a, annex table 4). More than half of Korea's FDI stock is in the manufacturing sector (table I.3). By destination, the United States is the largest host country, with a two-fifths share. Asia hosts a little less than that. About one tenth of Korean FDI is located in Europe. Korean firms have started a few very big projects in Central and Eastern Europe recently, most of which are not yet reflected in flow and stock data. When these projects are completed at the end of this century, the European share in the country's outward FDI is likely to rise.

The overwhelming bulk of Korean outward FDI is undertaken by large Korean firms, *chaebols* (UN-TCMD, 1993, p. 43). This is a consequence of a high level of market concentration within the Korean domestic manufacturing sector. The primary motive of *chaebols* in investing beyond Asia has been to gain market shares in host countries or gaining access to new technologies and skills, rather than exploiting low cost advantages (cheap labour and land). The latter has been more important for FDI in neighbouring Asian countries, especially as far as small and medium-sized enterprises are concerned.

The United Kingdom is the most favoured investment destination for Korean comapnies in the European Union. They had invested until recently in England and Northern Ireland. The LG Group is going to receive nearly $300 million subsidy from the Welsh agencies for establishing their two plants in Wales (a semiconductor plant and a consumer electronics plant with investments of £1.7 billion ($2.34 billion)) which are expected to create 6100 jobs. Wales is expecting a truck and heavy equipment plant from Halla group, another Korean *chaebol*.[a]

---

[a]   John Burton, Roland Adburgham and Stefan Wagstyl, "LG to announce £1.7 bn complex" *Financial Times*, 10 July 1996, p. 8.

Box 5. Singapore

Singapore's economic growth is dependent on its ability to access foreign markets. Traditionally this was achieved through exports. Rising costs of labour and perceived threats of protectionism in its export markets have encouraged Singapore's firms to invest abroad. By 1995, the total outward stock of Singapore had grown to $ 37 billion.[a] Most of this (56 per cent) is located in Asian developing economies, especially its traditional host economies, Malaysia and Hong Kong. The European Union hosts nearly 8 per cent of Singapore's FDI stock, with the United Kingdom absorbing more than half of it. The other most important destination in the European Union is the Netherlands. Recently IPC Corporation of Singapore has acquired a minority capital participation in a German company, Hagenuk Telecom GmbH, specializing in the production of mobile telephones. Both the partners aim at expanding the activities to other related products.

Among all the leading Asian investors, Singapore has invested the lowest share of its FDI stock in the United States (7 per cent), although Singapore is the second largest developing host country of the United States FDI in Asia. Singapore is the largest Asian investor in the Russian Federation.

More than half of Singapore's total FDI abroad is in financial services; the manufacturing sector has attracted only 20 per cent. In the case of the European Union, manufacturing accounted for only 3 per cent of Singapore's outward stock of FDI in 1994, and financial institutions for as much as 84 per cent (table II.8).

The domestic economy of Singapore is dominated by foreign affiliates. Some of them have shifted their labour intensive segments of production to neighbouring countries offering relatively cheap labour. A good part -- perhaps as much as half (Low, Ramstetter and Yeung, forthcoming) -- of the country's outward FDI is undertaken by foreign affiliates located in Singapore.

---

[a]   Investment in paid-up shares and attributable reserves. 1994 and 1995 stock on balance-of-payments basis were $11.0 billion and $13.8 billion, respectively.

Table I.3. Sectoral structure of outward FDI from selected Asian developing economies, various years
(Percentage)

Sector/industry	Hong Kong[a] (Stock, 1990)	Republic of Korea (Cumulated flows, 1960-Feb. 1996)	Malaysia[a] (Cumulated approvals, 1990-1995)	Philippines (Cumulated flows, 1973-Feb. 1996)	Singapore[b] (Stock, 1994)	Taiwan Province of China (Cumulated flows, 1959-1992)	Thailand (Average annual flows, 1970-1993)
Total (Million dollars)	..	11 270	..	6 297	37 319	5 650	979
Primary sector	..	8.0	..	16.5	..	0.3	0.5
Manufacturing	..	57.5	..	53.7	20.2	56.7	30.9
Food, beverage, tobacco	9.2	..	2.0	6.1	..	3.5	4.3
Textiles, leather	10.6	..	5.9	2.2	..	4.4	3.7
Paper, printing	4.4	..	1.1	..	..	2.0	..
Chemicals	7.6	..	12.3	9.8	..	12.6	0.7
Coal and petroluem products	..	..	22.2	13.2	..	..	..
Non-metallic	..	..	6.0	..	..	3.7	8.6 [c]
Metal products	10.6	..	16.6	4.9	..	8.1	..
Mechanical equipment	30.4	..	2.8	2.3	..	0.5	..
Electric/electronic	10.1	..	20.2	..	..	18.7	9.9
Motor vehicles	..	..	..	..	..	..	1.6
Other transport	3.7	..	2.0 [d]	4.0	..	..	..
Other manufacturing	13.4	..	8.8 [e]	11.3	..	3.2	2.1
Services	..	34.5	..	29.8	..	42.9	68.7
Construction	..	1.9	..	1.1	1.2	1.1	2.0
Trade	..	21.5	..	5.5	..	5.9	4.5
Transport, storage	..	0.7	..	0.2	4.2	0.6	4.2
Finance, insurance	..	-	..	13.7	63.6	24.8	35.7
Communication	..	-	..	1.8	..	-	..
Other	..	10.4	..	7.5	9.7	10.4	22.2

Source: UNCTAD, FDI database.

a   Manufacturing industries in percent of total manufacturing.
b   Investment in paid-up shares and attributable reserves. Not including intra-company loans and investment by financial institutions.
c   Includes metal products.
d   Including motor vehicles.
e   Including wood products, furniture, rubber and plastic products, sicentific and measuring equipment and miscellaneous.

Box 6. Malaysia

Malaysian FDI outflows jumped from less than half a billion dollars (average of 1990-1992: $478 million) a year to $1.9 billion in 1993-1995 (UNCTAD-DTCI, 1996a, annex table 2). About two fifths of Malaysian FDI is concentrated in Asia. There is a major shift in the importance of Asian destinations in FDI outflows from Malaysia. Before 1987, Singapore used to top the list of host countries. Since 1988, Malaysian firms have been investing more in Taiwan Province of China than in Singapore. Between 1985 and 1994, one fifth of all Malaysian FDI flows went to Taiwan Province of China, whereas Singapore received only 7 per cent. Another important feature of Malaysian FDI abroad is its high level of investment in Japan, which absorbed more than one fifth of the country's FDI flows since 1985. Other Asian developing countries located substantially lesser proportion of their FDI in Japan. The share of the European Union (16 per cent) is also higher in Malaysian FDI outflows than in those of other major Asian developing countries. France and the United Kingdom received more than half of flows to the European Union.

According to the survey of firms holding significant equity ownership abroad, about seven tenths of Malaysian FDI at the end of May 1993 was in finance, insurance, real estate and business services; another one tenth was in trade and hotels. Only seven per cent was invested in overseas manufacturing industries (Malaysian Industrial Development Authority, 1995).

respective figures for Singapore in 1994 and 1995. Thailand was positioned between these extremes. Outward FDI stocks remained marginal until 1985, but soared subsequently, underlining the fact that Thailand is emerging as an important investor country in the 1990s.

Similar discrepancies characterize other low income Asian developing countries. South Asia did not participate to any significant extent in Asia's boom of outward FDI.[6] This is in sharp contrast to China, which increased its share in worldwide FDI outflows from less than 0.5 per cent until 1991 to an average of 1.3 per cent in 1991-1995. As a matter of fact, China outperformed all other Asian developing economies except Hong Kong in terms of FDI outflows in 1991-1995 and ranked third (behind Hong Kong and Taiwan Province of China) with respect to outward FDI stocks in 1995.

As concerns the sectoral structure of outward FDI of Asian developing economies, the services sector accounts for a significant share in the total outward FDI of all economies which report the relevant information (table I.3). Within the services sector, finance and insurance are of particular importance in the case of Taiwan Province of China and Thailand. In the case of the Republic of Korea, however, outward FDI in trade accounted for most of the services FDI.

Box 7. Thailand

Most of the Thai outward FDI is of very recent origin. About nine-tenth of its accumulated stock was invested after 1990.[a] Even though Thai outward FDI flows rose in 1995 by about 50 per cent over the previous year, its FDI abroad is still modest, compared with other leading Asian investors. In the 1980s, Thai FDI was mostly concentrated in Hong Kong, the United States and Singapore. Recent FDI outflows have been more diversified. Within Asia, the Philippines, China and Indochina have attracted sizeable portions of new investment, which suggests that Thai FDI is taking advantage of the relatively lower production costs in these countries. The shares of traditional hosts of Thai FDI (Hong Kong and Singapore) have considerably retreated in 1995 compared with previous years.

The European Union hosted one-tenth of Thai stock in 1995, up from about 3 per cent in 1994. More than half of it is located in Germany. The second largest host of Thai equity capital is the United Kingdom with more than one-fifth share. Thai FDI stock in the European Union rose nearly fourfold in 1995 compared with 1994; most of the additional investments were placed in Germany. More than four-fifths of Thai FDI in the European Union is in services, as compared to a three-fifth share of this sector in total outward FDI of Thailand in 1995. More than half of it is in "investment" industry, which may include portfolio investment. Real estate (housing, hotels and restaurants, etc.) absorbed the same share of Thai FDI stock in the European Union (12 per cent) as in total FDI stock of Thailand. Thai firms have so far paid little attention to building their own trade distribution networks in the European Union as well as in other regions. The share of trade amounted to 8 per cent of Thai FDI in the European Union and 5 per cent in the case of FDI in the world as a whole. Thai FDI in the industrial sector of the European Union is valued at about $27 million. Most of it is in food (37 per cent) and metal based and non-metallic (44 per cent) industry. Practically all FDI in the food industry in Germany was undertaken in 1995. Investments in metal based and non-metallic industry are in Italy, originating from 1991. This suggests that there are only a few investments in these industries in the European Union.

---

[a]   UNCTAD, FDI database.

Box 8. China

China's FDI outflows rose in 1992 and 1993 to more than $4 billion a year, from less than $1 billion a year earlier; flows for 1995 are estimated at $2.5 billion. China was the second largest investor among Asian developing countries on a flow basis (UNCTAD-DTCI, 1996a, annex table 2). As compared to this, two thirds of China's FDI are located in Hong Kong. However, China's FDI requires a careful interpretation because Chinese affiliates in Hong Kong have often been used for acquiring foreign capital through listing in Hong Kong Stock Exchange and for "round tripping" (Zhan, 1995, p. 91). Chinese outward FDI is high also as compared to other countries at similar stages of development. Moreover, it is targeted relatively more at more developed countries (Zhang and van den Bulke, 1996, p. 410), seeking market access and technology, and is not motivated so much by a desire to gain access to low cost production abroad (Zhan, 1995, p. 88), since China itself has an ample supply of cheap labour and land.

The European Union hosts only 2 per cent of China's outward FDI. The average size of Chinese affiliates or joint ventures abroad is very small, though China has a few very big non-trade subsidiaries, e.g., the Portland Aluminium Smelter Company in Australia, UA Agri-Chemicals in the United States and Hierroperu SA in Peru.

The big push in Chinese FDI abroad came after the 1992 reform of state owned enterprises which granted their managers greater decision-making authority. Since then they seem to have increased their strategic alliances and investments abroad to strengthen their competitiveness.

Foreign direct investment in manufacturing was undertaken in various industries. Electric and electronic equipment figured most prominently among manufacturing industries in Taiwan Province of China and Thailand. In the former case, chemicals and metal products rank next in relative importance. The data on Thailand suggest a declining concentration of outward FDI in electrical and electronic equipment, when comparing cumulative flows in 1970-1993 with more recent outflows in 1991-1993.[7] The share of this industry in manufacturing FDI outflows was considerably lower in 1991-1993 (12 per cent) than in 1970-1993 (32 per cent). On the other hand, FDI outflows in metal-based and non-metallic industries figured much more prominently in 1991-1993 than before. Accumulated approvals in Malaysia show a fairly diversified structure of outward FDI in manufacturing in 1990-1995. In the case of Hong Kong, mechanical equipment represented the most important industry in terms of overall outward FDI stocks in 1990. However, several other industries (including textiles, leather and clothing; metal products; electric and electronic equipment each) accounted for more than 10 per cent of outward FDI stocks in all host countries taken together.

2. Internationalization of investment activities

The developments portrayed so far show the increasing role of Asian developing economies as foreign investors. Two additional questions need to be examined: first, to what extent has outward FDI contributed to the internationalization of the Asian developing economies' overall investment activity? Second, does the FDI boom reflect the participation of Asian developing economies in *globalized* production through FDI outflows extending beyond the Asian region, or does it rather reflect closer networking at the *regional* level?

Asian developing economies are, indeed, increasing the degree of internationalisation of their investment, as revealed by the ratio of FDI outflows to gross domestic fixed capital formation (table I.4). The average ratio for all Asian developing countries is still small by the standards of industrialised countries. Likewise, Asian TNCs are still lagging behind their developed countries counterparts when comparing the degree of transnationalization (table 1.5 and European Commission and UNCTAD-DTCI, 1996, p. 11). However, the ratio of FDI outflows to fixed capital formation of Asian developing countries is clearly above the ratio for developing countries in other regions, notably Latin America; a smilar picture emerges at the level of firms (table I.5).

But the degree to which investment activity is internationalized differs considerably between individual Asian developing countries. In light of their rather small FDI outflows, it is not surprising that the degree of investment internationalization is low in countries such as India, Indonesia and the Philippines. By contrast, Singapore has the highest degree of international investment activity in 1991-1995 (table I.4) followed by Malaysia and Taiwan Province of China; in fact, the degree of investment internationalization of that economy is considerably higher than the world average than that of Japan, and roughly comparable with that of the United States. China, the Republic of Korea and Thailand rank in between these extremes. While they did not belong to the first generation of Asian developing economies that internationalized their investment strategies, they caught up considerably in the 1990s, particularly China.

As concerns the second question, most FDI by Asian developing economies clearly takes place in the Asian region, i.e., it does not have a global orientation (table I.6). In fact, 37 per

Table I.4. Asian developing economies: ratio of FDI outflows to gross fixed capital formation, 1980-1995[a]

(Percentage)

Region/economy	1980-1985	1986-1990	1991-1995
South, East and Southeast Asian NIEs	0.4	1.8	4.3
Hong Kong	5.3	15.0	60.4
Korea, Republic of	0.3	0.6	1.6
Singapore	1.8	8.0	9.5
Taiwan Province of China	0.4	12.7	5.9
ASEAN(4)			
Indonesia	–	–	–
Malaysia	2.5	3.1	6.9
Philippines	0.1	–	–
Thailand	–	0.4	0.8
China	0.2	0.5	2.1
India	–	–	–
Memorandum:			
World	1.8	4.0	4.4
All developed countries	2.8	5.6	5.6
Japan	1.3	4.1	2.0
European Union	4.1	8.8	7.9
United States	2.0	2.8	6.6
All developing countries	0.4	1.3	2.9
Latin America	0.3	0.9	1.1

Source: UNCTAD, FDI database.

[a]   Annual averages.

Table I.5. Asian TNCs among the 50 largest TNCs based in developing economies, 1993

Economy/industry	Number of TNCs	Assets		Sales		Employment		Transnationa- lization index[a]
		Foreign	Total	Foreign	Total	Foreign	Total	
		(Million dollars)				(No. of employees)		(Percentage)
Hong Kong								
Diversified	5	.. [c]	29860	7 283	15132	.. [c]	278 164	24.4
Hotel	2	..	3 063	243	419	.. [c]	14 921	32.6
Republic of Korea [b]								
Electronics	3	.. [c]	102 723	.. [c]	89 989	.. [c]	406 103	15.9
Motor vehicles and parts	1	1 105	8 983	1 439	10 544	979	42 306	9.4
Construction	1	706	2 935	858	1 895	6 366	12 097	40.6
Petroleum refining	1	.. [c]	6 412	300	6 901	4	5 898	3.1
Trading	1	132	461	2 018	2 531	450	1 430	46.7
Diversified	1	102	1 641	88	1 345	820	5 832	8.9
Utilities	1	8	26 439	.. [c]	9 376	.. [c]	29 892	2.0
Malaysia								
Diversified	1	752	1 541	101	744	.. [c]	30 000	21.9
Food	1	419	2 829	1 493	2 738	6 500	30 000	30.3
Transport	1	137	1 758	331	639	286	2 837	23.2
Metals	1	20	1 060	54	901	1 400	18 500	5.1
Taiwan Province of China								
Electronics	3	1 208	5 816	2 029	5 631	11 163	37 102	29.0
Metals	1	.. [c]	6 215	476	2 355	6	9 601	8.8
Chemicals	1	327	1 906	233	1 491	60	3 645	11.5
Petroleum refining	1	263	12 942	156	10 075	27	21 780	1.2
Cement	1	.. [c]	1 365	55	614	200	1 376	11.0
Singapore								
Diversified	2	797	9 013	546	1 769	6 832	17 030	26.6
Electronics	1	104	232	280	292	432	1 261	58.3
Philippines								
Food	2	.. [c]	3 118	220	2 772	.. [c]	47 641	6.8
Memorandum:								
(All industries, billion dollars/ thousand employees)								
European Union TNCs	38	458	975	521	912	2 548	3 162	60.0
United States TNCs	32	415	1 535	453	1 175	1 781	4 762	34.3
Japanese TNCs	21	303	1 049	511	1 490	579	2 069	30.4
Latin America TNCs	17	8 581	60 861	6 849	40 432	20	321	12.0

Source: UNCTAD-DTCI, 1995, pp. 30-31; and European Commission and UNCTAD-DTCI, 1996, p. 11.

a   The index of transnationality is calculated as the average of the ratios of foreign assets to total assets, of foreign sales to total sales and of foreign employment to total employment.

b   The accounting standards of the Republic of Korea do not require the publication of consolidated financial statements including both domestic and foreign affiliates. The figures provided here are estimates of consolidated statements as provided by the companies in response to a survey by UNCTAD. Depending on the availability of the data on foreign components, the data for business group totals are used.

c   Data on foreign assets, foreign sales or foreign employment are suppressed to avoid the disclosure or are not available. In the case of non-availability of the data, they are estimated on the basis of other foreign component ratios.

cent of FDI inflows in nine Asian developing economies were accounted for by other Asian developing economies in 1994 (Services of the European Commission and UNCTAD-DTCI, 1996). This reflects the fact that since 1980, more than four fifths of the outward FDI stocks of the four NIEs taken together, as well as of ASEAN(4), were located in other Asian developing countries. This regional focus has since then remained strong -- with around two-thirds of the stock of the NIEs, ASEAN and China concentrated in Asian developing economies in 1992.

However, the direction of intra-regional FDI flows within East and South-East Asian developing economies has changed considerably since 1980. Now NIEs target nearly four fifths of their region's FDI outflows to China, whereas earlier in the past decade virtually all the outflows took place among themselves and ASEAN members (table I.6). Intra-NIEs FDI as a percentage of total FDI in Asia has decreased from 53 per cent in 1980 to 1 per cent in 1993, while the share of China increased from zero to 79 per cent. A similar development took place in ASEAN where intra-ASEAN flows fell from 89 per cent in 1980 to 3 per cent in 1993, whereas the share of China climbed from zero to 44 per cent during the same time. Though Viet Nam is a newcomer as a host country, it pulled in 30 per cent of ASEAN's regional FDI outflows in 1993. Its share in the NIEs' corresponding outflows was considerably lower (5 per cent); but in terms of absolute values, NIEs invested more than four times the amount invested by ASEAN (4) in Viet Nam in 1993. The largest investor in Viet Nam is Taiwan Province of China, followed by Hong Kong, Japan and Singapore (UNCTAD-DTCI, 1995, p. 55). Easy shipping access due to a long coast, cheap labour and good growth prospects with a domestic market of 70 million consumers have all proved very attractive for regional investors. Among the NIEs and ASEAN members, the latter have drawn more than four fifths of total Chinese FDI in these two groups of Asian countries (table I.6).

Table I.6. Intra-regional FDI flows in East and South-East Asian developing economies, 1989-1993

(Millions of dollars and percentage)

From To	Year	NIEs	ASEAN	China	Viet Nam	Total
NIEs	1980	145	128	..	..	273
		(53.1)	(46.9)			(100)
	1989	365	3139	4833	..	8337
		(4.3)	(37.7)	(58.0)		(100)
	1993	298	3959	21277	1427	26961
		(1.1)	(14.7)	(78.9)	(5.3)	(100)
ASEAN	1980	8	1	—	..	9
		(88.9)	(11.1)			(100)
	1989	18	164	16	..	198
		(9.1)	(82.8)	(8.1)		(100)
	1993	31	263	513	347	1154
		(2.7)	(22.8)	(44.4)	(30.1)	(100)
China	1980	—	5	..	..	5
			(100)			(100)
	1989	41	39	..	..	80
		(51.2)	(48.8)			(100)
	1993	52	244	..	..	296
		(17.6)	(82.4)			(100)

Source: Wallraf, 1996.

Nevertheless, a somewhat more globalized pattern of FDI stocks is beginning to emerge,[8] although the degree to which FDI patterns have become globalised differ considerably from country to country. While the investment stocks of Hong Kong, Malaysia and the Philippines continue to be concentrated with more than 80 per cent in neighbouring countries, the remaining share of outward FDI stocks is largely located in North America (in the case of Hong Kong and the Philippines) and Australia (in the case of Malaysia), whereas other destinations, including the European Union, were considerably less important. Singapore and Thailand locate about half of their FDI stocks outside other Asian developing countries. The focus of Thai FDI was on the United States, while the FDI stock of Singapore reveals a more diversified pattern in terms of locations outside the region. Among all investor countries under consideration, the regional focus was weakest for FDI from the Republic of Korea and Taiwan Province of China (table 1.7). Both countries locate more than a third of their outward FDI stocks in North America, with the rest of the world, too, accounting for considerable shares of both Korean and Taiwanese FDI.

In summary, the largest part of FDI of Asian developing economies is still concentrated in the same region. However, several Asian developing economies (Republic of Korea, Taiwan Province of China) have initially targeted North America as an investment location, when extending their FDI activities beyond Asia. Until 1992, FDI of Asian developing countries in the European Union typically remained of significantly less importance.[9] However, starting from extremely low levels, FDI in the European Union has gathered momentum recently. The

**Table I.7. Regional distribution of outward FDI stock of
Asian developing economies,[a] 1980 and 1992**

| | Total (Billion dollars) | | Of which (per cent) [b] | | | | | | | | | | | |
| | | | Asian developing countries | | Japan | | Australia [c] | | North America | | European Union | | Rest of the world | |
Economy	1980	1992	1980	1992	1980	1992	1980	1992	1980	1992	1980	1992	1980	1992
China	0.1	1.0	25	72	2	1	..	0	49	17	2	11	22	..
NIEs	5.2	64.4	83	69	1	1	4	4	5	14	2	4	4	8
Hong Kong	4.1	42.4	89	84	2	1	4	3	5	9	1	3	..	..
Korea, Republic of	0.2	5.6	22	32	1	2	2	4	17	38	30	7	28	18
Singapore	0.8	10.8	76	48	..	-	4	11	2	9	3	7	16	24
Taiwan Province of China	0.1	5.6	38	35	1	-	1	-	43	34	-	2	17	29
ASEAN(4)	0.8	6.1	84	63	..	-	5	6	11	10	-	20	-	1
Indonesia	0.04	2.4	98	40	..	-	3	3	-2	7	1	49	..	..
Malaysia	0.5	2.1	89	82	..	..	7	13	3	5	..	-	..	..
Philippines	0.3	0.9	74	90	..	..	..	-	26	8	-	2	..	..
Thailand	0.01	0.7	51	50	..	1	..	1	46	35	3	5	1	8

Source: Chia, 1995.

[a]   Total stocks are not fully consistent with data in table I.1 of this study.
[b]   Due to rounding, figures may not add up to 100.
[c]   Including New Zealand.

Republic of Korea, Singapore and, somewhat surprisingly, China were the frontrunners in this respect, if the European Union's share in overall FDI stocks is taken as a yardstick. Other Asian developing countries, including Thailand, have followed suit. It remains to be seen whether the creation and evolution of APEC will shift this pattern to a significant extent.

Notes

1   For a recent overview, see Schultz, 1996.

2   In descending order: United States, United Kingdom, Germany, the Netherlands, France, Canada, and Switzerland; see UNCTAD-DTCI, 1995, annex table 4.

3   Most interestingly, the share of labour intensive production of textiles, leather and clothing in total FDI stocks in 1993 was only half its share in 1984, whereas FDI in electric and electronic equipment gathered momentum.

4   In the following, Singapore is considered under Asian NIEs and excluded from ASEAN.

5   Data for outward FDI from Hong Kong in table I.1 are underestimated because they include only China and the United States for its investment destination.

6   Investment outflows from India, Pakistan and Sri Lanka taken together amounted to an annual average of $18 million in 1986-1990 and only $5 million in 1991-1995 (UNCTAD, FDI database).

7   In this context, it must be noted that a shift of Thailand's outward FDI towards manufacturing has been taking place. The decline of the services sector's share in total FDI outflows is mainly because FDI in finance, insurance and business services lost substantially in relative importance. Financial services, insurance and business services accounted for about 90 per cent of Thailand's cumulative outward FDI flows during 1970-1990.

8   China was a major exception in this respect. It has to be taken into account, however, that outward FDI stock of China was very low in 1980.

9   The large share of the European Union in Korean outward FDI stocks in 1980 is mainly due to the fairly low overall FDI stocks of the Republic of Korea at that time.

Chapter II

ASIAN FOREIGN DIRECT INVESTMENT IN THE EUROPEAN UNION

The European Union is the world's largest host region for FDI, having absorbed 38 per cent of global inflows and 39 per cent of total stock in 1995 (table II.1). This stock share is nearly twice that of the United States, the next largest FDI recipient. This chapter deals with the locational attractiveness of Europe for Asian TNCs. After considering Japan briefly,[1] the focus will mainly be on the four NIEs.

Table II.1. Inward FDI in the European Union, 1980-1995

(Millions of dollars and percentage)

Country	Flows (annual average)			Stocks		
	1980-1985	1986-1990	1991-1995	1980	1985	1995
European Union	15 658	59 650	81 586	184 960	226 493	1 028 070
Share in the world (Per cent)	28.2	38.1	37.8	38.4	30.8	38.7
Austria	213	454	874	4 459	6 122	14 034
Belgium and Luxembourg	1 189	4 673	9 594	7 306	8 840	84 605
Denmark	82	595	2 530	4 193	3 613	21 841
Finland	77	489	684	540	1 339	6 610
France	2 343	8 075	19 001	22 617	33 392	162 423
Germany	910	2 534	2 544	36 630	36 926	134 002
Greece	500	764	1 025	4 524	8 309	19 143
Ireland	198	65	94	3 749	4 649	5 442
Italy	984	3 876	3 160	8 892	18 976	64 696
Netherlands	1 647	6 370	6 942	19 167	24 952	102 598
Portugal	182	1 195	1 696	1 102	1 339	6 873
Spain	1 724	7 491	10 305	5 141	8 939	128 859
Sweden	283	1 438	6 015	3 626	5 071	32 805
United Kingdom	5 327	21 633	17 122	63 014	64 028	244 141
Memorandum						
World	55 543	156 467	215 971	481 907	734 928	2 658 633
Developed countries	37 872	129 739	140 496	373 548	537 984	1 937 968
Share in the world (Per cent)	68.2	82.9	65.1	77.5	73.2	72.9
United States	18 305	53 356	40 973	83 046	184 615	579 103
Share in the world (Per cent)	33.0	34.1	19.0	17.2	25.1	21.8
Japan	326	321	1 280	3 270	4 740	17 831
Share in the world (Per cent)	0.6	0.2	0.6	0.7	0.6	0.7
Developing countries	17 654	26 605	69 525	108 271	196 764	688 866
Share in the world (Per cent)	31.8	17.0	32.2	22.5	26.8	25.9
Central and Eastern Europe	17	122	5 950	87	180	31 800
Share in the world (Per cent)	0.03	0.08	2.76	0.02	0.02	1.20

Source: UNCTAD, FDI database.

A. Foreign direct investment from Japan

Japanese FDI in the European Union is concentrated in the United Kingdom and the Benelux countries. In 1995, the United Kingdom hosted two fifths of all Japanese FDI stock in the European Union, up from less than one third in 1988 (table II.2). In the Benelux countries, the Dutch share increased considerably during 1980-1995, whereas the combined share of Belgium and Luxembourg declined. The three members of Benelux together host presently one third of all Japanese FDI stock in the European Union. Germany has attracted a comparatively smaller portion of Japanese FDI, although it is a major competitor for Japanese TNCs in world trade. The Southern periphery (Greece, Portugal and Spain) of the European Union has also not proven very attractive for Japanese TNCs (their combined share is 0.7 per cent of Japanese global FDI stock in 1995).

Infrastructure, especially that related to financial institutions, seems to have played a major role in the locational choice of initial Japanese FDI in the European Union, which was subsequently strengthened by economies of agglomeration of Japanese affiliates in the host economies. Most Japanese FDI in the European Union is in trade-related activities (commerce) and financial institutions (table II.3). It is well known that Japanese banking affiliates in the most important financial centre of Europe, London, command a sizeable portion of syndicated

Table II.2. Japanese FDI in European Union and Central and Eastern Europe, 1980-1995

(Millions of dollars and percentage)

Country	Flows (annual average)			Stocks		
	1983-86	1987-90	1991-95	1980	1988	1995
World total (Million dollars)	13 210	51 210	40 286	61 815	186 894	512 240
Of which (Per cent)						
European Union	14.8	20.5	18.1	8.3	13.9	18.0
Austria	-	-	0.1	0.1	0.1	0.1
Belgium and Luxembourg	4.4	2.1	1.1	3.5	3.6	1.9
Denmark	-	-	-	-	-	-
Finland	-	-	-	-	-	-
France	0.8	1.6	1.9	1.0	0.9	1.5
Germany	1.4	1.5	1.9	1.5	1.3	1.7
Greece	0.1	-	-	0.2	0.1	-
Ireland	0.3	0.1	0.7	0.3	0.2	0.4
Italy	0.2	0.3	0.5	0.2	0.2	0.4
Netherlands	3.5	5.1	4.0	1.0	3.0	4.1
Portugal	-	0.1	-	-	-	0.1
Spain	0.7	0.6	0.6	0.5	0.6	0.6
Sweden	-	-	0.1	-	-	-
United Kingdom	3.5	9.0	7.1	-	4.0	7.2
Central and Eastern Europe[a]	-	-	0.2	0.3	0.1	0.1
Memorandum:						
United States	40.7	46.4	42.4	26.8	38.4	42.2
South and South-East Asia	13.7	12.6	20.1	26.6	17.2	17.2

Source: UNCTAD, FDI database.

[a]   Includes the Commonwealth of Independent States.

Table II.3. The sectoral distribution of Japanese FDI flows in selected European countries, 1981-1994

(Percentage)

Sector/industry	France		Germany		Italy		Luxembourg		Netherlands		Portugal	Spain	United Kingdom	
	1981-85	1990-94	1981-85	1990-94	1981-85	1990-94	1981-85	1990-94	1981-85	1990-94	1990-94	1990-94	1981-85	1990-94
Total (million dollars)	433	3493	844	4613	1111	1115	1111	616	1389	9375	149	1421	1132	18038
Primary sector	-	0.2	-	0.1	-	-	-	-	-	0.4	-	0.5	0.4	1.1
Agriculture and forestry	-	0.2	-	0.1	-	-	-	-	-	0.4	-	0.4	-	-
Fisheries	-	-	-	-	-	-	-	-	-	-	-	-	-	-
Mining	-	-	-	-	-	-	-	-	-	0.1	-	0.1	0.4	1.1
Manufacturing sector	35.6	38.8	19.1	33.8	0.4	54.3	-	15.3	8.9	33.5	59.7	63.8	20.3	23.9
Foodstuffs	4.8	6.4	0.1	0.3	-	-	-	-	0.2	0.7	1.3	-	0.4	0.6
Textiles	6.0	2.5	-	2.2	-	18.2	-	-	-	1.2	35.6	1.3	0.2	1.4
Lumber and pulp	-	-	-	1.0	-	-	-	-	-	-	-	0.6	-	-
Chemicals	2.3	6.3	2.4	9.0	-	0.6	-	-	4.2	9.2	2.0	10.1	-	0.7
Iron and steel/nonferrous metals	0.2	3.1	-	0.3	-	0.2	-	-	2.2	1.6	17.4	3.7	0.2	0.4
Machinery	5.5	10.7	2.4	9.0	-	8.9	-	10.7	0.3	3.4	-	10.7	3.1	1.7
Electronic industry	9.2	4.8	9.5	10.9	-	9.0	-	1.8	0.2	10.9	-	20.5	10.2	10.1
Transport equipment	0.5	2.1	0.9	-	-	2.1	-	-	-	5.0	4.0	6.3	2.3	7.6
Other	7.2	2.9	3.6	1.1	-	15.2	-	2.8	1.4	1.4	-	10.6	4.0	1.4
Services sector	64.9	61.0	81.3	66.0	99.6	45.3	-	85.2	90.9	66.0	40.3	36.0	79.3	75.0
Construction	-	-	1.3	0.1	-	-	-	-	0.4	0.5	-	0.1	1.3	0.8
Commerce	45.5	15.7	55.3	33.0	-	26.8	-	3.4	28.8	14.9	4.0	10.4	27.1	11.3
Finance and insurance	1.8	3.7	2.6	17.0	95.9	2.7	-	73.4	58.4	26.8	1.3	2.2	45.3	30.8
Transportation	-	-	0.1	0.6	-	-	-	3.4	0.4	1.6	-	0.5	0.1	0.3
Real estate	2.1	21.2	0.1	7.7	1.8	7.4	-	-	0.4	15.4	7.4	8.4	1.0	21.8
Others [a]	15.5	20.4	21.8	7.6	2.0	8.4	-	5.0	2.4	6.8	27.5	14.4	4.5	10.0

Source: data provided by the Ministry of Finance.

a　Includes other services and branches.

business. Between 1981-1985 and 1990-1994, Japanese FDI in these two industries of the United Kingdom increased ninefold, but their shares declined from 72 per cent to 42 per cent. In the services sector, the most notable growth of Japanese FDI in the United Kingdom was registered in real estate; in manufacturing, it was in transport equipment.

The Netherlands, as the next largest host country of Japanese FDI in the European Union, has also proven very attractive for trading and financial TNCs of Japan. But again the shares of these two services sectors have declined, which applies also to other European countries (table II.3). In view of the Single Market Programme of the European Union, Japanese TNCs have strengthened their foothold in the manufacturing sector, whereby the choice of industries has differed among countries. In the Netherlands, Japanese TNCs have favoured chemical and electrical/electronic industries, whereas in Germany they have preferred chemicals and machinery for their increased investments. In France, it is metals industry. The Southern countries of the European Union (Italy, Spain and Portugal) have generally attracted more Japanese FDI in the manufacturing sector than in services.

B. Foreign direct investment from Asian developing countries

1. Trends

The European Union is not a favourite location for Asian TNCs, attracting less than one-tenth of Asia's FDI. As noted above, some Asian developing economies have paid somewhat greater attention to the European Union, when outward FDI stocks in 1992 are compared with stocks in 1980 (table I.7). However, the share of the European Union in total FDI stocks has typically remained rather small. The minor role of the European Union as a recipient of FDI from Asian developing economies is also evident when home country data are considered (table II.4). The European Union attracted 7 per cent of overall FDI outflows from South, East and South-East Asia as a whole in 1983-1988. This share declined to 5 per cent in the early 1990s. As concerning outward FDI stocks of South, East and South-East Asia, the European Union's share remained nearly constant at about 4 per cent.

Table II.4. FDI by South, East and South-East Asia in the European Union, United States and Japan, 1983-1995

(Billions of dollars and percentage)

Region/country	Inflows (annual average)		Stocks	
	1983-1988	1990-1995	1985	1995
Total FDI by South, East and South-East Asia (value)	3.3	23.4	5.7	164.6
European Union	7.1	4.8 ª	4.1	4.2 ᵇ
United States	6.9	4.4 ᶜ	19.8	5.4 ᵈ
Japan ᵉ	1.4 ᶠ	1.0 ᵍ	4.1 ᶠ	1.1 ʰ

Sources: UNCTAD, FDI database and OECD, 1994 and 1995.

a 1990-1993.
b 1993.
c 1990-1994.
g 1991-1995. Data for the countries other than Hong Kong became available only after 1991. If the data for Hong Kong only are taken, the share is 0.2 per cent.
h 1990 stock from Hong Kong plus 1991-1995 flows from South, East and South-East Asia.

d 1994.
e On approval/notification basis.
f Only Hong Kong.

As compared with the European Union, outward investment by South, East and South-East Asia has a longer tradition in the United States. This is reflected in the much higher share that the United States held in outward FDI stock of South, East and South-East Asia in 1985 (20 per cent versus 4 per cent for the European Union; table II.4). However, the United States share declined considerably thereafter until 1995, when it exceeded the European Union share by less than 2 percentage points. The flow data are in line with the proposition that the European Union has gained attractiveness for FDI from Asia relative to the United States (table II.4). While both the European Union and the United States attracted a similar share (of about 7 per cent) in total FDI from this region in 1983-1988, the United States fell significantly behind the European Union in 1990-1993. The European Union also received significantly higher FDI inflows from South, East and South-East Asia than Japan since the mid-1980s. As a consequence, the European Union's share in total outward FDI stock of this region was four times higher than Japan's share in 1995, whereas the European Union and Japan had been equally important hosts of FDI stock of Asian developing economies in 1985.

As far as individual economies are concerned, Hong Kong is the most important investor among Asian developing economies in the European Union (OECD, 1995). Hong Kong ranked first in terms of both inward FDI stock in 1993 and inward FDI flows in 1990-1993. Hong Kong is closely followed by the Republic of Korea with regard to FDI stock data as of 1993, while Singapore ranks third by a high margin. However, FDI inflows into the European Union in 1990-1993 suggest that Taiwan Province of China is catching up quickly; during this period, FDI inflows from this economy were still lower than inflows from Hong Kong, but Taiwan Province of China clearly outperformed all other Asian developing economies.

Looking from the perspective of the European Union, non-Japanese Asian FDI inflows and stocks are as yet very small (table II.5). Although both of the above Asian shares have increased since the 1980s, they remain about or below the one per cent level. In contrast to the European Union, the Asian share in United States inflows is lower, but its share in FDI stock is higher, reflecting a longer tradition of Asian equity involvement in the United States; however, this may be given new impetus by the APEC efforts on freer trade and mobility of direct investments.[2] The distribution of Asian developing economies' FDI in the European Union shows that especially the United Kingdom has benefited from such investment. According to host country data, about two fifths of FDI stock held by Asian developing economies in the European Union is located in that country (OECD, 1995). Germany accounts for one third, and the Netherlands ranks next, with a share of one fifth. Not surprisingly, this pattern reflects the distribution of FDI in the European Union as based on outward FDI data of individual Asian host economies:

- Singapore's outward FDI stock in the European Union in 1994 was heavily concentrated on the United Kingdom; the Netherlands ranked second (Singapore, Department of Statistics, various years).

- Likewise, the United Kingdom attracted most of the FDI from Taiwan Province of China in the European Union. Germany and the Netherlands followed, though by a huge margin (Taiwan Province of China, Investment Commission, various years).

- The United Kingdom, too, led the list of host countries for Thailand in terms of stock in 1994. The share of the Netherlands amounted to one quarter, while the rest was mainly in Germany and France.[3]

- A somewhat different distribution exists with regard to Malaysia's outward FDI in the European Union. France emerged as the most important host of accumulated FDI flows in 1985-1994, followed by the United Kingdom. Germany and the Netherlands ranked third and fourth, but these two host countries received roughly one third of Malaysia's FDI in France and the United Kingdom (Malaysian Industrial Development Authority, various years).

- China's outward FDI appears to be less skewed towards particular European Union countries. France and Germany figure most prominently. But the United Kingdom, the Netherlands, Italy and, to a lesser extent, Belgium (together with Luxembourg) also received considerable FDI from China (China Resources, 1995).

Whether Asian investors would seek direct market presence in the United States or would prefer to serve its domestic market through production in Mexico (which has a preferential access to the United States market through NAFTA and at the same time offers locational factor price advantages) is an open question.

In Japan, the Asian investors have a higher share of around 6 per cent of FDI inflows than in the European Union and the United States (table II.5). This is simply because total inflow of FDI in Japan is relatively low, yielding a higher percentage for very small amounts of capital inflows from Asian countries. From the sole point of view of production costs, Japan is not at all a competitive location for Asian investors. Furthermore, Asian investments in distribution networks remain largely at bay as most of exports as well as imports in Japan is through its own trading houses. It should be noted, however, that FDI from Asian firms has been growing since 1993 to take advantage of decreasing asset prices and weakening position of a number of small and medium-sized enterprises after the burst of the "bubble" economy.

Table II.5. Share of South, East and South-East Asia in the inward FDI of European Union, United States and Japan, 1983-1995

(Percentage)

Economy	Flows		Stocks	
	1983-1990	1990-1995	1985	1995
European Union	0.9	1.1 [a]	0.1	0.5 [b]
United States	0.7	2.4 [c]	0.6	1.3 [d]
Japan [e]	3.3 [f]	6.3 [g]	4.0 [f]	4.6 [h]

Sources: UNCTAD, FDI database; and OECD, 1994 and 1995.

a   1990-1993.
b   1993.
c   1990-1994.
g   1991-1995.

d   1994.
e   On approval/notification basis.
f   Only Hong Kong.

g   1991-1995. Data for the countries other than Hong Kong became available only after 1991. If the data for Hong Kong only are taken, the share is 1.2 per cent.
h   1990 stock from Hong Kong plus 1991-1995 flows from South, East and South-East Asia.

Although less important as an investment target than Japan and the United States until recently (table II.5), the importance of Asian FDI in the European Union cannot be ignored. They contribute to employment and value added. For example, in Germany, 262 affiliates of developing Asian TNCs produced a DM8 billion worth of turnover and employed 8,000 persons in 1994.[4] Most importantly, inward FDI promotes exports of home countries and, thereby, contribute to a more efficient allocation of resources, price stability and consumer's welfare in host countries. The linkages established between foreign and domestic firms prove useful for exports by the host country.

2. Sectoral distribution

A first impression of the sectoral distribution of recent FDI projects by the Asian NIEs in European countries suggests the following (table II.6):

- Projects in manufacturing and services were of similar importance for the European Union as a whole (as well as for EFTA).

- Foreign direct investment in manufacturing was heavily biased towards the electronics industry, which accounted for three quarters of all manufacturing projects of the four Asian NIEs in the European Union. Projects in textiles, clothing, leather and footwear, as well as in chemicals and the production of toys, followed by a great margin.

- The distribution of projects within the services sector was much less concentrated than in manufacturing. Investment in trade figured most prominently, but FDI in financial institutions was only slightly less important. In addition, Asian NIEs engaged in quite a number of projects in other service industries such as sea transport, hotels and telecommunications.

- Projects in both manufacturing and services prefered the United Kingdom and Germany, followed by France and the Netherlands. The same ranking of European Union host countries prevailed with regard to the single most important manufacturing industry, i.e., electronics.

- Major host countries in the European Union attracted a similar number of FDI projects from Asian NIEs in both manufacturing and services. The only exception was France, where manufacturing projects (all but one in electronics) accounted for two thirds of the total number of projects.

- The United Kingdom hosted Asian FDI projects in all major services industries. In the services sector of Germany, the focus of investors from Asian NIEs was clearly on trade and, to a lesser extent, finance and sea transport.

Trade accounted for almost all FDI stock held by Hong Kong in Germany in 1992 (table II.7). While Hong Kong represented an extreme case, the share of trade in total FDI stock (including manufacturing, for which separate figures are not disclosed) exceeded 50 per cent

Table II.6. Number of FDI projects by the four Asian NIEs in European Union and EFTA countries, 1993

Sector/industry	EU											EFTA		
	Total	Denmark	France	Germany	Greece	Ireland	Italy	Netherlands	Portugal	Spain	United Kingdom	Total	Austria	Switzerland
Primary sector	3	-	-	-	-	-	-	1	-	-	2	-	-	-
Manufacturing[a]	83	1	15	25	-	4	2	5	2	2	27	4	-	4
Electronics	64	1	14	18	-	2	2	3	1	1	22	1	-	1
Textiles, clothing, leather, footwear	5	-	-	2	-	1	-	1	-	-	1	-	-	-
Transport equipment	2	-	-	1	-	-	-	-	-	1	-	-	-	-
Chemicals	3	-	-	1	-	-	-	-	1	-	1	-	-	-
Toys	3	-	1	-	-	1	-	-	-	-	1	-	-	-
Clocks, watches	-	-	-	-	-	-	-	-	-	-	-	3	-	3
Bicycles	2	-	-	1	-	-	-	1	-	-	-	-	-	-
Aircraft	1	-	-	-	-	-	-	-	-	-	1	-	-	-
Machinery	1	-	-	1	-	-	-	-	-	-	-	-	-	-
Paper, printing	2	-	-	1	-	-	-	-	-	-	1	-	-	-
Services[a]	77	-	7	26	2	2	-	6	1	4	29	5	3	2
Trade	26	-	3	11	1	-	-	1	-	4	6	-	-	-
Finance	22	-	2	7	-	-	-	5	-	-	8	2	1	1
Sea transport	9	-	1	6	-	1	-	-	-	-	1	-	-	-
Hotels	6	-	-	1	-	-	-	-	-	-	5	2	1	1
Telecommunication	6	-	-	1	1	-	-	-	1	-	3	1	1	-
Insurance	4	-	1	-	-	-	-	-	-	-	3	-	-	-
Real estate	3	-	-	-	-	-	-	-	-	-	3	-	-	-
Other	1	-	-	-	-	1	-	-	-	-	-	-	-	-
Total	163	1	22	51	2	6	2	12	3	6	58	9	3	6

Source: Kögel and Gälli, 1994.

a Manufacturing industries and services listed in descending order with regard to the total number of FDI projects in all European countries (including Eastern and Central Europe).

in the case of the three other Asian NIEs as well (see box 9 on the role of FDI in trade with regard to marketing).

Table II.7. Share of services in total FDI stock held by Asian developing economies in Germany,[a] 1992

(Percentage)

Industry	Asian NIEs				Other Asian developing economies		
	Hong Kong	Republic of Korea	Singapore	Taiwan Province of China	China	Malaysia	Thailand
Trade	91.9	55.8	57.9	56.4	41.8	x	8.8
Transportation, communication	2.3	x	x	x	25.5	–	–
Finance	–	36.2	–	x	x	–	x
Memorandum:							
Total (DM million)	86	448	19	149	98	X	34

Source: Schultz, 1995, on the basis of data from the Deutsche Bundesbank.

a   The share of manufacturing is not considered in this table because of the lack of disclosed information for this sector; "x" stands for not disclosed for confidentiality reasons.

Box 9. Marketing by Asian NIEs in Europe: the role of trade-supporting FDI

Foreign direct investment in trade typically accounts for a significant share of Asian NIEs' overall FDI in European countries. However, the role of FDI in helping Asian companies to penetrate European markets has various facets. Some Asian governments initiated the establishment of distribution centres, in order to promote exports to Europe. The Republic of Korea opened its first distribution centre in Europe in Rotterdam in September 1989 (Deutsch-Koreanische Industrie- und Handelskammer, 1990, p. 27). It is rather unlikely, however, that this project involved direct investment by privately owned Korean firms to any significant extent. Likewise, the state-run China-Hong Kong Development agency established the so-called "China-City" in Amsterdam in 1989; the major aim was to support Chinese producers in entering European Union-markets (Schultz, 1995). Besides trade-related public investment of Asian developing countries in Europe, trading companies based in Asian NIEs extended their operations through investing in European countries. In the late 1980s, large Korean trading companies assessed the possibility to set up distribution systems in Europe (Deutsch-Koreanische Industrie- und Handelskammer, 1990, p.28). Moreover, wholesale and retail activities accounted for a significant proportion of Hong Kong's FDI in Europe. Notable projects included the following (Kögel and Gällie, 1994, pp. 22-23; see also box 2):

• Dickson Concepts Ltd., a Hong Kong-based trading company, invested $101 million in the acquisition of Harvey Nichols, a leading department store in London, in 1991.

• Industrial Equity Pacific Ltd. held minority shares in various department stores in Paris since 1988, and took control of a group of distribution centres for automobiles produced by Rover in the United Kingdom.

• Another leading trading company based in Hong Kong, Jardine Matheson Holdings Ltd., established several foreign affiliates in Europe. In 1990, one of these foreign affiliates (Dairy Farm International) acquired a group of more than 100 food stores in Spain. Another one (Jardine International Motor) acquired the distribution network of a French company, which was engaged in the marketing of automobiles.

• Goldlion Holding Ltd., which marketed clothing items, established its European headquarters in Düsseldorf (Goldlion Europe GmbH).

/...

(Box 9, cont'd)

Trade-related FDI activities were also undertaken by Asian manufacturers, for whom exports to the European Union figured prominently. But the majority of exporting firms has not established production facilities in Europe so far. However, many exporters invested in representative offices, sales networks and warehouses. The city of Hamburg, for example, hosts about 20 representative offices of firms based in Hong Kong. Korean manufacturers of automobiles (Hyundai, Kia Motors Corp.) set up distribution channels, in order to penetrate European markets through exports. Reportedly, foreign trade-related FDI projects accounted for the largest *number* of Korean outward FDI projects in the 1980s, while the average *amount* (in terms of dollar) was relatively small (Lee and Lee, 1992, pp. 97-98). More recent data suggest, however, that this pattern has changed in the 1990s (Cho, 1992, table 4). The average amount involved in FDI projects subsumed under the category "international trade" exceeded $3 million in the period from 1990 to June 1992; the average amount involved in FDI projects in manufacturing was actually lower in this period ($2.3 million).

Finally, Asian manufacturers that already had established production facilities in European countries devoted part of their FDI outflows to marketing activities. Investment in manufacturing industries and in marketing are thus closely intertwined. For example, many of the Korean and Taiwan Province of China-based electronics firms with production bases in Europe undertook additional FDI with regard to marketing, distribution, storage and after-sales service (Kögel and Gälli, 1994, p. 20). Korean Goldstar opened a distribution centre in Germany in September 1989, which marketed microwave ovens, colour TVs and video recorders produced by Goldstar in Germany and the United Kingdom. Samsung's initial engagement in Portugal was in the form of a joint venture with the Portuguese marketing firm Emacet (holding 35 per cent of shares) and the wholesaler MRI (10 per cent of shares), in order to promote the marketing of Samsung's products in Portugal and other European countries (Choi, 1991, pp. 108-112). For the same reason, Samsung founded marketing subsidiaries in Germany (Samsung Electronics GmbH) in 1982, and in the United Kingdom (Samsung Electronics U.K. Ltd.) in 1984. Likewise, Taiwanese FDI in trade was closely linked to its FDI in electronics. For example, the conglomerate Kunnan was strongly engaged in marketing PCs through an exclusive dealers network of about 60 agencies in France.

As concerns Hong Kong, investors reportedly focussed on marketing and business services in Europe and North America (Kögel and Gälli, 1994, p. 21). Hong Kong's involvement in manufacturing in European host countries appears to be dominated by the electronics industry, followed by textile and clothing (Kögel and Gälli, 1994, pp. 21-22). Hong Kong-based companies engaged in European Union countries included:

- In the United Kingdom: Universal Toys, which acquired its Matchbox Toys plant in Essex already in 1982;[5] Hutchison Whampoa Ltd., whose subsidiary Hutchison Telecom entered a joint venture in the mobile phone business, and which acquired Microtel Communications from British Aerospace as well as Millicom Cellular; Peninsular Knitter in clothing; QPL International Holding, which established two affiliates producing electronic components in Wales in 1992.

- In Germany: Hutchison Telecom holds a 68 per cent share in ABC Telecom and a 86 per cent share in Hutchison Mobilfunk GmbH.

- In France: Great Wall Electronics Ltd., which formed a joint venture with a French holding company for producing colour TVs; Starlight International Ltd., which started to produce colour TVs in 1994.

- In Denmark: Allen Industries Ltd., which increased its production of diskettes from 0.8 to 3 million per month since late 1992.

Singapore provides data on the sectoral structure of FDI stocks held in Europe as a whole and in the two most important European host countries (the Netherlands and the United Kingdom). Detailed statistics on the distribution of FDI within manufacturing are lacking. Reportedly, the focus of Singapore's FDI in manufacturing was on electronics (Schultz, 1995, p. 78; Kögel and Gälli, 1994, p. 23). For example, the Singaporean company Mayor PTE established a plant for the production of electronic components in Wales. On the whole, however, manufacturing is playing a minor role in Singapore's FDI activities in Europe (table II.8). Investment stocks held in the Netherlands were almost exclusively in finance. This industry also dominated Singapore's FDI in the United Kingdom and in Europe as a whole. The United Kingdom also attracted considerable FDI from Singapore in business services. Furthermore, two state-owned companies (Government of Singapore Investment Corp. and Temasek Holding) indirectly acquired a 30 per cent share in the second largest British hotel group, Mount Charlotte, through their large-scale investment in Brierley Investments Ltd., a conglomerate based in New Zealand, in 1991 (Schultz, 1995). Singapore's engagement in the British hotel business received another push in 1993, when two hotels were acquired in London. Transportation ranked second behind finance in other European host countries.

Table II.8. Singapore: outward FDI stock, by industry, in European countries, 1994

(Percentage)

Industry	Europe	Netherlands	United Kingdom	Other
Manufacturing	3.0	0.5	1.6	8.6
Construction	–	–	–	–
Commerce	1.3	0.6	0.6	3.4
Transport	5.0	–	0.9	18.2
Finance	84.3	98.9	83.9	68.9
Real estate	0.6	–	0.9	0.5
Business services	4.9	–	10.4	0.1
Memorandum:				
Total (Million Singapore dollars)	3 923	1 093	1 842	989

Source: Ministry of Trade and Industry, Department of Statistics, *Singapore's Investment Abroad*, various issues.

In contrast to Singapore, FDI in manufacturing was much more important with regard to the engagement of firms from the Republic of Korea and Taiwan Province of China in the European Union. In the case of the former, it appears that manufacturing accounted for 45 per cent of the country's FDI stock held in the European Union in 1990.[6] This share declined slightly to 42 per cent by 1993 (table II.9; figures in parentheses).

The relative importance of manufacturing differed remarkably between individual European Union hosts of Korean FDI (Min, 1991, p. 180). Stock data for 1990 reveal that the Republic of Korea's engagement was (almost) exclusively in manufacturing in Ireland (100 per cent), Portugal (100 per cent), Belgium (97 per cent), and Spain (95 per cent). It was less prominent in France (51 per cent), Italy (38 per cent), the United Kingdom (28 per cent) and Germany (18 per cent). And it was non-existent in the Netherlands. In other words, Korean investors frequently preferred low wage locations in Central and Eastern Europe where they established production facilities through FDI in the 1980s.[7] By contrast, the focus of Korean investors was on marketing activities in advanced core economies of the European Union. By establishing trading networks through FDI, Korean investors strengthened their foothold in the larger national markets of the European Union. This mainly refers to Korean trading companies and automobile producers (Hyundai, Kia Motors) (Schultz, 1995, p. 63; see also box 9 above).

It is interesting to note, however, that the differences in the sectoral structure of Korean FDI, which emerged between various European Union host countries before 1990, has become less pronounced in subsequent years. This is indicated by the sectoral structure of FDI outflows from the Republic of Korea to major European Union countries in 1991-93 (table II.8). It is only in Germany that Korean FDI was still almost exclusively in trading activities.[8] Investment in manufacturing became considerably more important than before in the United Kingdom (box 4), and particularly in the Netherlands. At the same time, a major shift towards FDI in trade occurred in Spain.

Some information is available on the relative importance of specific manufacturing industries in Korean FDI from cumulated flows to the European Union as a whole during 1980-1990 (Min, 1991, p. 153). During this period, the ranking was as follows (in per cent of total FDI outflows in manufacturing):

electrical and electronic products	: 73.4
transport equipment	: 12.7
chemicals	: 7.2
machinery	: 3.2
wood and paper products	: 0.5
food products	: 0.2
others	: 2.8

Table II.9. Republic of Korea: FDI outflows to European countries, by sector, cumulated flows in 1991-1993

(Percentage)

Sector	Europe[a]		France	Germany	Netherlands	Spain	United Kingdom
Forestry, fishery	0.4	(0.3)	-	-	-	-	-
Mining	0.3	(8.1)	-	-	-	-	-
Manufacturing	40.7	(41.9)	39.3	12.8	58.8	29.8	37.6
Services	56.9	(49.6)	60.8	84.8	41.2	70.2	62.4
Construction	-	(-)	-	-	-	-	-
Trade	56.3	(48.1)	59.2	83.8	41.2	72.3	62.1
Transportation	0.1	(0.2)	-	0.4	-	-	-0.1
Finance, insurance	-	(..)	-	-	-	-	-
Real estate	0.5	(..)	1.5	0.6	-	-2.1	0.5
Memorandum:							
Total (Million dollars)	414.9	(560.4)	72.5	120.1	8.5	9.4	107.8

Source: Schultz, 1995, on the basis of data from the Bank of Korea; Ministry of Finance, 1994.

[a] In parentheses: distribution of outward FDI stocks on investment basis as of end 1993.

This ranking is very similar to the pattern of FDI projects in manufacturing by Asian NIEs in the European Union (table II.6). This refers in particular to the prominence of electronics (also box 10).

Box 10. FDI by Korean manufacturers of electronics in Europe

Manufacturers of electronics were among the frontrunners among Korean investors in Europe. Samsung Electronics pioneered this development by producing colour TVs in Portugal. A major wave of FDI projects by Korean producers of electronics, notably by LG, followed in the late 1980s (see accompanied table). Production facilities were located in both Portugal, Spain and Turkey and other European countries (France, Germany and the United Kingdom). Competition between Korean investors on European markets was fierce, since their production was focussed on a similar set of electronic products, notably video recorders, colour TVs and microwave ovens.

Production facilities of Korean manufacturers of electronics in European countries, as of early 1990

Company	Location	Start of production	Investment Million dollars	Investment Korean share	Principal products (Per cent)
LG	Germany	1987	3.4	100	Colour TV, VTR
	Turkey	1988	5.9	25	Microwave ovens
	United Kingdom	1989	6.0	100	Microwave ovens
	Spain	1989	..	..	Colour TV
Samsung Electronics	Portugal	End 1970s[a]	7.0	55	Colour TV
	United Kingdom	1987	5.0	100	Colour TV, VTR, microwave ovens
	Spain	1989	7.2	90	Colour TV, VTR
	Turkey	Under construction	2.7	51	Colour TV
	Hungary	under construction	5.0	35	TV
Daewoo Electronics	France	1988	9.0	51	Microwave ovens
	United Kingdom	1989	34.0	100	VTR
	Hungary	Under construction	..	..	..
Saehan Media	Ireland	1987	22.5	100	Video tapes

Source: Deutsch-Koreanische Industrie- und Handelskammer, 1990.

a   According to Choi, 1991, p. 109, Samsung Elektronica Portuguesa was founded in September 1983.

Competition further increased when major Korean investors expanded their operations. Prominent examples include: [a]

- LG planned to increase the capacity of its producltion in Turkey from 100.000 to 400.000 microwave ovens per year (and in the United Kingdom from 150.000 to 300.000 microwave ovens). The German subsidiary Goldstar Europe GmbH in Worms announced in 1990 to increase its production of video recorders by 50-100 per cent until the ned of 1993. In July 1996, LG announced a massive £1.7 billion electronics complex in South Wales. Two factories will produce semiconductors and television parts.[b]

- Samsung established facilities to produce 300.000 TVs in the United Kingdom, 200.000 in Turkey and 100.000 in Hungary, it also invested in the Czech Republic.

- Daewoo Electronics founded Daewoo Electronics Deutschland GmbH in Frankfurt in 1992 to serve as a centre for its European operations. In the early 1990s, Daewoo had the capacity to produce 300.000 microwave ovens in Europe, 500.000 video recorders in Northern Ireland, and 400.000 colour TVs in France.

/...

(Box 10, cont'd)

The FDI strategies of Korean producers of electronics in Europe revealed some new trends. First, production became more diversified. Particularly, the production of computers and computer parts gained momentum. As a result, Korean investors challenged Taiwanese competitors that had already established production facilities in the European Union exactly in this segment of the electronics industry (Kögel and Gälli, 1994, p. 21). For example, Samsung cooperated with Texas Instruments to start producing microchips in Portugal in 1993. New product lines also included CD players, magnetic tapes (by Samsung in Scotland), and refrigerators (by Samsung in Hungary and by LG in Italy). Second, Korean investors acquired production facilities by taking part in privatization programmes. Examples in the eastern part of Germany include: Hyundai acquired a firm producing semi-conductors; Korean Data Systems concluded a joint venture and started to produce PC monitors in late 1993; Samsung acquired in early 1993 a firm which used to produce TVs in the eastern part of Berlin, and supplied Korean and Japanese TV producers in Europe with TV tubes. Third, major producers of electronics such as LG, Daewoo and Samsung encouraged Korean input suppliers to follow suit in establishing production facilities in Europe (Deutsch-Koreanische Industrie- und Handelskakmmer, 1990, p. 30). This move rendered it easier to meet local content requirements which European host countries had imposed on Korean producers of electronics. Finally, Korean investors optimized their production and cost structure by relocating production facilities within Europe. Samsung shifted its production of colour TVs from Portugal and Spain to the United Kingdom. At the same time, the production of video recorders was relocated to Spain, and Samsung's production facilities in Portugal supplied parts and components to its assembly plants throughout Europe.[c]

The Internal Market programme of the European Union proved to be a major attraction for Korean FDI in electronics. More precisely, FDI was considered the best way to secure access to the crucially important European market, which, for example, accounted for a third of world demand for colour TVs (Choi, 1991, p. 109). The pioneers among Korean investors induced their Korean competitors to follow suit. A further stimulus was provided by European Union trade barriers against Korean exports of electronics, and by the fear of Korean exporters that the Internal Market programme would result in a "fortress Europe". As a matter of fact, Korean exporters of video reorcers, TV sets and TV tubes, CD players, and microwave ovens all had suffered from protectionist measures (especially anti-dumping measures) (for details, see Choi, 1991, p. 47). Hence, it was not just by pure coincidence that Korean producers of electronics were among the frontrunners in investing in the European Union.

A host of factors influenced the decision on where to locate production facilities in Europe.[d] It seems that Samsung's first investment in Portugal was induced by relatively low wage costs in this country which was soon to become a European Union member. Likewise, Northern Ireland was considered by Carmen Electronics, producing radios for automobiles, to be a cost effective platform for supplying the Single European Market. Locations at the European Union periphery also benefitted from tax incentives and subsidised interest rates offered to foreign investors. As shown above, however, more advanced European Union countries also attracted substantial FDI from Korean producers of electronics. Arguably, this was because investors wanted to produce where local demand for electronic products was relatively large. Furthermore, Korean FDI in Europe increasingly involved investment in research and development, in which more advanced European Union countries should have locational advantages.

---

[a]   For details, see Deutsch-Koreanische Industrie- und Handelskammer, 1990, p. 33, as well as Kögel and Gälli, 1994, pp. 24-27.
[b]   John Burton and Stefan Wagstyl, "European access lures Korean business", *Financial Times*, 10 July 1996, p. 8.
[c]   *Business Week*, 24 December 1992.
[d]   For a discussion of specific cases, see Choi, Ki-Chul, 1991, pp. 108-112, as well as Kögel and Gälli, 1994. See also "South Korea: Trade and Investment", *For Eastern Economic Review*, 10 June 1996 and O'Neil (forthcoming).

As in the case of the Republic of Korea, the electronics industry and the transport-equipment industry figure most prominently in FDI in manufacturing by firms from Taiwan Province of China in the European Union (table II.10). Nevertheless, accumulated outflows in 1959-1993 point to a different behaviour of Taiwanese investors as compared to Korean investors:

- As concerns the industry structure of FDI in manufacturing, FDI in transport equipment exceeded FDI in electronic and electric appliances by a factor of 2.6, if Europe as a whole is looked at as a host of Taiwanese FDI.

- The pattern for Europe as a whole is largely determined by the United Kingdom. In this host country, Taiwanese FDI in manufacturing was strongly concentrated on transport equipment. By contrast, the dominance of the electronics industry, observed for manufacturing FDI of the Republic of Korea in Europe, is also to be observed for manufacturing FDI of Taiwan Province of China in less important European Union host countries such as France, Germany and the Netherlands.

- Firms undertook considerable FDI in the textile industry of European countries, whereas this industry did not play any significant role in the case of the Republic of Korea. Investment in the textile industry was frequently a means to circumvent restrictive export quotas (Kögel and Gälli, 1994, p. 20). Due to high labour costs in some European countries, FDI in the labour intensive textile industry was not located there, but rather in peripheral countries where wages were relatively low.

- Investment in manufacturing played a more important role than for the Republic of Korea's overall engagement in Europe: the share of manufacturing in cumulated FDI outflows to Europe in 1959-1993 was 57 per cent (table II.10), while the share of manufacturing in total Korean FDI stocks held in Europe by end 1993 was only 42 per cent (table II.9). Particularly in the United Kingdom, but also in Germany, the relative importance of manufacturing FDI was considerably higher in the case of Taiwan Province of China than in the case of the Republic of Korea.[9]

- Taiwan Province of China and the Republic of Korea differ with regard to the structure of their FDI activities in the services sectors of European host countries. As concerns services, the Korean engagement was almost exclusively in trade (table II.9). By contrast, firms from Taiwan Province of China engaged less in trade than in other services (except for the Netherlands). Investment in banking and insurance figured prominently, especially in France.[10]

- Finally, small and medium-sized firms participated significantly in outward FDI, whereas large conglomerates dominated outward FDI by the Republic of Korea. In fact, most of Taiwan Province of China's outward FDI was undertaken by such firm (Schultz, 1995, p. 68). As a consequence, the average investment outlays involved in Taiwanese FDI projects were relatively small (about $1 million).[11] Nevertheless, econometric tests revealed that the propensity to invest abroad was positively related to the size of firms in Taiwan Province of China (for details, see Chen, 1992).

Table II.10. Taiwan Province of China: approved outward FDI by industry,
in European countries, cumulated flows in 1959-1993

(Percentage)

Industry	Europe	France	Germany	Netherlands	United Kingdom
Agriculture, forestry	-	-	-	-	-
Fishery, animal husbandry	-	-	-	-	-
Mining	-	-	-	-	-
Food, beverages	-	-	-	-	-
Textiles	7.29	-	-	-	-
Garment, footwear	-	-	-	-	-
Leather and fur products	-	-	-	-	-
Lumber and bamboo products	-	-	-	-	-
Paper products	-	-	-	-	-
Chemicals	0.11	-	0.53	-	0.12
Rubber products	0.02	-	-	-	0.04
Plastic products	0.15	-	1.94	-	-
Non-metallic products	-	-	-	-	-
Basic metals, metal products	0.06	-	0.77	-	-
Machinery	0.01	-	0.16	-	-
Electronic and electric appliances	13.75	19.81	31.31	14.31	15.67
Transport equipment	35.69	-	-	-	62.53
Precision instruments	0.26	-	3.27	-	-
Construction	0.04	-	-	-	-
Wholesale, retail	1.18	-	1.84	6.47	0.27
Trade	10.60	24.70	25.27	48.26	3.60
Transportation, storage	-	-	-	-	-
Banking, insurance	15.27	46.92	-	30.32	0.66
Other services	15.51	8.58	34.92	0.07	17.10
Memorandum:					
Total (Million dollars)	477.3	11.7	37.7	34.3	272.4

Source: Investment Commission (Taiwan Province of China), 1993.

Notes

[1]   Japan's outward FDI performance has been subject of considerable study: see, e.g., Nunnenkamp et al., 1994 and Michalski, 1995.

[2]   APEC Ministerial Meeting in November 1994 agreed on an APEC Concord of Non-binding Investment Principles (UNCTAD-DTCI, 1996a). They envisage, among other things, transparency of investment laws and regulations, non-discrimination of member countries, national treatment and minimization of performance requirements.

[3]   OECD, 1994; and information provided by the Bank of Thailand.

[4]   Data are provided by Deutsche Bundesbank.

[5]   Generally, Hong Kong's investors preferred acquisitions in the earlier phase of their engagement in Europe. This has changed more recently, with FDI in the form of joint ventures gaining prominence.

[6]   Min, 1991, p. 180, derived from Bank of Korea data. For the sectoral structure of the Republic of Korea's outward FDI in Asia, North America and OECD countries as a whole, see Lee and Lee (1992, pp. 97-106), Choi (1991, p. 12) and Min (1991, appendix table 2). See Deutsch-

Koreanische Industrie- und Handelskammer (1990, pp. 66-92) for a detailed list of Korean investors in North America and Europe as of June 1989; this source provides information on location, date of approval, product area, ownership structure, and amount of investment of Korean FDI projects.

7   For the same line of reasoning, see Choi, 1991, pp. 93-97.

8   However, Korean firms initiated manufacturing FDI projects in the eastern part of the country, partly by participating in the privatisation of state-owned enterprises. Manufacturing industries in which Korean FDI took place included electronics, machinery and textiles (Schultz, 1995, p. 62; Kögel and Gälli, 1994, p. 24).

9   By contrast, investors from the Republic of Korea focussed more strongly on FDI in manufacturing than Taiwanese investors in the case of France. Likewise, Taiwanese FDI in manufacturing was relatively modest in the case of the Netherlands.

10   It was mainly in 1990-1992 that Europe attracted considerable FDI flows from Taiwan Province of China in banking and insurance (Schultz, 1995, p. 68). Investment by firms from Taiwan Province of China in the European Union since the late 1980s was to take advantage of the Single European Market (Chia, 1995, p. 11; Kögel and Gälli, 1994, p. 28).

11   For the Republic of Korea, the average scale of FDI projects was about $2 million, if outward FDI at February 1996 is divided by the number of projects. The average size of Korean FDI projects in Europe amounted to about $3 million at the end of 1993.

ASIAN FOREIGN DIRECT INVESTMENT IN CENTRAL AND EASTERN EUROPE

The countries of Central and Eastern Europe offer unique opportunities for investment locations for Asian firms for a variety reasons:

- A primary motive of Asian firms for local European manufacturing lies in overcoming current and expected import protection. Since many countries of Central and Eastern Europe (Bulgaria, Czech Republic, Hungary, Poland, Romania, Slovakia, Slovenia and the Baltic states) have preferential access to the internal market of the European Union under their "Europe Agreements", Asian firms can avoid to some extent European Union import restrictions by producing in these countries, and exporting from there to the member countries of the European Union. Central and Eastern Europe offers a favourable entry point into the European Union market, with privatization programmes frequently facilitating the process.

- Asian firms can maintain their cost advantage vis-à-vis domestic European Union producers by locating their plants in Central and Eastern Europe. Wage and land costs in these countries -- compared to those in the member countries of the European Union -- are very low, and are likely to remain lower in the foreseeable future. Wage costs per hour range from $1 in Romania and Bulgaria to between $2.50 to $3.50 in the Visegrad states, compared with nearly $29 in Germany; total costs of production can be one half to two thirds less in Romania or Bulgaria compared with Western European countries.[1]

- Local demand in Central and Eastern Eureope for manufactured consumer goods is strong and production in these markets gives Asian firms a cost edge. Some of them (Czech Republic, Hungary, Poland and Slovakia) have free trade agreement among themselves, so that scale economies can be achieved.

- Economic and political conditions have stabilized, creating a more favourable environment for FDI.

A comparison of the Asian shares in total inward FDI in the region (table III.1) with those in European Union inward FDI (table II.4) suggests that, indeed, Asian developing countries have seized the investment opportunities in this region, while, interestingly, Japanese TNCs apparently have not (box 11) . The highest share (14 per cent) recorded for the Asian developing countries is in the FDI stock in the Russian Federation. About half of it is accounted for by Singapore. Another two fifths are owned by Chinese firms. China has a comparatively large number of foreign affiliates not only in the Russian Federation, but also in other countries of the region. Most of these are probably related to earlier representations of Chinese state

Box 11. Why is Japanese FDI so small in Central and Eastern Europe?

A pattern of Japanese FDI that places special weight on the United States and East and South-East Asia, as well as Western Europe, makes other regions small host receipients. Central and Eastern Europe, in particular, is such a region, accounting for only 0.2 per cent of Japanese FDI stock worldwide by March 1996.[a]

Regardless of the nationality of TNCs, market-seeking FDI in Central and Eastern Europe is low, either because of small populations in most countries and/or low purchasing power. Furthermore, cost-productivity configurations, another "pull" factor for FDI, are more attractive in other regions, as is the general economic performance. Finally, Central and Eastern Europe competes, of course, with other host regions for FDI; Asia, in particular is the most preferred location for Japanese investors in developing countries.[b] Still, a number of specific factors explain the exceptionally small FDI from Japan in Central and Eastern Europe:

- *A limited Japanese support-services network.* Japanese trading companies (*sogo shosha*), which have played a vital role in initiating and organizing Japanese FDI abroad (Kojima and Ozawa, 1984), are far less represented in Central and Eastern Europe than in the rest of the world. Japanese trading companies have approximately 5,500 foreign affiliates world-wide; only about 60 of them are located in Central and Eastern Europe (Toyo Keizai, 1996). The small presence of Japanese banking affiliates (only 2 out of 1,150 Japanese foreign banking (including insurance) affiliates are located in Central and Eastern Europe) is also a limiting factor; in countries in which domestic financial sector is underdeveloped, the provision of banking services by Japanese affiliates is particularly important, especially since Japanese TNCs tend to use their own banking affiliates.[c] The assistance for undertaking FDI abroad provided by the Government of Japan is also skewed in favour of other regions. The Japan External Trade Organization has a world-wide network of 79 offices (in 1996) to assist Japanese firms in the conduct of their business; but only five in Central and Eastern Europe, compared with 16 in South, East and South-East Asia.[d]

- *Weak linkage between official development assistance and FDI.* Japanese official development assistance and FDI are closely linked in some developing countries because a part of Japan's aid is tied to the purchase of Japanese products, or is associated with investment-facilitating activities, such as infrastructure development. In 1993, Central and Eastern Europe received only 1.5 per cent of Japan's bilateral official development assistance, a substantial part of which (76 per cent of the total in 1993) is in the form of grant aid for humanitarian purposes (Japan, Ministry of Foreign Affairs, 1995). Furthermore, Japan's assistance to Central and Eastern Europe countries is channelled through multilateral organizations, such as the EBRD, and has not led to higher Japanese FDI.

- *Moderate trade relations.* Weak trade relations between Japan on the one hand and Central and Eastern Europe on the other have certainly not facilitated FDI, neither as a sequential nor as a complementary activity. During 1990-1994, Central and Eastern Europe accounted for only 0.7 per cent of Japanese exports.

- *Availability of similar resources in other regions.* Japanese labour-intensive investments typically take place in neighbouring Asian countries, not only because of low labour costs and relatively skilled labour, but also because of a familiarity with Aisa's business culture. For natural resource-seeking FDI, Asia, Canada and Oceania have been the main host regions. Although Central and Eastern Europe has abundant cheap labour, Asia's geographical proximity to Japan means lower transportation costs for goods exported back to Japan. This is an important consideration, given that 15 per cent of sales of all Japanese affiliates abroad were made to Japan in fiscal year 1993 (MITI, 1995, table 2-13-13).

- *Psychological distance.* Although geographical distances have been significantly reduced due to technological developments in communications and transportation, Japan's psychological distance to Central and Eastern Europe, especially when compared with Asia, is greater. In some geographically distant countries in Latin America, a large influx of Japanese immigrants has made psychological distances smaller.

/...

(Box 11, cont'd)

Despite these factors, there are several ways of changing Japanese investors' negative impressions of this region as FDI locations. Unfamiliarity with this region's markets is an important drawback for Japanese investors. Japanese affiliates in Western Europe may play a role as catalyst by educating their parent firms or even by investing directly in these regions. In fact, this is already happening: examples are Fujitsu's investment in Poland via ICL, a Japanese affiliate in the United Kingdom; Kyocera's investment in the Czech Republic through its affiliate, AVX in the United Kingdom; and Alps Electric's in the Czech Republic through its affiliate in Ireland. The possible enlargement of the European Union to include some countries in Central and Eastern Europe may strengthen this trend as do the association agreements.

A possible source of future FDI are Japanese small and medium-sized enterprises (which account for some 15 per cent of Japan's outward FDI stock and for about half of Japan's equity investment cases (UNCTAD-DTCI, 1993). Traditionally, these firms have preferred to locate in Asia; but rising costs there are making that less attractive. In fact, the number of affiliates of Japanese small and medium-sized enterpirses that withdrew from Asia exceeded that of newly established affiliates in 1994.[e] In this respect Central and Eastern Europe may become more attractive to them, a possibility further encouraged by the governments of this region which try to attract FDI from small and medium-sized enterprises by giving them special preferences.

Source: UNCTAD-DTCI, 1996a.

a   This figure is low compared with 5 per cent for the European Union (1993) and even 0.4 per cent for the United States (1994).
b   Looking at the medium (the next three years) and the long term (10 years ahead), eight out of the 10 most preferred countries for Japanese TNCs are in Asia (the remaining two being in developed countries) (Export-Import Bank of Japan, 1996). One reason is that the operations of Japanese affiliates in that region are very profitable: in fiscal year 1994, the ratio of current income to sales of Japanese affiliates in that region was 4.1 per cent, compared, for example, with 1.9 per cent in the United States and 1.2 per cent in Europe (MITI, 1996).
c   For example, one fifth of funds raised by Japanese affiliates in host countries were through affiliates of Japanese banks in the same countries in 1992 (MITI, 1994, table 2-21-12).
d   Data provided by the Japan External Trade Organization.
e   *Nihon Keizai Shimbun*, 9 May 1996, based on a survey by MITI. There were 92 affiliates of small and medium-sized TNCs that withdrew in 1994, while 86 affiliates were established by them.

Table III.1. FDI of Asian developing economies in Central and Eastern Europe, latest available year

(Millions of dollars and percentage)

| Host country | Year | Accumulated FDI | | | Main investing economy |
		Total	From Asian economies	Share	
Estonia	1993	188	2.9	1.5	China ($ 2 million)
Hungary	1993	5 802	29.0	0.5	Republic of Korea ($ 23 million) China ($ 6 million)
Latvia	1994	315	0.5	0.2	China ($ 0.5 million)
Lithuania	1994	174	4.0	0.6	Hong Kong Republic of Korea China
Poland	1994	4 321	43.0	1.0	China ($ 25 million) Singapore ($ 13 million) Republic of Korea ($5 million)
Romania	1995	1 595	159.1	10.0	Republic of Korea ($ 159 million)
Slovakia	1995	923	10.7	1.2	Republic of Korea ($11 million)
Russian Federation	1994	2 919	403.6	13.8	Singapore ($195 million) China ($164 million) Hong Kong ($12 million) Republic of Korea ($11 million) Democratic People's Republic of Korea ($ 10 million) Taiwan Province of China ($ 5 million)

Sources: UNCTAD-DTCI, based on UNECE, various issues; PlanEcon Report, various issues; and national official sources.

enterprises which have now been designated as affiliates. More firms from Asian countries are active in the Russian Federation than in any other country of the region. This is probably due to the large domestic market and a vast reservoir of natural resources, in addition to a common border with China as well as relatively intensive trade relations with countries such as India.

Romania is the next largest host country for Asian FDI, both in terms of absolute amounts (1995: $159 million) and the Asian share in total inward FDI stock (1995: 10 per cent). In contrast to the Russian Federation, the entire amount of Asian FDI in Romania stems from only one country, the Republic of Korea. The selection of Romania by the Korean car manufacturer Daewoo, and very recently the acquisition by the same firm of the Polish car companies FS Lublin and FSO (box 12), are a reflection of Daewoo's efforts to access the European Union internal market through already existing firms rather than establishing entirely new manufacturing plants. This clearly reveals that the transport-equipment industry represents a major area in which Asian investors benefitted from privatization programmes. In other countries with Europe Agreements -- such as Hungary -- local car manufacturers had already entered into partnership or cooperation agreements with well established automobile TNCs from the Triad. Apart from the European Union market, the local markets in Central and Eastern Europe are also attractive for Daewoo as the demand for cars in lower price segments is likely to continue to rise in the foreseeable future. Total demand for cars in this region rose in 1995 by 7.3 per cent to about 604,000 units. It is expected to increase by 10 per cent a year, to reach more than 1 million units in the year 2000, compared with only 2 to 4 per cent a year growth of car demand in Western Europe.[2]

The Republic of Korea is the largest Asian investor in Central and Eastern Europe, accounting for one third of total Asian FDI stock in this region (table I.18). Singapore and China follow rather closely. Whereas Singapore's FDI is concentrated in the Russian Federation, Korean and Chinese FDI are regionally diversified. The most distinctive feature distinguishing these two countries is the average size of their investment projects. Chinese firms have many more foreign affiliates in Central and Eastern Europe than any other Asian country, and the average size of Chinese affiliates is small. Korean FDI is concentrated in relatively few projects, yielding, therefore, a higher average affiliate size. These large projects also attract investments by small and medium-sized enterprises from the Republic of Korea. (The German car manufacturer VW's acquisition of a majority share in Skoda's capital in Czech Republic, for example, led to FDI by at least 50 German small and medium-sized enterprises in that country, mainly as suppliers of components.) Daewoo's involvement in Romania and Poland is very recent. How many of Korean small and medium-sized enterprises will follow it in these countries would depend also on their integration in Daewoo's production process at home. Daewoo has already organised some visits to Romania by some of its leading components suppliers in the Republic of Korea, and of Romanian components producers to the Republic of Korea.

As far as the sectoral distribution of all Asian FDI in Central and East Europe is concerned, the available information suggests that, in the manufacturing sector, the electronic industry has drawn the largest number of investors from Asian developing countries (table III.2). This is consistent with the competitive advantage of Asian firms in this industry and the fact that some electronic goods have faced import restrictions in the European Union.

Box 12. The Korean car producer Daewoo in Central and Eastern Europe

Daewoo is one of the biggest industrial groups in the Republic of Korea, and its third largest carmaker. It has decided to make Central and Eastern Europe the centrepiece of its vehicle-producing operations for all of Europe. In the past two years, Daewoo assumed control of four formerly state-owned Central and Eastern Europe car manufacturers: Rodae in Romania; FS Lublin and FSO in Poland; and Avia, the Czech truck maker. In addition it has already built a car plant in Uzbekistan (see accompanied table).

Korea's vehicle makers' overseas production operation, 1996

Maker	Host country	Model	Production per annum (thousands)	Start year	Remarks
Hyundai	Netherlands	3.5 , 6 ton truck	2	1995	Country's first to produce CVs in Europe.
Kia	Germany	Sportage	30	1995	Karman, first in Europe.
Daewoo	Romania	Cielo	200	1995	Established a joint venture, Rodae with 51 per cent stake.
	Uzbekistan	Cielo, light car	200	1996	Contract in February 1993, holding 50 per cent stake.
	Poland	Cielo	90	1997	Takeover FSL holding 61 per cent stake and FSO holding 70 per cent.
	Czech Republic	Truck	100	1997	Takeover Avia with 50.2 per cent stake.

Source: KERI, *The Automobile Economic Weekly*, 19 September 1995.

Olteit had a joint venture with the French firm Citroën until 1991. Daewoo bought a 51 per cent stake for $158 million in 1994, giving the Republic of Korea the leading place among foreign investors in Romania, outranking the United States and European Union members. Daewoo plans to invest $900 million in the modernisation and expansion of Olteit until the year 2000. The first kit assembly of Daewoo Cielo began in Craiova, Romania, early 1990. The local content is presently only about 15 per cent, to be raised to at least 60 per cent in the coming years. The production is expected to be gradually increased to 150,000 units a year in the first phase. Later the production capacity is envisaged to be raised to 200,000 units, and a second model will be introduced. The Romanian factory is expected to supply motor and gear boxes to the factory in Uzbekistan. About 50 per cent of total production is planned to be exported to other countries in Central and Eastern Europe, and to the European Union.

Another step by Daewoo to penetrate Romania's industrial sector was taken in May 1996, when it signed an agreement to acquire 51 per cent in the 2 Mai shipyard at Mangalia, a major Black Sea port of Romania. It is Romania's second biggest shipyard, with a capacity to build and repair ships of 200,000 deadweight tonnes. Romania has 12 shipyards, and hopes to boost quality and productivity through Daewoo's cooperation. Daewoo has plans to enter into banking, tourism and the rail sectors of Romania.

In Poland, Daewoo has acquired a 70 per cent stake in Fabryka Samochadow Osobowych (FSO) and 51 per cent in FS Lublin with an envisaged total FDI of $1.5 billion until the end of this century. The final amounts for modernisation and development of the Polish outdated plants may be higher. Daewoo has been allowed to import the main components, whereas some European Union firms (such as Fiat which has a production unit in Bielsko Biala) do not have the same privilege.

Daewoo Electronic Manufacturing in Poland produces colour television sets in Proszkow, 40 km away from Warsaw. It is building a factory there to manufacture washing machines, refrigerators and car radios. Furthermore, Daewoo is planning to acquire a stake in banks, build hotels and invest in Polish steel plants as well as the aircraft industry. Some other Korean firms which are active in Poland are Lucky Goldstar Group, Samsung and Hyundai.[a]

---

a   "Auslandsinvestitionen: Ausgangsbasis für Ostmitteleuropa. Südkoreanische Unternehmen ergreifen die Initiative", *Handelsblatt*, 4 June 1996.

**Table III.2. Sectoral distribution of Asian NIEs' selected FDI projects in
Central and Eastern Europe, 1993**

(Number)

Sector/industry	Czech Republic	Hungary	Latvia	Poland	Russian Federation	Slovakia	Ukraine
Raw materials	-	-	-	-	1	-	-
Manufacturing	2	7	2	5	6	1	2
Electronic	2	5	-	4	2	1	2
Leather, footwear	-	-	2	-	2	-	-
Transport equipment	-	1	-	-	1	-	-
Chemicals	-	1	-	-	-	-	-
Aircraft	-	-	-	-	1	-	-
Machinery	-	-	-	1	-	-	-
Services	1	3	1	-	2	2	1
Trade	1	2	-	-	2	2	1
Banking, insurance	-	1	-	-	-	-	-
Telecommunication	-	-	1	-	-	-	-

Source: Kögel and Gälli, 1994.

CONCLUSIONS TO PART ONE

Asia has emerged as a dynamic global investor of equity capital. Its shares of the world's outward FDI stock rose more than that of the European Union, while that of the United States declined. Most of the Asian FDI stock is, of course, owned by Japanese investors. But the greater dynamism in terms of growth has been developed by the Asian developing countries. Three of the NIEs have become net outward investors. Asian developing countries proved to be the major driving force for the recovery of FDI outflows from the FDI-recession in 1991-1992, contributing about two thirds of additional outflows in 1993-1994.

The European Union, though the largest host to FDI in the world, has received so far a very small portion of non-Japanese Asian FDI. Most FDI by the Asian developing countries is still intra-regional, although there is a trend towards a greater geographical dispersion.

Hong Kong is the largest Asian home economy. Its FDI exceeded even that of Japan in 1995, for the third consecutive year. About more than one half of all FDI from Asian developing countries originated in 1995 in Hong Kong.

The Republic of Korea and Malaysia are also fast growing outward investors. Korean FDI is geographically more diversified. Another distinguishing feature of its FDI is that most of it has been undertaken by its big industrial conglomerates which dominate the domestic manufacturing sector. One of them, the car maker Daewoo, has chosen Central and Eastern Europe as the most important stepping stone for accessing European market. Since 1994, Daewoo has acquired control of formerly state-owned car plants in the Czech Republic, Poland and Romania, and of the second biggest shipyard of Romania. Transnational corporations from other Asian developing countries have also recognized the usefulness of Central and Eastern

Europe as a low-cost production base, and as a good platform for relatively unrestricted entry in the European Union internal market of goods. Moreover, local demand for manufactured consumer goods in Central and Eastern Europe is projected to rise strongly, providing further encouragement for them to invest in the region.

Notes

1   "Zentraleuropa - Als kostengünstiger Standort von der weltweiten Autoindustrie geschätzt", *Handelsblatt*, 24 August 1995.

2   Kevin Done, "A drive into the fast lane," *Financial Times*, 28 February 1996.

PART TWO

WHAT DRIVES ASIAN FOREIGN DIRECT INVESTMENT
IN THE EUROPEAN UNION?

Part One has shown that outward foreign direct investment (FDI) from Asian developing economies has been quite dynamic, but that its presence in the European Union and Central and Eastern Europe is relatively low. Developing Asian economies accounted for only 1 per cent of inward FDI flows into the European Union during 1990-1993 (table II.5), and less than 0.2 per cent of gross fixed capital formation there, in 1992-1993. In relation to the Asian presence in terms of exports to Europe, FDI is also relatively low (see chapter VI). Moreover, as Part One shows, Europe accounts for a small proportion of outward FDI flows from Asian economies, with the major part focusing on other Asian economies. In a sense, Asia appears to be "neglecting" Europe in its internationalization process. On the surface, this seems to mirror the neglect of Asia by European transnational corporations (TNCs) (Services of the European Commission and UNCTAD-DTCI, 1996): only 3 per cent of European investment stocks were held in Asia in 1993 ($27 billion), even though Asia is now the world's fastest growing market and the most dynamic base for export production.

However, this picture of "mutual neglect" hides a basic asymmetry: European economies are highly industrialized, and their firms are experienced overseas investors. Asian developing countries are relative newcomers in the industrial and FDI field, with a smaller, narrower base of advantages that they can exploit, and much less knowledge of what international production involves and what it means to operate abroad, let alone in more developed economies. Thus, while it is appropriate to refer to European firms "neglecting" Asia as far as FDI is concerned, Asian firms are beginning to discover Europe. While European firms have failed to build upon a long-standing base in Asia, Asian firms are just at the beginning of their entry into Europe.

Chapter IV reviews explanations for the low FDI presence of Asian investors in Europe. Chapter V analyses why it may be desirable for Asia to raise its FDI in the European Union. Chapter VI examines the relationship between trade and FDI, first to trace the relative export and FDI performance of Asian countries in Europe, and, second, to see what export patterns show for the competitive position of potential Asian investors in Europe. The last section of the chapter looks at the underlying determinants of FDI competitiveness of Asian countries.

WHY IS ASIAN FOREIGN DIRECT INVESTMENT IN EUROPE LOW?

The reasons for Asia's low FDI presence in Europe can be of four types: competitive limitations on the part of Asian firms; their orientation towards destinations other than Europe; constraints to investing in Europe because of regulations or policies in Europe; and constraints to FDI because of home country policies.

A. Competitive limitations of Asian investors

Competing within a domestic market calls for certain competencies, which have to be higher the greater the exposure to import competition or to affiliates of TNCs from more advanced economies. Exporting from the home base may call for an even broader range of competencies, since a firm has to collect new information, as well as has to bear the costs of transporting products and establishing a market presence in an unknown market. Setting up an affiliate abroad, and facing other enterprises on their home ground, carries higher risks and greater costs than both: it involves overcoming higher "transaction costs" because of, among other things, differences in language, culture, laws and regulations, supplier networks and government and business connections.

While, for established TNCs, these difficulties diminish with experience and growth, for relative new-comers they may still be an important handicap. To offset this, investors must possess a competitive edge that enables them to operate profitably as TNCs despite higher transaction costs. This edge has to be more pronounced in host countries that are more advanced than the home country in terms of, e.g., the level of technology, product differentiation, quality standards and more rapidly changing consumer tastes. Thus, for Asian firms to invest in the mature industrial countries in Europe calls for relatively highly developed capabilities, especially where investment involves the setting up of productive or service facilities for which the investor provides technology, management, marketing and other skills. In terms of the "investment development path" theory (Dunning, 1993), which explains the growth of FDI as a function of the relative competitive advantages and location costs of host and home countries, growing outward FDI by Asian economies is driven by the rising advantages of its firms and the locational attractions of Europe.

Where an investment involves buying into existing companies with no transfer of skills or know-how, purchasing real estate, or setting up a marketing branch to handle existing exports, the transaction does not necessarily require special "ownership" or competitive advantages by the investor. However, to the extent that Asian FDI in productive industries is concerned, the competitive base of the investor assumes a vital significance. In this context, perhaps what is surprising is not how little Asian firms invest in European productive sectors but how much. The growth of such FDI in the recent past shows how rapidly the production base of Asian economies has grown, and how some Asian enterprises have reached, even surpassed, world levels of capabilities. Thus, the low level of FDI is less significant than its growth.

However, the kinds of capabilities built up by many Asian enterprises are not always suited to undertaking FDI in (the productive sectors of) Europe. In many cases, their advantages may be much more effectively exploited in countries that are at similar or lower levels of development, such as countries in Asia or other developing regions that have lower wages, simpler industrial structures and comparable levels of technological capability. Clearly, this is the main explanation for the geographical pattern of Asian FDI described in Part One.

The level of development also partly explains the sectoral pattern of Asian FDI in Europe which, to a large extent, takes place in services such as trading (related to exports from Asia), real estate and hotels/restaurants, and does not require highly developed ownership advantages on the part of investors. Of course, some services FDI does require specific competitive capabilities, such as advanced financial or communications activities, and growing Asian FDI of this type reflects the accumulation of the relevant skills and experience. Some of the FDI from Hong Kong and Singapore falls into this category.

Many Asian enterprises that have developed the capability to invest in more advanced economies are relatively new to international investment. They have not yet developed the globalization strategies of more mature TNCs and do not yet view Europe as a potential site for global sourcing in an integrated production strategy, but only, or mainly, as a market to be tapped by setting up a local production presence. To the extent that this is so (and there are emerging signs of globalization in a few of the larger Asian investors), it may be holding back their FDI presence in Europe.

B. Orientation towards other destinations

Asian investment intentions in Europe need to be seen in the context of a realignment in global FDI which generally favours Asia. Clearly this shift is accentuated for Asian TNCs which are now the preponderant investors in developing Asia. Both these facts are reflected in tables IV.1 and IV.2: in particular Europe is placed behind South, East and South-East Asia and North America as a past and future investment target for Asian and non-Asian firms (table IV.1).

There is, of course, some variability in the priority accorded to Europe by Asian firms, depending on origin and industry. Firms from Japan and the Republic of Korea are more interested in Europe than any other Asian firms because of their global orientation.[1] Taiwanese firms are somewhat more orientated towards Asia; Chinese FDI in developed countries has hitherto been concentrated in North America, but it is likely to swing towards Europe over the next few years (chapter II). The same may also be true for ASEAN firms, but at the moment they are concentrating their efforts on other ASEAN countries, China, India and other nearby countries such as Myanmar and Cambodia.

Table IV.1. Geographical investment priorities of firms based in Asia, Western Europe and North America[a]

	Asia		Western Europe		North America	
Destination priority	Past	Future	Past	Future	Past	Future
Western Europe	1.1	1.3	2.6	2.3	2.2	1.9
North America	2.0	1.8	2.0	1.8	2.4	2.1
Japan	0.9	1.0	0.7	0.6	1.0	0.9
South, East and South-East Asia	3.1	3.2	1.5	2.3	1.9	2.3
Latin America	0.6	0.7	0.8	1.2	1.4	2.0
Africa	0.2	0.3	0.2	0.2	0.1	0.2
Central and Eastern Europe	0.6	0.8	1.2	1.7	0.6	1.2

Source: Hatem, 1996.

a   Excludes the country of origin.

Note: This table is based on replies from 260 companies, one third of which were from Asia, including Japan. The responses to this question were scaled from 0 to 4. 0 = low or nil priority. 4 = high priority. The above figures are the simple numerical averages of responses obtained.

Table IV.2. Parent companies' priority regional markets

(Number of responses)

	Japanese (68[a])		European (18[a])		United States (21[a])	
Region	High priority[b]	Medium priority[b]	High priority[b]	Medium priority[b]	High priority[b]	Medium priority[b]
Europe:						
European Union	5	23	8	3	6	6
Eastern Europe	1	4	1	5	1	5
Americas:						
North America	18	25	7	2	14	3
Central and South America	1	9	2	5	4	10
Africa and West Asia:						
West Asia	1	7	1	1	1	4
South Africa	-	4	-	2	-	3
Other Africa	-	4	-	1	-	3
Asia:						
China, Hong Kong and Taiwan Province of China	44	18	6	9	13	7
ASEAN	55	10	9	6	6	8
North East Asia	11	15	2	2	4	4
South Asia	4	21	4	2	3	3
Central Asia	3	8	1	2	1	3

Source: ASEAN Foreign Direct Investment Database.

a   Number of firms responding to question.
b   High priority regions received rankings of "1" or "2"; medium priority regions received rankings of "3" or "4".

The orientation of Asian developing economy FDI towards other economies within the Asian region is a result of much greater familiarity with the business conditions, costs and opportunities within the region. Despite the differences in language, culture and legal systems, operational conditions and problems tend to be similar. In addition, many business communities in various countries, in particular those of Chinese origin, have close personal and cultural ties with each other. The markets are booming. Labour costs are low. Some countries are rich in natural resources. There is a growing liberalization of trade and investment regimes, increasing political commitment to closer regional economic relations and freer flows of products and factors of production, and a growing desire to develop technologies and skills on a regional basis. All these developments are conducive to greater FDI within the region, and reinforce the natural "gravitational" factors that lead outward investors to start with nearer and more familiar locations.

However, even among developed destinations, as Part One has shown, most leading Asian investors have been more inclined to invest in other regions (mainly North America) than in Europe. Although there is increasing interest in investing in Europe, FDI stocks are still clearly biased towards other regions. The reasons for this are partly historical, but also have a strong economic basis.

The historical reasons have to do with the pattern of cultural, political, aid and other linkages with the United States in the period since World War Two. While Europe had long-standing links with many Asian economies in an earlier period, these links had grown weaker by the time the industrial development of the region started. Certainly, Japan and the newly industrializing economies (NIEs) that led the development surge had closer relations with North America than with Europe, and the Korean War strengthened these relations.

The economic reasons are closely related to the historical ones. Particularly much of the expansion of manufactured exports from the Asian NIEs was directed at the United States market, and United States buyers and subcontractors had close relations with Asian firms, making investing in the United States a natural process. Communications were well established, and there were close personal links in terms of Asians living and studying in the United States. Japan's FDI in developed countries also started in the United States and then entered Europe, and the developing Asian economies are following suit. There was perhaps a greater familiarity with the United States way of "doing business"; certainly, there was less diversity of language, culture, legal systems and so on in the United States than in Europe. The European market was, and is, much more fragmented than that of the United States, and the resulting transaction costs (internal costs of transport, communication, currency transfer, conformance to standards and so on) are considerably higher.

These transaction costs are falling as the European market becomes more unified, but they remain relatively high. It is more costly for Asian investors to collect information on local markets, suppliers, laws and regulations, standards, institutions and business practices in Europe (and certainly in Central and Eastern Europe) than in the United States or Asia, and this tends to inhibit FDI, especially by smaller firms.

C. Regulatory constraints to Asian foreign direct investment in the European Union

Apart from the transaction costs of investing in Europe, it is conceivable that constraints posed by European governments to inward investment, both in general and to Asian investments in particular, could explain the low Asian FDI in Europe. But most European governments have liberalized their regulatory frameworks for FDI to a very large extent, with "liberalization" defined as a process, which "includes the avoidance of discriminatory market-distorting measures by tempering or eliminating restrictions on, and special incentives to, TNCs by governments, the establishment of certain positive standards of (equal) treatment and protection of foreign affiliates and the introduction of certain controls and prudent supervision to ensure the proper functioning of the market" (UNCTAD-DTCI, 1994, p. 288). On this basis, the policies of individual European Union countries are quite "liberal", indeed, with only a modicum of impediments to foreign investors. (For recent changes in regulation, see annex table 1.) The large number of incentives available to foreign investors (even though their effects are very limited -- see UNCTAD-DTCI, 1996b) underlines that the main objective of national governments is to create a favourable investment climate.

Nevertheless, some impediments to investment exist. They include restrictions on investment and also relate to standards of treatment. In terms of the former (and underlining again their limited importance) the chief impediments that remain relate mainly to:

- In some countries, inward FDI is subject to notification or authorization (Belgium, France and Spain), due to specific circumstances involving legal, safety or health considerations.

- Management-participation requirements in Scandinavian countries, Switzerland and, to a lesser extent, Italy. In these countries, management-participation requirements (normally, that foreign firms must employ a preponderance of local or European Union citizens) are quite restrictive and can constitute a significant barrier to foreign entry.

- Sectoral restrictions are found mostly in the services sector and natural resources (table IV.3). In a number of industries foreign investors have limited access (e.g., because of ceilings or performance requirements), entry is granted on a reciprocity basis, or no FDI is permitted. Many of the restricted sectors (road and rail transport, energy, water, gas or electricity distribution) are not important for Asian investors at this time, though they may be in the future. In others, such as finance and telecommunications, Asian enterprises have invested in the European Union in spite of restrictions; for these investors problems may arise from the European Union or national competition policies and regulations regarding mergers and acquisitions (Agarwal et al., 1994, pp. 298-301). However, these regulatory measures are so far not great hindrance to FDI since Asian investments are generally for market access.

- Other impediments in the manufacturing sector include:

  - requirements for foreign investors (usually in electronics and automobiles) to comply with "voluntary" local content requirements;

- different manufacturing and consumer standards between European Union member countries, although these are being ameliorated by single-market-related measures;
- access to European Union/national research-and-development programmes, although not precluded, is sometimes difficult for foreign companies;
- differences in the extent and openness of government procurement which is likely to be of some importance in telecommunications and construction; and
- trade between Eastern and Western Europe faces some restrictions, which may deter Asian investors that wish to locate their production facilities in Central and Eastern Europe with a view to selling in Western European markets.
- Obstacles are also posed by the complexity of visa requirements and residence permits for expatriate personnel. The latter are particularly problematic for South-East and South Asian business people who wish to travel to a number of European countries. Additional obstacles include the limited availability of good quality, cheap labour with the skills necessary to interact with Asian business people. Land costs, the need to find partners, and a general limited European awareness of developments in Asia and the concomitant dismissal of Asian practices and potentialities by European business all pose problems for Asian investors interested in establishing themselves in Europe.

Once established, foreign affiliates are accorded genuine national treatment,[2] and Asian investors do not face any discriminatory treatment. This is backed by a network of bilateral double-taxation agreements and, in a few countries, "unilateral" tax-credit facilities. It is worth mentioning that, although most European countries have double-taxation treaties with Asian economies, there are some gaps. Only the United Kingdom has treaties with all 10 ASEM Asian economies (European Commission and UNCTAD-DTCI, 1996, table III.1). Brunei Darussalam and Viet Nam are usually not treaty partners; and two countries (Portugal and Greece) do not have treaties with any of the ASEM partner countries.

Policies related to inward FDI are generally the purview of national governments, rather than the European Union as a whole, although they increasingly have to comply with European Union directives affecting inward FDI policy (e.g., the directives on parent-subsidiary taxation, cross-border mergers and the harmonisation of exchange controls). One particular issue concerns intra-European competition as regards certain rules and policies, which can be problematic from both a national (e.g., because of the cost of incentives) and a corporate (e.g., because of consequent difficulties in operating across Europe) perspective. Some of these difficulties could diminish if there were more of a European Union-wide approach towards FDI, which would reduce or eliminate any overlapping or diverging policies that may exist (tables IV.4 and IV.5). From the point of view of Asian and other foreign investors, such a policy would be beneficial because it would increase European Union-wide transparency in laws, regulations and administrative practices and, thereby, reduce transaction costs.

Table IV.3. Sectoral restrictions[a] on FDI in the European Union, 1992

Country	Banking	Insurance	Radio broad-casting	Telecom-munica-tion post & telephone services	Road	Rail	Air	Maritime	Mining	Oil and/or gas	Fishing and fish processing	Real estate	Tourists	Audio visual work (incl. film film distribution)	Publishing	Public utilities (incl. energy water, gas, electricity distribution)	Gambling, casiono, lottos and lotteries, etc.
Belgium	R	R		L	C	C	L	L		C	L	L	R	C			
Denmark	R	R		L	C	C	L	L			L					C	
France	LR	LR	L	L	R	C	L	L	L	R	L[a]		R	R	LR	L	L
Germany	LR	LR	L	L	C	C	LR	L[a]	L								C
Greece	LR	LR	L	C	C	C	C	L	L	C	L	L	R			C	C
Ireland	LR	LR	C	C		C	C	LR			C					C	
Italy	LR	LR		C	C	C	LR	L	R		L		R			C	C
Luxembourg		L	C	C	L	L	L									C	
Netherlands	LR	L	L	L	C	C	L	L			L					C	
Portugal	LR	L	L	C		C	C	R				L				C	
Spain	R	R	L	L	C	C	L	L								C	
United Kingdom	R	R	L	L	C	C	L	L	L		L		L			C	L

Source: OECD, 1992.

a   This table covers mainly measures related to establishment that are regarded as restrictions in the sense of the OECD Code of Liberalisation of Capital Movement and not covered by the general authorization procedures. If there are no restrictions, cells are left blank.

Key   :   L=Limited;   R=Reciprocity;   C=Closed (including monopolies).

Table IV.4. The business environment for foreign investors in the European Union and Switzerland

Country	Restrictions on form of business organisation	Exchange controls	Local participation or management requirements	Availability of general incentives (e.g., grants, subsidies, loan guarantees).
Austria	No restrictions.	No restrictions.	No restrictions.	Wide variety available at federal, provincial and municipal levels.
Belgium	No restrictions.	No restrictions.	No restrictions.	Wide variety available.
Denmark	No restrictions.	Some restrictions (minimal).	All managers and at least a half of the directors of a Danish registered company must reside in the EU or be EU nationals resident in other member states (an exemption is possible). There is a similar, less restrictive, rule for branches.	Some
Finland	No restrictions.	Authorised bank must be used.	The managing director and at least a half of the founders and members of the board of directors of a limited liability company must be citizens of the Nordic countries or of other countries of the EEA (an exemption is possible). The manager of a branch must reside in Finland.	Some
France	No restrictions.	Some FDI has to be declared to the authorities.	No restrictions.	Wide variety available.
Germany	No restrictions, except for investments near Greece's frontiers.	Some reporting requirements.	No restrictions.	A wide variety including a number of incentives for the eastern states, including higher financing guarantees, grants, subsidies and financing of public programmes.
Greece		No restrictions, but repatriation of profits must be made via Greek Banks.	A few exceptions.	A wide variety of incentives which may be combined in specified ways.
Ireland	No restrictions.	No restrictions.	No restrictions.	Some incentives.
Italy	No restrictions.	Some reporting requirements.	A few exceptions.	Wide variety available.
Luxembourg	No restrictions.	No restrictions.	No restrictions.	Some incentives.
Netherlands	No restrictions.	No restrictions, but capital movement must be through an authorized Dutch institution.	No restrictions.	Wide variety available.
Portugal	No restrictions.	Some reporting requirements.	No restrictions.	Wide variety available.
Spain	No restrictions.	Some verification requirements.	No restrictions	Wide variety available.
Sweden	No restrictions.	No restrictions, but capital movement must be through an authorised Swedish institution.	Foreign citizens have to register their business with the Patent and Registration Office. A foreign business' representative must be resident in Sweden, as must the managing director and at least half of the directors of a corporation. Residents of the EEA can be managing directors or directors.	Wide variety available.
Switzerland	No restrictions.	No restrictions.	The majority of a corporation's board of directors must be Swiss citizens. The directors must hold at least one share.	Some
United Kingdom	No restrictions.	No restrictions.	No restrictions.	Some

Sources: UNCTAD, based principally on data supplied by Deloitte Touche Tohmatsu International, Arthur Andersen and Deutsche Morgan Grenfell and annex table 5.

Table IV.5. Incentives in the European Union and Switzerland

Country	Tax incentives available	Eligibility for incentives	Taxation of resident entities	Double taxation treaties with Asian countries
Austria	Some	Technology content, job creation, regional location in Austria.	As for Austrian firms on worldwide income, subject to double tax treaties.	China, India, Japan, Pakistan, Republic of Korea, all ASEAN except Brunei Darussalam, Singapore and Viet Nam.
Belgium	Some	Variable, e.g. for SMEs, distribution centres.	As for Belgian firms, but special rules for, for example, companies located in tax havens, conduit companies, investment companies. Different treatment of branches and subsidiaries.	China, India, Japan, Pakistan, Repubic of Korea, Sri Lanka, all ASEAN except Brunei Darussalam and Viet Nam.
Denmark	Some	Regional location in Denmark, R&D, exports.	Different for branches and subsidiaries, based on world-wide rates for the latter, subject to double tax treaties.	China, India, Japan, Republic of Korea, Sri Lanka, all ASEAN except Brunei Darussalam and Viet Nam.
Finland	None	Regional location in Finland, R&D, training.	Different for branches and subsidiaries, based on world-wide rates for the latter, subject to double tax treaties.	China, India, Japan, Republic of Korea, Sri Lanka, all ASEAN except Brunei Darussalam and Viet Nam.
France	Various. For example, the headquarters of a foreign international group of companies may receive favourable tax treatment under certain circumstances. French based companies whose activity is exclusively in holding participation interests in foreign companies get special treatment.	Regional location in France, high technology industries, exports and training.	As for French companies, subject to double tax treaties. Branches and subsidiaries are treated the same. With official permission profits and losses of foreign operations can be included in taxable profits.	Bangladesh, China, India, Japan, Pakistan, Republic of Korea, Sri Lanka, all ASEAN except Brunei Darussalam.
Germany	Some. In the eastern states there are special depreciation rates, real estate valuations are lower and special provisions for newly constructed housing and municipal trade tax...	Development of the eastern states, R&D in new technologies, product innovation, environ-mental protection, training for the disadvantaged, exports.	As for German companies on worldwide income, subject to double tax treaties.	Bangladesh, China, India, Japan, Pakistan, Repubic of Korea, Sri Lanka, all ASEAN except Brunei Darussalam and Viet Nam.
Greece	A wide variety of incentives which may be combined in specified ways.	Manufacturing enterprises, tourism, software development and advanced technologies, business plans and Law 89 offices (branches established in Greece solely for administration purposes).	As for Greek companies on worldwide income, subject to double tax treaties, but complicated by many types of incentives/entities.	India. None of the ASEM Asian countries.
Ireland	A wide variety, including a total exemption from tax on patent royalties (in combina-tion with tax treaties).	Manufacturing and financial enterprises, including mutual funds for non-residents.	As for Irish companies on worldwide income, subject to double tax treaties.	Japan, Pakistan, Republic of Korea.

/...

(Table IV.5, cont'd)

Country	Tax incentives available	Eligibility for incentives	Taxation of resident entities	Double taxation treaties with Asian countries
Italy	A wide variety of tax incentives.	Regional location in Italy, new businesses, new employment	As for Italian companies on worldwide income, subject to double tax treaties. Taxes abroad are liable against Italian tax payable. Branches and subsidiaries are broadly treated the same.	China, India, Japan, Republic of Korea, Pakistan, all ASEAN except Brunei Darussalam, Indonesia and Vietnam.
Luxembourg	A wide variety of tax incentives.	Holding companies, collective investment, coordination companies, reinsurance companies.	As Luxembourg copmanies on worldwide income, subject to double tax treaties. A credit can be received for foreign taxes which can be offset against local tax paid. Branches and subsidiaries are treated differently.	China, Japan, Republic of Korea, Indonesia.
Netherlands	Some, for small-scale investments.	Regional location in the Netherlands, research and innovation, education and training.	As Dutch companies on worldwide income, subject to double tax treaties. Foreign income is normally exempted.	China, Japan, Republic of Korea, all ASEAN except Brunei Darussalam and Viet Nam..
Portugal	A wide variety of tax incentives, extra provision in Madeira.	Regional location in Portugal, exports, industrial sector, energy, venture capital companies, tourism.	As Portuguese companies on worldwide income, subject to tax treaties. Foreign income can be set off against Portuguese corporate tax.	None of the ASEM Asian countries.
Spain	Some	Regional location in Spain, SMEs.	As Spanish companies on worldwide income, subject to tax treaties. Foreign income can be set off against Spanish corporate tax.	China, Japan, Republic of Korea, Philippines.
Sweden	Wide variety available.	Regional location in Sweden, R&D, training.	As Swedish companies. There are numerous double tax treaties; even in their absence the unilateral tax credit facilitates the avoidance of double taxation.	Bangladesh, China, India, Japan, Pakistan, Republic of Korea, Sri Lanka, all ASEAN except Brunei Darussalam.
Switzerland	Some, mainly by cantons.	New enterprises, management services, international coor-dinating activities, interna-tional headquarters operations.	As Swiss companies on their worldwide income, excluding income from a foreign permanent establishment or foreign real estate. The Direct Federal Tax Law (promulgated on 1 January 1995) requires the cantons to harmonise their tax laws by 2001.	China, Japan, Republic of Korea, Indonesia, Malaysia, Singapore.
United Kingdom	Some	Regional location in the UK, new technology, major projects in the national interest.	As UK companies on their worldwide income, subject to double taxation treaties.	Pakistan, Republic of Korea, Sri Lanka, all ASEAN countries.

Sources: UNCTAD, based principally on data supplied by Deloitte Touche Tohmatsu International, Arthur Andersen and Deutsche Morgan Grenfell and annex table 5.

Note: Incentives are normally available to both domestic and foreign companies.

D. Asian restrictions on outward foreign direct investment

Asian economies' policies towards outward FDI vary widely in scope and structure (annex table 2). This reflects considerable differences in terms of levels of development, factor endowments and national objectives. Any analysis of these policies is best undertaken by dividing these countries into three groups: Japan, the NIEs and other Asia.

Japanese policies towards outward investment are now higly liberal. Only financial institutions require authorization for overseas investment; some restrictions on overseas involvement apply to companies involved in the fishing, leather and pearl-culture industries. Beyond this, the Government's stance is one of support for outward investment. This includes generous provision of information services and technical assistance, financial assistance and insurance (table IV.6); in addition, there are special provisions for small and medium-sized enterprises. A number of Japanese organizations are involved in providing this support, especially the Export-Import Bank of Japan (EXIM), the Japan Overseas Development Corporation (JODC) and the Japan External Trade Organisation (JETRO).

The NIEs also permit and, to a certain extent, facilitate, outward FDI to various degrees, depending on their level of development, industrial structure and policy stance (for a detailed example, see box 13) (UNCTAD-DTCI, 1995). In the case of the Republic of Korea, for example, the liberalization of outward FDI policies is fairly advanced (UNCTAD-DTCI, 1995); the adoption of a "negative list" system in 1994 means that outward FDI is restricted in only a few business areas. The chaebols' competitiveness in industries like automobiles, shipbuilding, electronics and petrochemicals has meant that they have invested heavily overseas;[3] Korean small and medium-sized enterprises mainly invest in South-East Asia and would need considerable support in order to orient their activities to Europe (Shin, 1996). Recently, however, the Government of the Republic of Korea adopted legislation to limit foreign borrowing by its large TNCs, in response to a sharp rise of Korean outward FDI after the relaxation of foreign financing in September 1992, accompanied by a rise in foreign debt. Wishing to avert a rapid growth of such debt, the Government introduced ceilings on foreign loans. The new rules require firms to finance at least 20 per cent of their foreign investments with domestic funds; the rules also limit payment guarantees by parent companies to the value of their total net worth. Old investments were not affected by these rules.

Most other developing Asian economies permit outward FDI within the context of their national objectives and resource availability.[4] In a number of cases, policies are codified in specific rules and regulations, as in China, in the "Provisional regulation for approval procedures and administration of non-trade related outward FDI" of 1985, the "Administration of foreign exchange for outward investment" of 1989 and the "Approval procedures and administration of overseas investment" adopted in 1993 (box 14) (UNCTAD-DTCI, 1995). In other cases, policies are in the process of being generated or implemented. In order to help Thai investors, for example, the Thai Board of Investment (BOI), chaired by the Prime Minister, has recently approved a proposal to establish the Thailand Overseas Investment Promotion Board (TOIPB), chaired by the Prime Minister. The TOIPB is intended to promote overseas investment through tax, financial, technical and legal strategies. Although there is no formal

Table IV.6. Overseas investment-assistance measures in Japan

Taxation system	Finance	Investment insurance guarantee	Subsidies for training and survey expenses	Information services
1. Reserve for Overseas Investment loss/ Special Taxation Measures to compensate for Risk of Investment in LDCs (inclusion of a fixed percentage of the investment/ loan amount (set aside as reserve) for an overseas subsidiary in the loss account)	1. Export-Import Bank of Japan: - Provision of long term finance for overseas investment by Japanese enterprises - Capital investment in joint ventures involving Japanese enterprises	1. Overseas Investment Insurance: i. Eligible Investment (1) Acquisition of shares, etc. (2) Acquisition of claims pertaining to long-term loans to a foreign corporation whose management is substantially controlled by a Japanese corporation (3) Acquisition of rights related to real estate etc. (4) Assumption of surety obligation pertaining to long-term debts incurred a foreign corporation whose management is substantially controlled by a Japanese corporation ii. Percentage of Indemnity (1) Political risks (war, expropriation and transfer): 95% (2) Commercial risk (bankruptcy): 40%	1. Training scheme for foreign engineers (mainly from the private sector) (75% government subsidy provided for the AOTS)	- Japan External Trade Organization (JETRO) - Asia Technology Cooperation Association - Institute of Developing Economies (IDE) - The Association for Overseas Technical Scholarship (AOTS) - Overseas Fishery Cooperative Foundation (OFCF) - Overseas Economic Cooperation Fund (OECF)
2. Allowances for Foreign Taxation (elimination of international dual taxation): - Direct deduction of the amount paid in foreign taxes by overseas branches from the corporation tax payable in Japan - Deduction of the dividend tax and others among the foreign tax paid by an overseas subsidiary from the corporation tax payable in Japan - Tax spacing credit	2. Overseas Economic Cooperation Fund: - Capital investment or loans for projects of Japanese private enterprises in LDCs (economic cooperation projects	2. Overseas United Loan Insurance: i. Eligible Investment (1) Acquisition of claims pertaining to long-term loans to foreign governments or foreign corporations (excluding a corporation whose management is substantially controlled by a Japanese corporation) (2) Assumption of surety obligation pertaining to long-term debts incurred by foreign governments or foreign corporations (excluding a corporation whose management is substantially controlled by a Japanese corporation)	2. Commissioning of private organizations to conduct studies on overseas investment-related issues	- Japan Overseas Educational Services - Japan Overseas Development Corporation (JODC) - Overseas Japanese Medical Fund - Metal Mining Agency of Japan (MMAJ) - International Development Center of Japan - Japan International Cooperation Agency (JICA) - International Consulting Services Association - The Japan Commercial Arbitration Association
3. Transfer Price Taxation System: - Special taxation arrangements concerning trade with related businesses overseas - Special income tax arrangements for specified subsidiary abroad	3. Japan Overseas Development Corporation: - Cooperation Fund for Overseas Investment by Small Businesses	ii. Percentage of indemnity (1) Political risks (war, expropriation, transfer, etc.) 97.5% (when contributing to the reflux of capital) 95% (general case) (2) Commercial risks (bankruptcy and delay of six months or more in the performance of obligations) 90% (other than bonds) 40% (bonds)	3. Surveys by the MITI on the overseas business activities of Japanese enterprises	- People's Finance Corporation - Shoko Chukin Bank (Bank of Commerce and Industrial Cooperatives) - Japan National Oil Corporation (JNOC) - Small Business Finance Corporation - Japan Small Business Corporation - Japan International Development Organization Ltd. (JAIDO)
4. Overseas Contribution Taxation System: Special loss account for a parent company which makes donations to the activities of its overseas subsidiaries to contribute to the interests of the host country	4. Japan International Cooperation Agency: - Loans for projects of Japanese private enterprises in LDCs	3. Insurance System of Export-Import Bank of Japan: (1) Guarantee of debt service for loans of Japanese financial institutions for overseas investment (capital investment, loans and direct investment projects etc.) (2) Guarantee of debt service for loans of Japanese financial institutions for overseas subsidiaries, joint ventures and joint-venture partners (foreign governments and government organizations, etc.) (3) Coverage of guarantee provided by Japanese enterprises for debt service for loans taken out by invested companies		- Japan Overseas Enterprises Association (JOEA) - The Japan Chamber of Commerce and Industry (JCCI) - Japan Productivity Center - Japan Consulting Institute - The Export-Import Bank of Japan (JEXIM) - Institute for International Studies and Training (IIST) (Note: Investment guidance, finance, training and seminars, etc. are also provided.)
	5. Small Business Finance Corporation; People's Finance Corporation; Central Bank for Commercial and Industrial Cooperatives (Shoko Chukin Bank): - Loans for foreign direct investment overseas by small businesses	4. Bilateral Investment Protection Agreements: - with Egypt: 1977 - with Sri Lanka: 1982 - with China: 1988 - with Turkey: 1992		

Source: MITI, 1994.

Box 13. The experience of Taiwan Province of China

Four stages mark the development of the outward FDI policy of Taiwan Province of China. Although the first recorded case of outward FDI (for a cement plant in Malaysia) occurred in 1959, the first official policy statement was promulgated in 1962 as "Regulations governing the screening and handling of outward investment and outward technical cooperation projects." Subsequently revised four times, this regulation remains the main policy instrument governing outward FDI. Its initial content and application was strict, setting rigid financial requirements for approval, including specified paid-in capital levels, low debt/equity ratios, and substantial recent net profit performance. These criteria essentially aimed at keeping most investment capital at home to develop the island s economy. In fact, only 123 outward FDI projects valued at under a total $50 million occurred between 1962-1978 (Taiwan Province of China, economic affairs authorities, 1993).

A second stage, from 1979-1984, was characterized by active promotion of outward FDI, motivated by a desire to secure natural resources for industrial use in the face of the energy crisis and global recession. The paid-in capital and debt/equity ratio requirements were relaxed and reinvestment restrictions were loosened. A 1979 "Statute for encouragement of investment" authorized a five-year tax-exemption for outward FDI solely in extractive industries involved in shipping natural resource products back to Taiwan Province of China. Fifty outward FDI projects worth a total of $84 million materialized during this period (Taiwan Province of China, economic affairs authorities, 1993).

The third stage, from mid-1984-1986, expanded promotional efforts, particularly to take advantage of the Caribbean Basin Initiative. The paid-in capital requirement was again cut, and the extractive industry tax incentive was broadened to incorporate similar projects by non-extractive firms. The same tax incentive was now also offered to FDI projects engaged in processing and selling agricultural or industrial raw materials products; transferring specifically identified technologies, and other identified product sales by enterprises. In addition, the Export-Import Bank initiated outward investment insurance and provided loans up to 70 per cent of the firm s aproved outward investment. Foreign direct investment facilitation services were also begun by an Industrial Development and Investment Center to organize and provide information and seminars for and about Taiwanese manufacturers interested in FDI. This three-year period recorded 77 outward investments totaling over $137 million (Taiwan Province of China, economic affairs authorities, 1993).

Finally, the fourth stage began in mid-1987 when the administration relaxed its foreign exchange controls and further revised the outward FDI regulations. Total capital stock requirements were eased and applications for most outward FDI projects under $5 million were simplified and accelerated. Approved projects are required to meet one of the following conditions considered to meet national interest criteria:

- acquiring needed natural resources or component parts for domestic industries;
- improving regional trade imbalances or maintain markets for domestic products;
- inducing imports of technical management or production know-how;
- supporting technical cooperation without harming national security or domestic industries;
- promoting international economic cooperation;
- assisting domestic industrial restructuring and product-quality upgrading; and
- indirectly transferring technology to the island through venture-capital operations.

Current (1996) outward investment-assistance measures include: publishing about 170 pamphlets to introduce investment climates of 42 countries to companies that are interested in investment abroad; establishing a data bank to provide essential information on joint ventures; rendering assistance in organizing missions to investigate the investment environment in foreign countries; helping outward investors from Taiwan Province of China to organize associations for mutual assistance; setting up Chinese schools in host countries; allowing 20 per cent investment credit for

/...

(Box 13, cont'd.)

approved outward investors through the Export-Import Bank; permitting remittance of foreign exchange earnings derived from overseas investments or technical cooperation projects back into the economy; consigning Taiwanese overseas offices to render necessary services to outward investors; and negotiating investment guarantee and double taxation agreements. As of the end of 1995, Singapore, Indonesia, the Philippines, Malaysia, Viet Nam, Thailand and nine other countries had signed investment guarantee agreements with Taiwan Province of China.

Two new things are worthy of mentioning among the latest assistance measures for outward investment from Taiwan Province of China. First, the Industrial Park Development Program assists Taiwanese investors in procuring land for the establishment of factories at cost in developing countries, with the aim of encouraging the investors to establish manufacturing bases in those countries. Taiwanese investors' factories and local small and medium-sized enterprises may get assistance in such fields as the procurement of parts, production, management, financing and technology transfer. Partnership between Taiwanese investors and local small and medium-sized enterprises will substantially increase the possibility of development of small and medium-sized enterprises in developing countries. Second, the Overseas Young Entrepreneur Training Program provides youth in developing countries with good opportunities for learning the industrial and managerial skills necessary for the setting-up, and successfully running small or medium businesses in their home countries. The Program is extected to upgrade the utilization of human resources, enhance the industrial development of developing countries, and strengthen private-sector interaction between Taiwan Province of China and recipient countries.

These changes and measures have contributed to record FDI outflows, with more than 2,000 approved projects valued at close to $8.9 billion by 1994 (Taiwan Province of China, Investment Commission, 1995).

Source: UNCTAD-DTCI, 1995, pp. 326-327 and information provided by Industrial Development and Investment Center in Taiwan Province of China.

Box 14. The experience of China

In spite of a number of concerns with respect to outward investment -- especially concerning excessive capital outflows at the expense of domestic investment; the perception that outward FDI did not contribute as much to national development as domestic investment; and the perception that Chinese companies lacked the experience necessary to operate effectively in international markets -- the Government of China began to allow outward FDI in 1979, as part of its broader "open policy." Outward investment was viewed as an important means of integrating China into the world economy, securing a stable supply of raw materials, improving export opportunities and strengthening economic relations with neighbouring countries. But because of its concerns, the Government s approach towards outward FDI was cautious. Specifically, it favoured investments in kind (equipment, know-how and manufacturing materials) to avoid excessive capital outflows. It also encouraged outward investments that would generate benefits for the domestic economy, such as resource and market seeking FDI.

Since the initial reforms were implemented in 1979, the approval process has been gradually liberalized. Prior to 1983, when the Ministry of Foreign Trade and Economic Cooperation (MOFTEC) became the focal point for the screening of outward FDI, the authority for approval of all outward FDI projects was highly centralized. After 1983, all projects remained subject to screening, but smaller projects and projects with Chinese equity in kind were subjected to less strenuous screening procedures. In addition, many investment projects simply escaped the screening process. Finally, the screening process is largely limited to original investments and, therefore, reinvested earnings by Chinese foreign affiliates that have passed the original screening process are usually not subject to subsequent further screening. Liberalization measures were codified in the "Provisional regulation for approval procedures and

/...

(Box 14, cont'd.)

administration of non-trade related outward FDI" of 1985, the "Administration of foreign exchange for outward investment" of 1989 and the "Approval procedures and administration of overseas investment" adopted in 1993.

The regulatory regime and approval process governing outward FDI involves different levels of government, depending upon the type, scale and location of investments being proposed. These include local authorities, MOFTEC, the State Planning Commission, the State Council, the Ministry of Finance, the Administration of State Assets and the State Foreign Exchange Administration. Projects worth more than $30 million are still subject to approval by the State Council. Projects valued between $1 million and $30 million, as well as projects involving government loans, or guarantees for foreign loans require the submission of a feasibility study to the State Planning Commission and the details of the project to MOFTEC. Projects valued under $1 million are approved by the Commission of Foreign Trade and Economic Cooperation or by the ministries responsible for the prospective investor.

In addition to this gradual liberalization of China s outward FDI regime, the Government started to promote some types of outward FDI beginning in the late 1980s. In general, all foreign affiliaes have been exempted from taxes for the first five years of their existence. After this period, foreign affiliates pay taxes on earnings of 20 per cent. In addition to these general incentives, the Government also started to promote outward FDI projects that could serve specific objectives. These included:

- channelling advanced technology and equipment back to China;
- securing stable sources of raw materials that cannot be sourced or are scarce in China;
- contributing to foreign exchange earnings and generating export opportunities;
- contributing to stronger economic ties with neighbouring countries and countries included in China development assistance programmes.

The methods by which the Government has promoted the above-mentioned types of outward FDI have included tax incentives, subsidies, national bank loans with preferential terms, and better access to the domestic market for goods produced by Chinese foreign affiliates.

The Government has also sought to link official development assistance (ODA) to FDI. It has done so by encouraging recipient governments to use ODA loans to attract Chinese investment in existing projects and by using ODA funds to establish joint ventures involving Chinese companies. Since 1991, ODA-related outward FDI projects have been established in a number of developing countries, especially in Africa. If prospective investors in the electronics and machinery industries plan to make their investments in kind, they are exempted from paying a "security deposit" (5 per cent of the value of the proposed investment) to the Government, and if proposed investments in these sectors are less than $1 million, they are exempted from the approval process.

The Government of China has also promoted FDI to Hong Kong. For example, in 1986 the China International Trust and Investment Corporation (CITIC) acquired the Ka Wah Bank, and China Merchants Holdings Ltd. acquired Union Bank. Other major investments in Hong Kong by Chinese companies have included the Bank of China Building ($130 million), the second harbour tunnel ($390 million), and the partial take-over of Cathay Pacific Airline by CITIC (a 12.5 per cent stake for $260 million).

While the general trend during the 1980s and the early 1990s has been a gradual liberalization of China s outward FDI regime, concern over the lack of government control beyond the initial screening process and the poor performance of some Chinese foreign affiliates have motivated the Government to strengthen its post-approval monitoring capabilities. However, this is not likely to decrease Chinese outward FDI significantly in the long term (although it may have a short-term dampening effect), given the Government s commitment to the ongoing internationalization of the Chinese economy and the important role that Chinese TNCs have played in this process since 1979.

Source: UNCTAD-DTCI, 1995, pp. 329-330.

legislation on outward investment, the amount of capital which can be remitted overseas is capped at $10 million; but approval for amounts above this can be received from the Bank of Thailand. The importance attached to outward FDI is indicated by the fact that ministers of Commerce and Industry, as well as the Secretary General of the BOI and the Presidents of the Federation of Thai Industries and the Thai Chamber of Commerce, are on the TOIPB Board.

Moreover, policies in some Asian developing economies towards outward FDI encourage intraregional FDI. Partly this is motivated by a strategy of tandem economic development among the countries of the region, partly by the limited availability of capital and foreign exchange (outward FDI in less developed economies does not require convertible foreign exchange to the same extent as FDI in developed economies) (Altomonte et al., 1996).

To conclude, three main limitations remain as far as outward FDI policies of Asian economies are concerned.

- First, a number of countries have only partially liberalized their outward FDI policies. To the extent that this limits opportunities for their enterprises to increase their competitiveness in international markets, governments may need to review their approach in this area.

- Second, support for outward FDI is generally modest. While Japan and the Republic of Korea have Export-Import banks and other organizations to support outward FDI, similar support in the other countries is not necessarily available and, if there is, the degree of such support varies from country to country.

- Third, support is seldom targeted to Europe.

Overall, however, the trend is clearly in the direction of liberalizing outward FDI policies, which puts firms into a position to explore and exploit investment opportunities abroad -- in the region, in Europe and in the rest of the world.

Notes

[1] From the Japanese TNCs' point of view, however, Europe is given a medium priority (table IV.2).

[2] Branches are usually treated differently because they do not have a separate legal identity from the parent company.

[3] "Good breeding", *The Economist*, 18 May 1995; "Do or die", *Far Eastern Economic Review*, 13 June 1995.

[4] Foreign exchange need not be a hindrance to FDI. Chinese TNCs, for example, often establish themselves in Hong Kong in order to garner capital resources for internationl investments. For a discussion of foreign-exchange contraints and outward FDI, see Altomonte et al., 1996.

Chapter V

WHY ASIA SHOULD INVEST IN EUROPE

A. Introduction

The growth of FDI by Asian economies is essentially a manifestation of their economic dynamism and the competitiveness of their firms. Most of these economies have enhanced their economic performance at historically unprecedented rates over the past three decades, a growth led mainly by exports of manufactured products. However, as earlier with more developed economies, the expansion of exports from Asia is being followed by the growth of outward investment. Exports and investment are largely complementary means of exploiting a growing competitive base. While the setting up of production facilities abroad can reduce the exports of the particular products from the home country, it can also lead to the upgrading of the production and export structure and add to overall export capacity, in some cases, the absence of FDI may even cause the loss of exports. Beyond that, FDI allows production to be located more efficiently than when confined to one economy, a vital consideration in a globalizing world economy; it allows producers to gear products more closely and quickly to changing consumer preferences in foreign markets; it enables them to tap into the base of skills and knowledge in host economies, especially when host countries have more advanced innovative capabilities than the home economy; it can help to deal with protectionist sentiment; it provides an avenue for investible resources to be allocated productively over a much broader area than if it were confined to the domestic economy; and it lets the home country, and its enterprises, behave more rationally in terms of diversifying their asset portfolio, distributing investments over a broader range of countries.

To quote the *World Investment Report 1995* (UNCTAD-DTCI, 1995, pp. 128-131):

"Foreign direct investment has become not only a means to access markets for final output, but also a means to access factors of production, particularly created assets, with a view to organising production internationally. Corporate executives are increasingly aware of the contribution of a portfolio of locational assets for their competitiveness ... Having access to foreign factors of production and, at the same time, being able to organise production internationally, has a number of advantages that bolster TNC competitiveness:

• Cost savings are achieved through the internationalization of activities within a TNC system where this allows members of the system *privileged access* to the firm's proprietary resources; the benefits of reduced transaction costs as compared to those of arm's length international transactions; better resource allocation and specialization; an intra-firm international division of labour; and economics of scale and scope.

- *Advantageous access* of foreign affiliates, through backward linkages, to a wider pool of assets and experience.

- A larger financial resource base due to access to larger markets.

- Resilience to shocks — for example, changes in exchange rates or cyclical conditions — is increased by the cross-border diversification of locational assets and the advantages of being active internationally through more than one modality.

Apart from the positive benefits achieved in these ways and from the interaction between them, an additional benefit may occur by pre-empting rival firms from access to the same assets....

In established industries and products in which competition is regional or global and the major competitors are well defined, the existence or the potential availability of locational assets makes the establishment of foreign affiliates a crucial component of the firm's ability to maintain competitiveness. For both small and large firms, and regardless of whether they are headquartered in large or small, developed or developing, countries, FDI can therefore contribute centrally to competitiveness."

All this underlines that, in today's world economy, outward FDI is an option that firms need to consider to maintain their competitiveness, and countries need to consider allowing to maintain a cohort of viable, internationally competitive enterprises.

B. Why invest in Europe?

The case for outward investment as an integral element of long-term growth and competitiveness is now widely accepted by Asian governments. What, however, are the reasons for seeking to invest in particular in Europe? There are several, some of immediate significance, others of a more long-term nature.

- *Market size and sophistication.* The sheer size of the European market is illustrated in table V.1, which shows total and per capita GDP in Asia and the European Union, as well as the three leading Central and Eastern Europe countries (the Czech Republic, Hungary and Poland). If Japan is excluded, Asia's market size in 1993 is only 28 per cent of that of the European Union. It is vital for any region with growth ambitions, especially Asian economies with their high dependence on exports to developed countries, to have a strong market presence in the latter region.

- Quite apart from this, the sophistication and differentiation of the European market offers a great stimulus to the competitiveness and upgrading of firms operating there. The average consumer in Europe is highly discriminating and demanding; tastes are highly fashion-conscious and change rapidly; and there are considerable differences in buying patterns and preferences between countries. This has two implications for Asian enterprises: first, having a direct manufacturing presence in the market may often be a necessary condition for competing in certain consumer products; second, exposure to a highly sophisticated market can itself be advantageous since it promotes design, quality, marketing and other capabilities that sharpen competitiveness.

- *Access to technology*. Setting up production facilities in Europe can provide access to a technology base that is important, as indicated by relatively higher research-and-development expenditures (table V.2). Small technology-based firms could be acquired by Asian investors (as did Korean and Taiwanese firms in the United States) (Hobday, 1995); and technology-based joint ventures and strategic alliances could be setup. Even if no direct link is established with local firms, simply placing manufacturing facilities in areas of high technology can provide significant spillover benefits through, e.g., the ability to recruit knowledgeable technical staff, interactions with technology institutions and flows of knowledge from suppliers and consultants.

Table V.1. Markets in Asia and Europe

Economy	Total GDP (Million dollars)			Per capita (Dollars)
	1985	1990	1993	1993
China	290 462	369 627	425 611	490
Hong Kong	30 730	59 670	89 997	18 060
India	175 710	254 540	225 431	300
Indonesia	86 470	107 290	144 707	740
Japan	1 327 900	2 942 890	4 214 204	31 490
Korea	86 180	236 400	330 831	7 660
Malaysia	31 270	42 400	64 450	3 140
Philippines	32 590	43 860	54 068	850
Singapore	17 470	34 600	55 153	19 850
Taiwan Province of China a	62 079	156 993	213 385	10 566
Thailand	38 240	80 170	124 862	2 110
Sub-total	2 179 101	4 328 440	5 942 699	
Belgium	79 080	192 390	210 576	21 650
Denmark	57 840	130 960	117 587	26 730
France	510 320	1 190 780	1 251 689	22 490
Germany	624 970	1 448 210	1 910 760	23 560
Greece	29 150	57 900	63 240	7 390
Ireland	18 430	42 500	42 962	13 000
Italy	358 670	1 090 750	991 386	19 840
Luxembourg	3 764	10 557	12 503	37 320
Netherlands	124 970	279 150	309 227	20 950
Portugal	20 430	56 820	85 665	9 139
Spain	164 250	491 240	478 582	13 590
United Kingdom	454 300	957 150	819 038	18 060
Sub-total	2 446 174	5 948 407	6 293 215	
Czech Republic	..	44 450	31 613	2 710
Hungary	20 560	32 920	38 099	3 350
Poland	70 439	63 590	85 853	2 260
Sub-total	90 999	140 960	155 565	

Sources: World Bank, 1987, 1992 and 1995; Asian Development Bank, 1994; OECD, 1995; and information provided by the UNCTAD Secretariat.

a   Data from Taiwan Province of China, Council for Economic Planning and Development, 1995.

- *Access to corporate culture and managerial methods.* If Asian companies are to become or remain global players, they need to utilize the most advanced managerial methods and innovative corporate cultures. Tie-ups with European companies are among a number of ways of achieving this.[1]

- *Participating in European research-and-development programmes.* Europe has large technology programmes, which mainly focus on fundamental research but can have important industrial applications. Though there may be some reluctance to allow foreign affiliates to participate in these programmes, over time this may be overcome. To benefit from such programmes would require Asian firms to be present within the European Union. There are several Asian firms that have the basic technological capability to participate in, and benefit from, advanced scientific research, and their participation would provide beneficial feedbacks to their home countries.

- *Locational advantages for efficiency-seeking investment.* Efficiency-seeking investment that is highly sensitive to labour costs will not be attracted to the European Union. However, the rates of wage increases, especially in the 1990s, are much higher in Asia than in the European Union (table V.3), and the labour cost differences are bound to erode over time. In fact, there exist lowwage areas within the European Union, and certainly in Central and Eastern Europe, where pay is well below levels in parts of Asia. Increasing labour market flexibility in Europe, combined with persisting unemployment and the shift to low-wage service employment, will further reduce wage differences. When combined with good infrastructure, access to high-quality suppliers and high levels of skill, many parts of Europe can be excellent sites for basing production aimed for world markets.[2] Especially in complex operations that are not labour-cost sensitive, Europe may well be cheaper than other sites, because of the high level of skill and experience of the workforce, and the range of specialized personnel and suppliers available.

The base of skills that exists in Europe, as reflected in enrolment in higher levels of education and particularly in technical fields, is substantial (see chapter VIII). In fact, enrolment data do not capture the reservoir of accumulated training, experience, interlinkages among firms and between firms and universities and research institutes, that feed into competitiveness.

Table V.2. Research-and-development expenditures in Europe, recent years

Country	Year	Share of GDP (Per cent)	Per capita (Dollars)
European Union			
Belgium	1990	1.7	264
Denmark	1991	1.8	427
France	1991	2.4	489
Germany	1989	2.8	572
Greece	1986	0.3	11
Ireland	1988	0.9	67
Italy	1990	1.3	219
Netherlands	1991	1.9	357
Portugal	1990	0.6	29
Spain	1990	0.9	99
United Kingdom	1991	2.1	348
Central and Eastern Europe			
Czech Republic	1991	1.8	44
Hungary	1992	1.1	33
Poland	1992	0.9	18

Source: UNESCO, *1995.*

- *Globalization*. Following from the previous point, and given the growing emergence of global production by TNCs the world over, Asian TNCs can also be expected to start integrating their operations across different regions of the world. In fact, remaining competitive internationally may require being established in each of the Triad markets. In this scenario, Europe could be the most efficient production base for supplying the world-wide operations of Asian TNCs with some high-technology products, components and services and for undertaking advanced research and development. The prospects for this would improve, as Asian enterprises gain experience in Europe of setting up local research centres, linking up with supply networks and establishing relations with research laboratories and universities. Japanese TNCs are already doing this; those from NIEs are following, with firms from the Republic of Korea such as Hyundai, Kia and Daewoo in automobiles to the fore.[3]

Table V.3. Average industrial wages

(Dollars per annum)

	Year			Growth rate (Per cent)	
Economy	1985	1990	1993	1985-93	1990-93
China	384	500	656	3.90	7.02
Hong Kong	4 808	9 161	13 220	7.49	9.60
India	1 298	1 592	1 230	-0.38	-6.25
Indonesia	921	925	1 128	1.46	5.09
Japan	13 644	26 368	37 854	7.56	9.46
Korea, Republic of	3 476	9 353	12 269	9.43	7.02
Malaysia	3 375	3 240	4 148	1.48	6.37
Philippines	1 257	1 968	2 433	4.83	5.45
Singapore	7 290	10 800	15 393	5.48	9.26
Taiwan Province of China	3 862	10 168	14 017	9.64	8.36
Thailand	2 422	3 523	4 661	4.79	7.25
Average	3 885	7 054	9 728	6.78	8.37
Average, excluding Japan	2 909	5 123	6 916	6.38	7.79
Belgium	10 617	22 774	24 702	6.22	2.05
Denmark	15 021	28 336	30 389	5.16	1.76
France	16 725	33 961	37 305	5.90	2.38
Germany[a]	17 563	38 487	43 735	6.73	3.25
Greece	7 281	14 319	15 917	5.75	2.68
Ireland	11 582	23 915	24 846	5.60	0.96
Italy	15 647	46 311	41 850	7.28	-2.50
Luxembourg	23 389	35 600	42 083	4.28	4.27
Netherlands	23 135	42 133	47 870	5.33	3.24
Portugal	4 541	10 237	11 999	7.19	4.05
Spain	12 852	24 205	22 647	4.13	-1.65
United Kingdom	14 579	25 249	25 776	4.15	0.52
Average	14 411	28 794	30 760	5.57	1.66
Czech Republic	2 264	2 396	..	..	..
Hungary	1 437	2 495	3 387	6.32	7.94
Poland	1 627	1 257	2 160	2.04	14.49
Average	1 776	2 049	2 774	3.24	7.86

Source: UNIDO, *1995*.

[a]   Western part of Germany only.

- *Overcoming protectionist pressures and sentiments.* One of the main reasons for Asian FDI in both Europe and the United States has been to relieve protectionist sentiments in these major markets for exports. If Asian enterprises continue to export to Europe from other bases and are perceived to threaten local employment, measures to limit their market access may well become irresistable. Investment in local manufacturing operations and creating local employment may be necessary for securing market shares in the future.

- *Increasing FDI specialization and cross-FDI flows.* Setting up facilities in activities in Europe where Asian firms have clear competitive advantages would in turn allow European enterprises to specialize more efficiently and so invest in their own areas of advantage in Asia. In other words, FDI could itself stimulate investment flows that are more bi-directional, so promoting overall investment, with greater technology exchange and less political resistance. This would benefit both parties.

- *Winning government contracts.* Increasing liberalization in such industries as construction and services in Europe, which were traditionally closed to foreign firms, may open up large areas for activity in such fields as infrastructure, entertainment, health provision, power generation, road transport and telecommunications. While the liberalization process still has some way to go, a production presence by Asian firms may be necessary —or at least improve the chances—to win contracts in these activities, and should form part of the long-term planning of firms.

- *Forging closer relations with European enterprises.* While it may be possible for Asian enterprises to forge close relations with European counterparts without having direct investment in Europe, a production presence in Europe may clearly offer strategic benefits. A strong competitive position by Asian firms in their home market may, for instance, induce European firms to enter into agreements with them more readily. Where European firms have strong locational advantages, say in Africa or Latin America, this could offer large benefits to Asian TNCs that seek to expand there.

- *Portfolio diversification.* Given the attractiveness of Europe, far-sighted global companies would seek to have an important part of their portfolio in Europe. There are several economies in Asia that are net outward investors, despite their relatively low levels of per capita income. This is not, of course, the only driving force in their outward investment, since their enterprises could invest overseas while other foreign sources are tapped for domestic investment. However, the very high savings rates in the region (table V.4) certainly provide a long-term macroeconomic reason for outward investment.

C. Conclusion: opportunities and potential

An analysis of Europe as a site for direct investment shows that there are several powerful reasons why Asian enterprises should look closely and carefully at opportunities there. In essence, Europe is too rich, technologically advanced and welcoming for any dynamic firm to be ignored. In a rapidly shrinking world, Europe must figure as an important site for global corporations. Its diversity itself offers challenges, which, if accepted, would improve the competitive position of Asian firms that enter there.

The realization of these opportunities depend very much on the capabilities of the home countries concerned and the competitive strength of the enterprises concerned. As discussed below, these vary considerably within Asia. Given the close inter-relationships between trade and FDI, a good (though incomplete) "snap-shot" of the investment opportunities open to any country is given by the pattern of its exports to Europe by its own enterprises. The success of exports immediately suggests the existence of a competitive advantage. Whether or not this advantage is sufficient to lead to FDI, and whether it should be exploited by means of setting up a facility in Europe, needs further examination. In some low technology areas, it may not be advantageous to invest directly in Europe to retain a competitive edge there; investment in sales outlets or design facilities may be sufficient. In others, FDI may be the preferred option. These cases include:

- Technologically complex activities, where setting up in Europe offers cost advantages as well as spillover benefits in terms of accessing new technologies and skills.
- Activities where proximity to final consumers (e.g., high fashion) is essential to a quick response and interaction with designers.
- Activities where close and continuous interaction with industrial buyers is essential for efficient sales and service (e.g., manufacturing equipment).
- Activities where a local production presence is of vital importance in winning large contracts (infrastructure projects).
- High technology services, such as telecommunications, transport, media and entertainment, complex financial services and other high-growth services areas, can only be contested by a local presence.
- Activities that provide large amounts of employment and backward linkages, i.e., where there is a high risk of protective barriers being established to exports (automobiles or consumer electronics).
- Activities that are not particularly complex or high-technology but where the high skill and flexible labour base in Central and Eastern Europe and parts of Southern Europe make for the most efficient sites (assembly operations, textiles and garments, sports goods, footwear, processed foods).
- Finally, where a globally integrated TNC system requires a presence in Europe.

Table V.4. Savings and investment, 1993

(Per cent of GDP)

Economy	Savings	Investment	Difference
China	40.2	41.2	-1.0
Hong Kong	28.9	28.3	0.6
India	23.8	24.1	-0.3
Indonesia	30.5	28.3	2.2
Japan	32.7	30.3	2.4
Korea, Republic of	34.7	34.3	0.4
Malaysia	38.1	33.2	4.9
Philippines	15.6	24.1	-8.5
Singapore	48.4	41.4	7.0
Taiwan Province of China a	26.8	24.7	2.1
Thailand	35.9	40	-4.1

Source: World Bank, 1987, 1992 and 1995; Asian Development Bank, 1994; and OECD, 1995.

a   Taiwan Province of China, Council for Economic Planning and Development, 1995.

It is difficult to pinpoint the most promising areas for Asian investment in Europe. Europe is "open for business" in an increasing range of areas, including some that were unthinkable a few years ago (e.g., infrastructure, various services), as well as conventional areas of industry and services. What is important is for Asian countries to identify their own capabilities and to encourage their enterprises to take up the challenge to invest in Europe. The next few chapters analyse the basis of those capabilities.

Notes

1   "Asia's new giants", *Business Week*, 27 November 1995, pp. 30-40.

2   For instance, Wales has been chosen for a proposed investment by the LG Group of Republic of Korea because wages there are apparently lower than in the home country.

3   See "Do or die", *Far Eastern Economic Review*, 13 June 1996, pp. 54-57.

Chapter VI

THE RELATIONSHIP BETWEEN ASIAN EXPORTS AND FOREIGN DIRECT INVESTMENT

A. Introduction

The relationship between trade and FDI has been seen to have two conflicting effects: for FDI to replace exports from the home country, or for it to complement export activity directly as well as indirectly (by improving the competitiveness of a country's firms). The former view was common in early discussions of outward FDI in "off-shore processing" activities by developed country TNCs, and it was much the concern of trade unions. It was partly based on a static view of the process of international competition, including the premise that existing competitive advantages would not change. It ignored the fact that those advantages were constantly challenged, and that setting up production facilities overseas enabled firms to exploit these advantages longer, to upgrade domestic activities and to service foreign markets better. This latter view is backed for industrialized countries by several empirical investigations.[1] Moreover, FDI in trade-related services is essential to supporting export development in several types of manufactures. Hence, the significant role of Asian FDI in the services sector of the European Union may well further increase Asian exports of manufactures to the European Union. Even within manufacturing, Asian investors in the European Union can promote exports by using inputs supplied from their home base.

What do the existing, admittedly imperfect, data show on the relative importance of FDI and trade in the economic relations between the European Union and the Asian developing economies? Bearing in mind that the relations between trade and FDI are complex and do not easily emerge from the data, a brief look at the experience of Japan, which has a relatively long tradition of investing in Europe, may offer some insights as to how FDI and trade relations of Asian developing economies with Europe are likely to develop.

B. Japan

The decline of Japan's FDI in the early 1990s notwithstanding, Japan's average annual FDI outflows to the European Union in 1991-1994 exceeded average annual outflows in 1980-1985 by a factor of six. Japanese FDI stock in the European Union rose from $2.4 billion in 1980 to $56.8 billion in 1994, accounting in the latter year for 6.2 per cent of total inward FDI stock in the European Union (UNCTAD-DTCI, 1996a, annex table 3). The share of Japanese FDI in total inflows in the European Union was about 6 per cent in 1991-1994, and accounted for about 1.6 per cent of gross fixed capital formation of all European Union countries. At the same time, Japanese manufactured exports to the European Union increased by a factor of 5 in 1980-1994 (table VI.1), bringing its share in total manufactured imports by European Union from 4.8 per cent in 1980 to 6.7 per cent in 1993.

The ratio of FDI flows to manufactured exports from Japan to the European Union rose steeply between 1983-1986 (8.3 per cent) and 1987-1990 (20.9 per cent). However, this ratio declined to 11.7 per cent in 1991-1993, when FDI flows to the European Union were curtailed, while manufactured exports continued to rise. Over the entire period, Japanese companies increasingly resorted to FDI as a means to access European Union markets, while exports remained the dominant vehicle for bringing goods to these markets. The evidence strongly suggests that Japan's FDI in the European Union has supplemented, rather than replaced, its exports to this region.

Complementarities between Japan's FDI in, and its exports to, the European Union may be attributed in large part to the major role of the services sector in Japan's FDI. Services (including construction) accounted for about three quarters of Japan's total FDI stock in Europe in fiscal year 1995, and for 76 per cent of its notified FDI flows to Europe in that year. But even within manufacturing, the available evidence points to complementarities between FDI and trade. For example, electrical and electronic equipment accounted for the largest share of total manufacturing FDI stock of Japan in the European Union (table VI.1): this industry figured most prominently in Japan's manufacturing exports in 1994, recorded export growth well above the average for total manufacturing, and increased its share in total European Union imports of electronics. Transport equipment is another industry in which European Union

Table VI.1. Structure of Japanese FDI[a] and exports to the European Union, 1994

(Billions of dollars and percentage)

Item	Value	Textiles[b]	Chemicals[c]	Metal products[d]	Machinery[e]	Electrical equipment[f]	Transport equipment[g]	Total manufacturing
FDI stock	21.2	6.5	13.9	4.0	16.3	28.3	17.7	100
FDI outflows	1.9	4.3	16.9	2.2	16.4	17.7	23.7	100
Exports	61.4	1.4	6.2	3.1	13.4	39.3	23.4	100
Memorandum:								
Exports of 1994 as ratio to exports of 1980	..	2.8	7.2	1.7	6.9	7.0	22.4	4.8
Exports of 1980 in per cent of total European Union imports	..	1.1	1.4	2.9	3.1	11.0	9.4	4.8
Exports of 1993 in per cent of total European Union imports	..	0.9	2.5	2.7	7.0	13.2	10.6	6.7

Sources: UNCTAD, FDI database; and UNCTAD, trade database.

[a]   FDI in Europe is based on notifications. Stocks are cumulative flows. Therefore, the data are different from those in the text which are based on balance-of-payments data. Fiscal year.

[b]   SITC 26 + 61; 65+84.

[c]   SITC 51-59.

[d]   SITC 66-69.

[e]   SITC 71-74.

[f]   SITC 75-77.

[g]   SITC 78+79.

import barriers could have and are believed by some to have led to a replacement of exports by FDI. However, the data suggest that FDI went together with persistent export growth, as Japan further increased its share in total European imports of transport equipment. Similar developments took place in the chemicals and machinery industries.

To summarize, the Japanese experience indicates that complementarities between FDI and trade may well dominate substitution effects. This is relevant to Asian developing economies, since Japan was the first target of protectionist measures of the European Union against imports from Asia.

C. Asian developing economies

Since FDI outflows from Asian developing economies to the European Union began to grow only recently, their share in total FDI stock was still less than one per cent in 1993, although their share in inflows has grown to above that figure (table VI.2). Their share in gross fixed capital formation has been even lower.

The picture looks different for exports by Asian developing economies to the European Union (table VI.2). This is not surprising, because they started their process of international integration by means of a strong export drive. Except for the Philippines, Asian economies raised their share in the total merchandise imports of the European Union during 1980-1993. China's share more than quadrupled, while that of Singapore, Taiwan Province of China, Indonesia and Thailand more than doubled.[2]

Table VI.2. Imports and inward FDI flows to the European Union from Asian developing economies

Economy	European Union imports from Asian developing economies (Per cent of total imports)[a]		Share in EU FDI inflows of FDI flows from Asian developing economies, 1992-1993[b]
	1980	1993	
China	0.36	1.64	0.04
NIEs	1.68	3.22	1.32
Hong Kong	0.65	0.86	0.64
Republic of Korea	0.38	0.72	0.17
Singapore	0.23	0.67	0.05
Taiwan Province of China	0.42	0.97	0.46
ASEAN(4)	0.96	1.71	0.06
Indonesia	0.23	0.46	-0.01
Malaysia	0.34	0.56	0.07
Philippines	0.16	0.16	-0.003
Thailand	0.23	0.53	0.002

Source: OECD trade database; OECD, 1995.

[a]   Total merchandise imports.
[b]   The calculation of these indicators is restricted to 1992-1993, since FDI inflows from individual Asian developing countries are not reported by many European Union host countries in previous years. As a result, large discrepancies prevail between reported inflows from South and East Asia as a whole on the one hand, and the sum of reported inflows from the nine Asian developing countries considered in this table on the other hand. For 1992-1993, this discrepancy is substantially reduced; reported inflows from South and East Asia exceeded inflows from the nine Asian developing countries by 22 per cent.

Import market shares increased relatively modestly for Hong Kong. At first sight, this may suggest a negative correlation between outward FDI and export growth, Hong Kong being the most important foreign investor among Asian developing economies in Europe. However, Hong Kong relocated much of its manufacturing capacity at the low-technology end to cheaper locations (like China), and upgraded its domestic export activity to higher value-added products and activities. Thus, outward FDI by Hong Kong, especially in trade-related services, may reflect more the growth of exports from China to the European Union.

The data on Taiwan Province of China also suggest that FDI and exports complement each other. Taiwan Province of China was among the best performers in European Union import markets and was also the second largest foreign investor there in this group. Similarly, China, the Republic of Korea and Thailand continued to expand their penetration of European markets through exports even after they began to invest there.

As in the case of Japan, FDI in trade-related services by Asian developing economies in the European Union is likely to support their export drive. This applies especially to Hong Kong and Singapore, whose FDI in the European Union is strongly concentrated in services. Such investments also account for significant shares of the FDI undertaken by firms from the Republic of Korea, Taiwan Province of China and Thailand.

It appears that complementarities between FDI and trade prevail also within the manufacturing sector. The electronics industry is a telling example in this respect. Electronics ranked first among manufacturing industries with respect to outward FDI in the European Union of almost all Asian developing economies. China, the Republic of Korea, Singapore, Taiwan Province of China, Malaysia and Thailand all recorded a substantial rise of their import market shares in electronics in the European Union (table VI.3). Moreover, an earlier study revealed a positive correlation, over time, between Korean exports and outward FDI to the European Union in the electronics industry.[3]

Transport equipment is another interesting case. This industry ranked high in FDI from the Republic of Korea and Taiwan Province of China in the European Union, and outward FDI went together with steeply rising import market shares of these two countries in the Union. The same pattern of significant outward FDI, together with a dynamic export performance in European markets, prevails in the chemical industry of the Republic of Korea, and in the metal industry of Malaysia and Thailand.

Some replacement of exports by outward FDI is likely to have occurred in the textile and clothing industry. Economies such as Hong Kong and Taiwan Province of China, which reported considerable outward FDI in this industry, experienced a decline in their shares in overall imports in the European Union of textiles and clothing. It is doubtful, however, that outward FDI was really the *cause* for less dynamic export growth. Import market shares in this industry declined for all Asian NIEs, and the magnitude of this decline does not appear to be closely linked to the significance of outward FDI. In contrast to Asian NIEs, lower-income Asian developing countries (especially China and Indonesia) gained considerable shares in European Union markets for textiles, leather and clothing. All this suggests that higher-income NIEs came under competitive pressure from lower-income Asian developing countries in the labour intensive production of textiles and clothing. They thus had little choice but to restructure manufacturing in favour of more (physical and human) capital-intensive industries, and to relocate production to lower wage areas. Outward FDI in textiles and clothing offered one way to promote industrial restructuring, and to extend the life of their competitive advantages. Hence, outward FDI was the consequence, rather than the cause, of a slowing export performance in European Union markets (and world markets in general) in labour-intensive industries such as textiles and clothing.

At this stage, the internationalization of Asian developing economies via FDI in, as compared with exports to, the European Union is lower than in the United States. More specifically, the ratio of FDI to exports was lower in the European Union than in the United States for all countries except Singapore (table VI.4).

Table VI.3. Import market shares of selected Asian economies in the European Union, by industry, 1980 and 1993

(Percentage)

Industry		China	Hong Kong	Republic of Korea	Singapore	Taiwan Province of China	Indonesia	Malaysia	Philippines	Thailand
Food, beverage,	1980	0.57	0.02	0.16	0.07	0.25	0.73	0.24	0.31	1.13
tobacco	1993	0.74	0.05	0.08	0.11	0.05	0.52	0.23	0.15	1.28
Paper and	1980	0.10	0.09	0.55	0.44	0.92	0.09	0.33	0.33	0.14
wood products	1993	0.64	0.15	0.13	0.25	0.38	1.57	0.42	0.17	0.23
Rubber	1980	0.03	0.03	1.02	0.15	0.98	0.00	0.19	0.00	0.12
products	1993	0.24	0.06	2.26	0.36	1.19	0.22	0.81	0.00	0.80
Non-metallic	1980	0.12	0.70	0.32	0.07	0.44	0.00	0.02	0.01	0.33
minerals	1993	1.17	1.01	0.16	0.20	0.64	0.07	0.36	0.10	1.06
Metal products	1980	0.35	0.84	0.65	0.12	1.18	0.00	0.02	0.00	0.13
	1993	2.61	0.75	1.08	0.32	3.02	0.13	0.22	0.06	0.23
Textiles, lea-	1980	1.58	4.78	2.54	0.38	1.32	0.12	0.28	0.35	0.53
ther, clothing[a]	1993	5.68	4.40	1.40	0.32	0.91	1.94	0.81	0.45	1.26
Chemicals	1980	0.43	0.01	0.05	0.03	0.06	0.03	0.01	0.00	0.01
	1993	0.74	0.06	0.34	0.16	0.21	0.06	0.08	0.01	0.03
Mechanical	1980	0.02	0.07	0.02	0.10	0.17	0.01	0.03	0.00	0.00
equipment[b]	1993	0.40	0.15	0.30	0.19	0.51	0.01	0.17	0.02	0.18
Electrical	1980	0.01	1.26	0.76	1.35	1.33	0.02	0.46	0.15	0.02
equipment[c]	1993	1.89	1.27	2.05	3.73	3.36	0.21	1.94	0.36	0.74
Transport	1980	0.00	0.02	0.08	0.11	0.08	0.00	0.03	0.03	0.01
equipment[d]	1993	0.07	0.03	0.81	0.17	0.55	0.03	0.15	0.00	0.06
Total manu-	1980	0.37	1.26	0.68	0.34	0.77	0.03	0.15	0.11	0.12
facturing	1993	2.12	1.22	1.01	0.94	1.38	0.46	0.63	0.18	0.54

Source: OECD trade database.

[a]   SITC 61, 65 and 84.
[b]   SITC 71-74.
[c]   SITC 75-77
[d]   SITC 78+79.

**Table VI.4. Ratio of FDI stock to merchandise exports in the
European Union and United States, selected Asian
developing economies, 1993**

(Percentage)

Economy	European Union	United States
China	1.5	2.1
Hong Kong	7.1	12.9
Korea, Republic of	4.0	10.7
Singapore	8.2	7.1
Taiwan Province of China	0.8	7.5
Malaysia	0.1	1.6
Philippines	1.2	1.7
Thailand	0.6	3.3

Sources: Chia, 1995; UNCTAD, 1994.

Notes

[1] See, for example, Nunnenkamp, Gundlach and Agarwal (1994) and the literature given there.

[2] Data for Hong Kong and Singapore have to be interpreted carefully. They include re-exports, which tend to dominate the data (their own exports account for around a quarter). For Hong Kong, the re-export figures also include substantial amounts of production in other Asian economies (mainly China) by its own TNCs, reflecting the effects of industrial restructuring via outward FDI.

[3] Min (1991, p. 157). The dominant role of the electronics industry in both outward FDI and exports of the Republic of Korea is also stressed by Schultz (1995, p. 63).

COMPETITIVE ADVANTAGES OF ASIAN ENTERPRISES IN TRADE

A. What are competitive advantages?

Competitive advantages are the firm-specific set of capabilities that enable individual firms to perform well in open markets. Some competitive advantages may be based on factors such as access to cheap labour or natural resources, and are shared by many firms. More relevant here are "ownership" advantages stemming from the "created assets" that firms obtain by developing particular knowledge, technologies and skills that enable them to do better than their rivals. Firms do not, moreover, become competitive on their own: they draw upon a range of tangible and intangible inputs from other firms and institutions around them, including for skilled personnel, technology, information, finance, contract production, research and training.

The process is one of intense interaction among firms, and between firms and institutions, with considerable spillover effects. Governments can play a crucial role in increasing the competitiveness of a country's firms, by providing the correct incentives and signals for firms to undertake the risky and costly task of developing competitive capabilities, and strengthening or creating factor markets and institutions to provide the inputs that firms cannot create in-house (Lall, 1996). The ability of an economy to capture and "internalize" some of the dynamic spillover effects that capability development creates, is one of the most important ingredients for sustained economic growth.

Why is this relevant to Asian FDI in Europe? Competitive advantages differ between *firms*, depending on their initial abilities and subsequent efforts to develop new advantages. They also vary by *industry*, with some industries performing better than others, depending on the resource base and the success of the firms concerned in building upon them. More importantly, they vary by *country*, depending on its set of capabilities and the specialization it has undertaken. These differences, in turn, show up in the patterns of outward FDI. Knowledge of underlying competitive advantages can help to explain and predict these patterns.

What then are the ownership advantages of Asian enterprises, and how do they differ by industry and nationality? The concern here is with *direct investment*, not with Asian firms buying shares in existing firms (which is akin to *portfolio* investment), without taking an interest in control, management and technology. For portfolio investment, no specific competitive advantages are required, and this is not addressed here. However, it is not easy to identify competitive advantages for direct investment. In many cases, the advantages are very firm or technology-specific. They are also liable to change rapidly. Available data tend, however, to be aggregated across industries and technologies, making identification difficult.

Since the advantages that govern outward FDI are often identical to those that determine export patterns, trade data provide an indication as to where competitive advantages can be found. This is especially true for manufacturing FDI, where exports and outward FDI are closely intertwined as alternative or complementary means of serving foreign markets.[1]

B. Competitive advantages in trade

Table VII.1 shows the export structure of the developing South, East and South-East Asian economies by destination (European Union and Central and Eastern Europe) and distribution by commodity group, and the rate of growth in each export category. The European Union's importance as a destination for Asian exports decreased between 1970 and 1980, but then regained some of its share over the 80s. This was the result of an annual rate of growth of total exports to the European Union from these economies of over 17 per cent. The rate of growth of exports to Central and Eastern Europe was under half of this, and the share of the latter region in Asian exports fell from nearly 2 per cent to 0.4 per cent.

The growth of exports to the European Union was highest in manufactures, growing at nearly 22 per cent per annum over 1970-1992. At the end of that period, manufactures constituted nearly 90 per cent of Asian exports to the European Union, and nearly 75 per cent of those to Central and Eastern Europe. The lowest growing were agricultural products and ores and minerals, reflecting the protection given to European agriculture, the nature of evolving comparative advantage in Asia, and the inherently slow growth of many resource-based exports.

**Table VII.1. Export structure of developing South, East and South-East Asian countries,
1970, 1980 and 1992**

Product	Year	Destination (Per cent) EU	Destination (Per cent) CEE [a]	Distribution (Per cent) EU	Distribution (Per cent) CEE [b]	Growth (Per cent) (1970-92) EU	Growth (Per cent) (1970-92) CEE [b]
All products	1970	17.1	1.9	100	100	17.2	8.1
	1980	15.6	0.5	100	100		
	1992	16.1	0.4	100	100		
All food	1970	23.0	2.3	28.4	26.1	9.9	5.1
	1980	20.3	0.7	16.3	32.5		
	1992	15.2	0.5	7.0	14.1		
Agricultural	1970	20.3	3	22.7	32.5	5.7	-3.6
	1980	17.3	2.2	9.9	19.8		
	1992	13.3	0.3	2.3	2.6		
Ores/minerals	1970	13.1	2.9	6.5	6.7	5.7	2.6
	1980	23.2	1.7	6.3	9.5		
	1992	6.8	0.3	0.7	2.1		
Fuels	1970	5.0	0.2	2.0	2.6	10.1	12.9
	1980	0.8	-	1.0	6.6		
	1992	1.3	-	0.5	6.8		
Manufactures	1970	15.5	1.3	39.5	31.9	21.5	12.3
	1980	19.5	0.4	63.7	29.5		
	1992	17.6	0.4	88.2	73.6		

Source: United Nations, 1994.

a   Not including former Soviet Union.
b   Including former Soviet Union.

Thus, the engine of Asia's competitivenes in Europe is likely to be in*manufacturing*, but this does not mean that this will necessarily be the largest area for its FDI activities there. On the contrary, for three sets of reasons, *services* may be more significant for several countries:

- Firms from those economies that have strong competitive positions *vis à vis* European firms in complex industries and are major investors in manufacturing, such as the Republic of Korea and Taiwan Province of China, are likely to invest in services such as trade and storage to support their export activity.
- Economies with competitive services firms, led by Hong Kong and Singapore, may invest directly in a range of "high-technology" services, such as finance, communications, media and retailing.
- Less industrialised countries with less competitive services firms, which do not invest significantly in manufacturing activity in Europe in the near future, may invest in less demanding services activities related to, e.g., trade and restaurants.

Table VII.2. Merchandise exports from Asian and European countries, 1993

Economy	Exports	
	Value (Billion dollars) (1993)	Growth (Per cent) (1980-93)
China	91.7	11.5
Hong Kong [a]	28.8	0.03
India	21.5	7.0
Indonesia	33.6	6.7
Japan	362.2	4.2
Korea, Republic of	82.2	12.3
Malaysia	47.1	12.6
Philippines	11.1	3.4
Singapore [b]	74.0	12.7
Taiwan Province of China	84.9	11.0
Thailand	36.8	15.5
Sub-Total	874.2	8.8
Belgium	112.5	4.5
Denmark	35.9	4.4
France	206.3	4.5
Germany	380.2	4.2
Greece	8.0	5.3
Ireland	28.6	9.0
Italy	168.5	4.3
Netherlands	139.1	4.7
Portugal	15.4	10.6
Spain	62.9	7.4
United Kingdom	180.6	4.0
Sub-Total EU	1 337.8	5.7
Czech Republic	12.9	..
Hungary [a]	8.9	2.3
Poland	14.0	2.8
Sub-Total CEE	35.8	2.55

Sources: World Bank, 1995; Asian Development Bank, 1994; *Hong Kong External Trade*, February 1996.

[a] Excludes re-exports.
[b] Includes re-exports.

Resource-based FDI from Asia is unlikely to be important in Europe (though it is significant within Asia).

In the long-term, the evolution of the competitive base in manufacturing is likely to most significantly affect the pattern of FDI, both directly in manufacturing itself, and indirectly via export-supporting service activities. To analyze the competitive base for this sort of ownership advantage in Asia, and to determine which countries are likely to drive manufacturing FDI, it is useful to look at some manufacturing competitiveness indicators as revealed by the trade data.

There is considerable variance in export performance between Asian economies (note that only the larger Asian economies, with substantial industrial bases, are considered here, since these have the most potential for FDI in Europe). Taking the top 11 exporters from the region in 1993, Japan dominates exports with 41 per cent of the total (table VII.2). Even if Japan is excluded, there is a high degree of concentration among the other economies. The most important exporters are China ($92 billion), Taiwan Province of China ($85 billion), Republic of Korea ($82 billion) and Singapore ($74 billion).[2] These four economies alone account for two-thirds of total non-Japanese exports from Asia ($333 billion). The three "new NIEs", Indonesia,

Malaysia and Thailand, are also substantial exporters, led by Malaysia. The highest rates of export growth are for Thailand, Singapore and Malaysia, followed by the Republic of Korea, Taiwan Province of China and China. By contrast, Hong Kong exports are stagnant. Exports from the Philippines have grown very slowly, and India and Indonesia have done only slightly better (although the Indonesian figure is misleading because its manufactured exports have grown very rapidly, at over 34 per cent per annum, while its other exports have stagnated).

The above data (for total merchandise exports) do not show the category of interest here, manufactured products; figure VII.1 shows the share of *manufactures* in total exports in 1993. The most advanced economies by this measure, after Japan, are the Republic of Korea, Taiwan Province of China and Hong Kong, with China and Singapore (whose re-exports include non-manufactures) close behind. The lowest are Indonesia and Malaysia, with India and Thailand in the middle range.

Table VII.3 shows the trends in manufactured exports by three groups of Asian developing economies from 1980 to 1994 to the world as a whole, and to the European Union and Central and Eastern Europe (excluding the former Soviet Union). The three developing economy groups are:

- *Developing Asia*: This group includes 12 economies, i.e., the NIEs (Hong Kong, Singapore, Republic of Korea, Taiwan Province of China), the ASEAN (4) (Indonesia, Malaysia, the Philippines, Thailand), plus India, China, Viet Nam and Brunei Dasussalam.
- *NIEs*. The four original NIEs, i.e., Hong Kong, Singapore, Republic of Korea and Taiwan Province of China.
- *Non-NIEs*. The eight other economies mentioned above.

Figure VII.1. Shares of manufactures in total merchandise exports from Asia, 1993

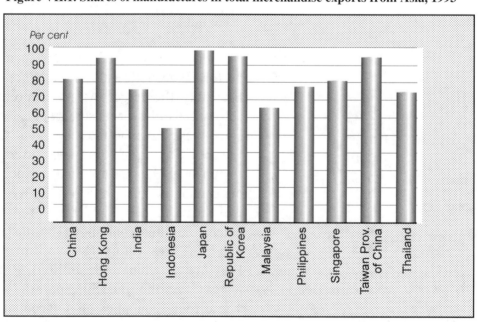

Source: UNCTAD, trade database.

These data show that the 12 Asian economies together expanded their manufactured exports to all destinations rapidly over this period, with a sharp acceleration in growth in the post-1985 period. The share of the European Union in their exports fell in the early part of the 1980s, but then recovered and reached nearly 15 per cent by 1994. Still a relatively small proportion, it should be expected to increase to reflect the share of the European Union in global GDP. The growth of exports by the non-NIEs was much faster than that of the NIEs: in the second period, it was twice as high. As a result, the share of the non-NIEs in the exports of the 12 countries rose from 16 per cent in 1980 to 42 per cent in 1994. This reflects the very rapid growth of exports by most of the new-NIEs and China, and the slow growth of exports by Hong Kong among the NIEs.

C. The technological basis of comparative advantage

However, manufactured exports alone are not a sufficient indicator to predict which countries are most likely to become investors in Europe, or of the types of activities they are likely to invest in. Two additional factors need to be taken into account:

- The *technological* capacities existing in these countries as these provide the basis for the competitiveness of manufacturers, as this affects both the overall ability to be outward investors and the activities in which they have advantages vis-á-vis European firms. Given the technological status of Europe, it is the Asian countries with most technologically advanced industries that are likely to be successful investors.

- The *role of domestic versus foreign firms* in the export activities of Asian economies. If, for example, the more sophisticated manufactured exports are largely driven by foreign affiliates, the ability of domestic firms to undertake FDI in Europe is likely to be low.

Table VII.3. Manufactured exports from developing Asia, 1980-1994

Exporting countries	1980 World	1980 EU	1980 CEE	1985 World	1985 EU	1985 CEE	1994 World	1994 EU	1994 CEE
				Values (Billion dollars)					
All Asia	65.1	8.8	0.17	102.7	10.0	0.48	486.1	70.2	2.41
NIEs	54.6	7.0	0.07	82.9	7.8	0.05	283.1	39.8	1.00
Non-NIEs	10.5	1.8	0.10	19.8	2.2	0.43	203.0	30.4	1.41
				Shares by destination					
All Asia	100	13.5	0.3	100	9.7	0.5	100	14.4	3.4
NIEs	100	12.8	0.1	100	9.4	0.1	100	14.1	0.4
Non-NIEs	100	17.1	1.0	100	11.1	2.2	100	15.0	o.7

	Rates of annual growth (Per cent)						
	1980-85 World	1980-85 EU	1980-85 CEE		1985-94 World	1985-94 EU	1985-94 CEE
All Asia	7.9	2.1	18.9		16.8	21.5	17.5
NIEs	7.2	1.8	-4.9		13.1	17.7	34.0
Non-NIEs	11.2	3.2	27.6		26.2	30.3	12.7

Source: UNCTAD, trade database.

How does the technological basis of competitiveness differ between Asian developing countries? A detailed breakdown, derived from the OECD, is by technological characteristics such as resource, labour and scale-intensive production, differentiated production and science-based production (table VII.4). The early growth of exports from developing countries tends to be in the first two kinds of industries, using local natural resources and cheap unskilled labour; interestingly, the initial FDI from Asian developing countries was also in these categories (Tolentino, 1993). However, Asian FDI in Europe is unlikely to be in these sectors. Unskilled labour is bound to remain cheaper in other regions of the world for the foreseeable future, though there may well be some instances where more skilled labour-intensive activities are transferred to parts of Europe (e.g., to Southern Europe or Central and Eastern Europe). It is in the others, scale intensive, differentiated and science-based activities, that Asian FDI in Europe is more likely, once competitive advantages are built up. What do the trade data suggest for the pattern of advantages?

Table VII.4. Technological basis of competitive advantage

Activity group	Major competitive factor	Examples
Resource-intensive	Access to natural resources	Aluminium smelting, oil refining
Labour-intensive	Costs of unskilled or semi-skilled labour	Garments, footwear, toys
Scale-intensive	Length of production runs	Steel, chemicals, automobiles, paper
Differentiated	Products tailored to varied demands	Machine tools, generating equipment
Science-based	Rapid application of science to technology	Electronics, biotechnology, medicines

Source: OECD, 1987.

Table VII.5 shows the breakdown by technological categories of world-wide manufactured exports by eight Asian economies over 1980-1992.[3]   In resource and labour-intensive activities, all economies, with the exception of Indonesia, show diminishing export shares. Those with the largest concentration of such exports in 1992 are China (65 per cent), Indonesia (78 per cent), Thailand (56 per cent) and India (78 per cent). While this sector may generate

Table VII.5. The technological basis of manufactured exports of eight Asian economies, 1980-1992

(Per cent of total)

Activity group	China 1985	China 1992	Republic of Korea 1980	Republic of Korea 1992	Taiwan Province of China 1980	Taiwan Province of China 1992	Singapore 1980	Singapore 1992
Resource-based	4.3	6.3	7.1	3.3	7.7	6.6	5.4	2.6
Labour-intensive	66.6	58.4	49.0	35.1	55.5	38.4	19.3	11.5
Scale-intensive	17.6	11.2	25.3	26.4	9.4	12.2	20.2	13.5
Differentiated	5.3	17.2	16.4	29.7	26	29.2	53.3	41.9
Science-based	0	1.1	2.1	5.4	1.2	13.5	1.8	30.5

Activity group	Indonesia 1980	Indonesia 1992	Malaysia 1980	Malaysia 1991	Thailand 1980	Thailand 1991	India 1980	India 1992
Resource-based	14.7	29.5	11.0	5.7	27.0	18.0	26.5	28.7
Labour-intensive	28.9	48.7	18.4	18.7	41.0	38.0	55.4	49.6
Scale-intensive	20.2	7.6	4.9	8.6	8.0	7.0	11.2	17.1
Differentiated	19.0	7.6	60.1	57.1	19.0	23.0	4.1	1.2
Science-based	0	0.9	3.8	9	0	10.0	2.8	3.4

Source: UNCTAD, based on United Nations trade data.

some FDI in Europe (for instance, a large textile group in Indonesia has set up a synthetic fibre plant in Ireland), it is unlikely to lead to sustained FDI in the European Union (but some such activity may be seen in Central and Eastern Europe). The remaining, more advanced activities, are concentrated in three NIEs (Republic of Korea, Taiwan Province of China and Singapore) and Malaysia.

Table VII.6 shows the same breakdown for manufactured exports over 1980-1994, and the relevant growth rates for 1985-1994, for the three groups of Asian economies. The data for the country groups show that the countries together follow the pattern of export-quality upgrading; reducing the share of resource and labour-intensive products, and raising that of more complex and technology-based products. The pattern holds for all destinations. The NIEs have more such upgrading than the non-NIEs, which experienced an increase in the share of labour-intensive exports to the world as a whole (but a reduction in the share of such exports to the European Union). The NIEs sell a higher proportion of science-based products to the European Union than to the world as a whole, but less scale-intensive and differentiated products. Taking the last two, differentiated and science-based products, as "high-technology" exports, figure VII.2 shows the differences between countries in 1992, and between groups of countries in 1994.

Table VII.6. The technological basis of Asian manufactured exports,
by country group, 1980, 1985 and 1994

Activity group	1980			1985			1994		
	World	EU	CEE	World	EU	CEE	World	EU	CEE
All Asia (Per cent distribution by technological basis)									
Resource-based	9.2	11.5	21.9	6.6	6.3	7.9	6.9	5.4	1.3
Labour-intensive	48.3	58.5	68.1	46.5	46.2	65.1	33.3	33.6	62.9
Scale-intensive	13.7	6.3	3.5	17.2	16.1	18.7	13.8	10.8	9.5
Differentiated	23.3	17.5	6.0	22.6	21.8	6.6	32.4	30.5	18.8
Science-based	5.5	6.2	0.5	7.0	9.6	1.7	13.5	19.7	7.5
NIEs (Per cent distribution by technological basis)									
Resource-based	6.6	7.2	-	5.1	4.0	-	4.6	2.0	1.0
Labour-intensive	50.3	59.6	88.6	46.3	45.3	74.6	26.7	24.6	33.3
Scale-intensive	14.0	6.1	2.0	17.9	16.8	3.9	16.4	11.9	13.3
Differentiated	22.8	19.5	8.4	22.3	21.9	15.2	35.1	33.2	36.3
Science-based	6.3	7.6	1.1	8.4	12.0	6.2	17.3	28.3	16.2
Non-NIEs (Per cent distribution by technological basis)									
Resource-based	23.0	28.7	37.8	13.4	14.5	8.9	10.3	9.9	1.5
Labour-intensive	40.5	54.7	53.3	49.3	50.2	63.9	43.0	45.5	84.3
Scale-intensive	12.7	6.9	4.6	14.7	14.2	20.6	10.5	9.5	7.1
Differentiated	22.1	8.7	4.2	20.8	19.9	5.5	27.6	26.4	5.5
Science-based	1.7	1.0	0.1	1.8	1.2	1.1	8.6	8.7	1.6

Annual growth rates 198519-94									
	All Asia			NIEs			Non-NIEs		
	World	EU	CEE	World	EU	CEE	World	EU	CEE
Resource-based	17.3	19.7	-1.9	11.9	9.7	-	23.0	25.4	-5.4
Labour-intensive	13.0	17.7	17.1	7.0	10.7	23.4	24.5	29.0	15.9
Scale-intensive	14.3	16.8	9.8	12.0	13.7	51.0	22.1	25.2	1.3
Differentiated	21.1	25.7	30.5	18.2	22.6	46.8	29.8	34.0	12.6
Science-based	24.7	30.6	36.4	21.5	28.2	47.2	47.4	58.8	17.1

Source: UNCTAD, trade database.

The most technology-intensive exporters in developing Asia are Singapore and Malaysia, followed by Taiwan Province of China and the Republic of Korea. However, these figures may give a misleading picture of their indigenous technological capabilities, since the contribution of foreign investors to their high-technology exports have not been taken into account. Both Singaporean and Malaysian manufactured exports are dominated by foreign affiliates, with 80-90 per cent of high-technology products coming from foreign affiliates. Thai exports of technology-intensive products are also dominated by foreign affiliates, with local firms playing a larger role in resource and labour-intensive activities. Chinese labour-intensive exports are largely under the control of investors from the other NIEs, mainly Hong Kong and Taiwan Province of China. By contrast, the share of foreign affiliates in exports from the Republic of Korea and Taiwan Province of China is relatively low, and the bulk of the high-technology products are manufactured by local firms. [4]

There are further interesting differences between the Republic of Korea and Taiwan Province of China. In the Republic of Korea, the industrial structure is dominated by a relatively small number of large private conglomerates (*chaebol*) which were encouraged by the Government to achieve economies of scale in complex technologies and to enter world markets with their own brand names. The Taiwanese structure, on the other hand, is dominated by a large number of small and medium-sized enterprises which are very flexible, skilled and technologically capable. They are able to export on their own and produce differentiated products to original-equipment manufacturer orders by foreign buyers and manufacturers.

Figure VII.2. Percentage shares of high-technology products in manufactured exports, 1992

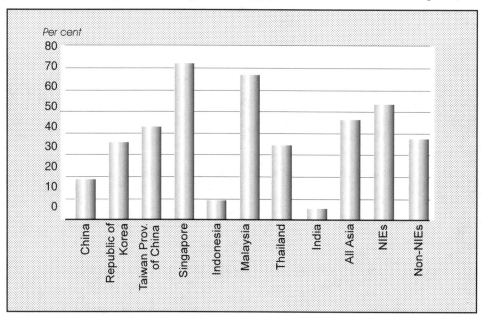

Source: UNCTAD, trade database.

Chaebols tend to have much more financial and research "muscle" than most Taiwanese firms, and so are likely to be larger overseas investors in complex activities in the longer term. This is reflected in the substantial investments that Korean *chaebol* are making in the United Kingdom and Central and Eastern Europe in such activities as consumer electronics, memory chips and automobiles. There are a few such Taiwanese investments in Europe, and their scale and scope are smaller. There are no comparable Hong Kong or Singaporean direct investments in complex industrial activities in Europe.

Notes

[1]   However, not all outward FDI reflects export-competitiveness patterns. Some may be based on advantages built up in import-substitution industrial activities (particularly for large economies like China and India with "heavy" industries that have built up considerable capabilities but do not export significantly). Some may be based on (and aimed to seek) "bought-in" advantages that rely on foreign partners to provie competitive assets. And some FDI may be based on the domestic experience of non-manufacturing activities such as services and resource extraction (agriculture, fishing and mining). Service and resource-based activities are in fact important parts of Asian FDI. Their competitive advantags are difficult to chart with available data, though some are themselves related to industrial development.

[2]   However, the Singapore figure is misleading because it includes re-exports. The Hong Kong figure excludes this, since national data are available for the two categories of exports separately.

[3]   Hong Kong data are not shown because disaggregated information is not available for its own exports. However, most Hong Kong investment in Europe is likely to be in real estate and trading services.

[4]   According to Ramstetter (1994), in 1991 foreign affiliates accounted for 24 per cent of manufactured exports from Hong Kong, 69 per cent from Malaysia, 91 per cent from Singapore and 17 per cent from Taiwan Province of China. The figure for the Republic of Korea is likely to be significantly lower than for Taiwan Province of China, since the former has relied less on inward FDI for its industrial development (Lall, 1995).

Chapter VIII

DETERMINANTS OF COMPETITIVE ADVANTAGES
OF ASIAN INVESTORS

The capabilities that are exploited through outward FDI result from a complex interaction of incentives, factor markets and institutions, all brought together by a mixture of market forces and government policies (Lall, 1996). Some of the basic ingredients of competitive success are: *human capital development* and *technological effort*. It is also important to consider *government support*, though this cannot be analysed fully here.

A. Human resources

The level of skills of the population is clearly a major determinant of a country's ability to engage in international competition, whether by trade or by FDI. One way to judge skill levels is to compare educational enrolment figures; this is not a perfect measure because the quality of education varies greatly across countries, and because skills are also formed on-the-job and by training that does not show up in enrolment data. Nevertheless, enrolment data are readily available on a comparative basis, and they show the main trends in skills development.

The Asian economies considered have virtually universal primary enrolment (though there is still considerable illiteracy in India, and to lesser extents in China, Indonesia and Malaysia) (table VIII.1). Secondary enrolment rates are very high in the NIEs, with the Republic of Korea and Taiwan Province of China matching developed country rates of near 90 per cent, with Hong Kong, Singapore and Philippines only slightly behind. At the tertiary level, the Republic of Korea and Taiwan Province of China again are near developed country levels (and ahead of Japan), followed by the Philippines, Hong Kong and Thailand. Singapore is, surprisingly, in the group of countries with low tertiary enrolments, and China is well behind, the result of a deliberate policy of fostering education at the lower and middle levels; this makes it the only economy in Asia with tertiary enrolment levels near those of sub-Saharan Africa, and may be a precursor to skill shortages in the medium to long term.

The lags recorded by Hong Kong, Singapore and Malaysia are somewhat balanced by the high proportions of their tertiary students that study overseas; in addition, Singapore places more emphasis on vocational training geared to industrial needs than other countries. The high enrolment levels in the Philippines, on the other hand, may be offset by problems of quality and relevance, which also may be found in a number of other countries, where rapid expansion of higher education has not been matched by the calibre of teachers and equipment, especially in the technical subjects.

The patterns of education seem to correspond to the picture of industrial competitiveness and export structures discussed above. The one exception appears to be Hong Kong, which has high levels of skill but a generally low-technology export structure and a rapidly contracting industrial sector; this may be explained by Hong Kong relocating these activities to mainland China, and by its moving into financial and other services, very skill-intensive activities. Singapore is also moving into high-technology services, but has managed to maintain high rates of industrial and manufactured exports growth.

When analyzing the determinants of economic competitiveness, higher level technical skills are more relevant than education in general. The data on tertiary-level students enrolled in various scientific and technical subjects in Asia, the European Union and three main Central and Eastern Europe countries show how wide the differences are between the Asian economies, and how some Asian economies, in particular the Republic of Korea and Taiwan Province of China, are far ahead of European Union countries in the creation of certain types of technology skills (table VIII.2). For example, with respect to enrolments in *all technical subjects* relative to the population, the norm in much of the European Union is around 1 per cent, with the three Central and Eastern European countries at 0.4 to 0.7 per cent. In Asia, the lowest figures (below 0.2 per cent) are recorded by India, China, Indonesia and Malaysia (although Malaysia has large numbers of university students overseas). These are all countries with relatively single export products, with the exception of Malaysia, which is basically engaged in electronics assembly (a low-technology operation in a high-technology industry) under the aegis of TNCs. In between are Thailand, Singapore and Hong Kong (0.4 to 0.6 per cent), which have more demanding export structures but with varying roles for domestic technology (Hong Kong and Singapore also have large numbers of students overseas). The Republic of Korea and Taiwan Province of China, by contrast, with 1.7 per cent and 1.5 per cent respectively, have much higher levels of enrolment in technical fields than the European countries, including the technological leaders. Interestingly, the Japanese figure, 0.6 per cent, is lower than the low end in Europe, and about one-third that of the Republic of Korea.

In *natural science*, the Asian economies are further behind Europe than in other technical subjects; the Republic of Korea has by far the highest proportion of enrolment in Asia, and in relation to Europe, the Republic of Korean

Table VIII.1. Educational enrolments, tertiary students abroad and adult literacy rate, 1990-1992

(Per cent of age group)

Economy	Primary	Secondary	Tertiary	Per cent tertiary students abroad	Literacy rate
China	121	51	2	3	79
Hong Kong	117	75	20	32	91
India	102	44	10	1	50
Indonesia	115	38	10	2	83
Japan	102	97	32	..	99
Republic of Korea	105	90	42	2	97
Malaysia	93	58	7	38	82
Philippines	109	74	28	0	94
Singapore	107	71	9 [a]	25	90
Taiwan Province of China	100	88	38	..	..
Thailand	97	33	19	1	94

Sources: World Bank, *1994 and 1995*; UNESCO, *Statistical Yearbook,* various issues; UNDP, *1995*; Taiwan Province of China, Council for Economic Planning and Development, 1995; and information provided by Singapore's Ministry of Education.

[a]   Estimate.

Table VIII.2. Tertiary level students in technical fields

(Numbers and percentage)

Economy	Year	Natural science		Maths and computer		Engineering		All technical subjects		Science, mathematics, computers & engineering		Ratio of engineers to scientists
		Numbers	Per cent of population	Numbers	Per cent of population	Numbers	Per cent of population	Numbers	Per cent of population	Per cent Tertiary	Per cent of population	
China	1993	95492	0.008	174862	0.015	1156735	0.098	1831966	0.155	31.7	0.12	12.11
Hong Kong	1992	5503	0.095	6661	0.115	14788	0.256	35068	0.607	30.3	0.47	2.69
India	1990	869119	0.102	13117	0.102	216837	0.025	1036707	0.122	24.5	0.13	0.25
Indonesia	1992	22394	0.012	20891	0.007	205086	0.109	315325	0.167	13.4	0.13	9.16
Japan	1991	59030	0.048	145948	0.017	488699	0.394	730637	0.590	19.6	0.46	8.28
Republic of Korea	1993	75778	0.172	4557	0.331	367846	0.834	730346	1.655	31.2	1.34	4.85
Malaysia	1990	8775	0.049	..	0.025	12693	0.071	32222	0.180	21.4	0.15	1.45
Philippines	1993	..	..	..	..	211859	0.327	..	..	..	..	..
Singapore	1994	1281	0.046	1420	0.051	13029	0.465	16767	0.599	20.4	0.56	10.17
Taiwan Province of China	1993	16823	0.080	32757	0.157	179094	0.857	303964	1.454	42.3	1.09	10.65
Thailand	1992	77098	0.135	1292	0.002	105149	0.185	249952	0.439	15.9	0.32	1.36
Sub-total Asia		1231293	0.048	401505	0.016	2971815	0.116	5282954	0.207	24.1	0.18	2.41
Belgium	1990	6886	0.067	4019	0.039	32640	0.316	99250	0.961	32.7	0.42	4.74
Denmark	1992	5732	0.111	6700	0.130	20614	0.399	54811	1.060	21.0	0.64	3.60
France	1991	266299	0.467	..	..	123514	0.217	614159	1.078	21.2	0.68	0.46
Germany	1993	310435	0.384	..	..	389182	0.481	805801	0.997	37.3	0.87	1.25
Greece	1991	8024	0.078	6837	0.066	27659	0.269	71176	0.692	21.7	0.41	3.45
Ireland	1992	14191	0.400	2554	0.072	13885	0.392	37234	1.050	28.3	0.86	0.98
Italy	1993	93761	0.164	64099	0.112	200749	0.351	610642	1.069	21.3	0.63	2.14
Netherlands	1992	16707	0.110	8742	0.058	..	..	137510	0.905	..	0.17	..
Portugal	1991	7260	0.019	10180	0.027	28404	0.074	60616	0.158	24.0	0.12	3.91
Spain	1992	82751	0.210	65807	0.167	176702	0.448	473159	1.199	23.7	0.82	2.14
United Kingdom	1992	105983	0.183	76430	0.132	219078	0.378	596404	1.029	26.3	0.69	2.07
Sub-total EU		918029	0.245	245368	0.065	1232427	0.328	3560762	0.949	25.1	0.64	1.34
Czech Rep.	1993	2600	0.025	3299	0.032	36847	0.358	56342	0.547	33.0	0.42	14.17
Hungary	1993	1776	0.017	1588	0.015	10614	0.103	41718	0.405	10.4	0.14	5.98
Poland	1993	19047	0.050	12819	0.033	119912	0.312	254769	0.662	20.3	0.39	6.30
Sub-total CEE		23423	0.040	17706	0.030	167373	0.283	352829	0.598	20.6	0.35	7.15

Sources: UNESCO, *1995*; Taiwan Province of China, Council for Economic Planning and Development, 1995; and information provided by Singapore's Ministry of Education.

Notes: All technical subjects include natural sciences, mathematics and computer science, medical, engineering, architecture, trade and crafts and transport and communications. No data available for Luxembourg.

figure is lower than France, Germany, Ireland, Spain and the United Kingdom, but higher than the others. In *mathematics and computer science*, the Republic of Korea leads not only the Asian economies but all the European countries as well. In *engineering* the lead of the Asian NIEs is particularly large. The Republic of Korea, Taiwan Province of China and Singapore all have higher enrolment rates than Germany, which has the highest rate in Europe. China's 1.16 million engineering enrolments are almost equal to the entire European Union's 1.23 million, though the former's size means that in relation to the size of the population the figure is only 0.1 per cent.

The Asian emphasis on engineering rather than science contrasts with Europe. There is clearly a difference in educational emphasis between the regions. While there may be an expectation that, as economies become more developed, more scientists would be needed than engineers (to conduct more basic research), this does not apply to Asia: the richest country, Japan, and the industrially most advanced NIEs (Republic of Korea and Taiwan Province of China) continue to have a predominance of engineers rather than scientists. There is thus a greater emphasis on the more practical aspects of technical education in Asia, which contributes to their industrial efficiency and export dynamism.

Finally, it is relevant to consider *vocational training* (table VIII.3). In Asia, the leader by far, in enrolments as a percentage of the population, is Taiwan Province of China (2.4 per cent), followed by Republic of Korea (1.9 per cent), Singapore (1.1 per cent), and then the others. The European countries also show large differences, with enrolment rates varying from 5 per cent (the Netherlands) to under one per cent (Ireland, Luxembourg and Portugal). The three Central and Eastern European countries place a lot of weight on vocational training, with ratios of 2-4 per cent of their populations.

These data may not necessarily indicate the quality and intensity of training for industrial-related worker skills across countries, since different countries use different means of

Table VIII.3. Vocational training enrolments
(Numbers and per cent of population)

Economy	Year	Population (Thousands)	Vocational training Numbers	Per cent of population
China	1993	1 178 400	5 724 200	0.5
Hong Kong	1987	5 777	45 943	0.8
India	1993	901 459	853 752	0.1
Indonesia	1992	188 740	1 430 527	0.8
Japan	1991	123 921	1 452 097	1.2
Republic of Korea	1994	44 131	851 495	1.9
Malaysia	1990	17 892	40 944	0.2
Philippines	..	..	..	..
Singapore a	1993	2 800	30 448	1.1
Taiwan Province of China	1993	20 994	513 659	2.4
Thailand	1992	56 972	448 174	0.8
Belgium	1985	10 331	374 335	3.6
Denmark	1992	5 170	153 987	3.0
France	1993	56 998	1 251 295	2.2
Germany	1993	80 857	2 264 244	2.8
Greece	1990	10 289	134 949	1.3
Ireland	1992	3 546	25 549	0.7
Italy	1993	57 127	1 789 922	3.1
Luxembourg	1987	10 331	14 790	0.1
Netherlands	1992	15 186	701 413	4.7
Portugal	1991	38 245	50 149	0.1
Spain	1993	39 452	1 169 409	3.0
United Kingdom	1992	57 971	586 000	1.0
Czech Rep.	1993	10 296	240 799	2.3
Hungary	1993	10 292	388 990	3.8
Poland	1993	38 460	1 505 465	3.9

Sources: UNESCO, *1995;* Taiwan Province of China, Council for Economic Planning and Development, 1995; and information provided by Singapore's Ministry of Education.

a   Include technical enrolments at secondary level and the Institute of Technical Education.

imparting such training, and the contents of the courses differs widely. Nevertheless, they do indicate that the European countries are generally well advanced in this respect, and, given their much longer experience of training, also have very large accumulated stocks of trained manpower. On top of this must be added skills learnt on the job and gained from enterprise-funded training programmes.

Employee training is growing rapidly in Asia. Japan is renowned for its investments in such training. In developing Asia, the Republic of Korea leads in terms of firm-level spending on training; the Government has levied a 5 per cent payroll training levy on larger firms for some two decades now. Singapore has a well-developed system of external training for employees, with the Government taking the lead in setting up advanced training centres (many in collaboration with TNCs and foreign governments) and giving financial incentives to firms to release employees for training. Taiwan Province of China has a range of institutions to help its small and medium-sized enterprises to upgrade worker skills. Other Asian countries lag in creating advanced industrial skills, though they are making strong attempts to catch up.

To conclude: inspite of great diversity, dramatic progress has been made on the part of NIEs in creating technical, especially engineering, skills to support the ownership advantages of their firms. The sheer pace of growth in tertiary technical education in the Republic of Korea and Taiwan Province of China, given their low starting point some four decades ago, is impressive indeed. The other NIEs have pockets of strength. The new NIEs and other Asian developing economies are lagging somewhat, and may face increasing difficulties in providing skills as their industrial structures become more technologically complex. This suggests that, in terms of the competitive advantages of firms in investing in Europe, firms from the two larger NIEs, the Republic of Korea and Taiwan Province of China, will dominate FDI in manufacturing activity, with firms from the smaller NIEs playing more of a role in service-related FDI. The other Asian countries will tend to have more specialised advantages in industrial niches, mainly in simpler technologies.

B. Technological capacities

Asian developing countries remain overwhelmingly dependent on imports of technology from the more mature industrial countries. Nevertheless, they undertake significant technological activities, to absorb complex technologies locally and to adapt and improve upon imported knowledge. The extent to which formal research and development is undertaken in each country depends upon the complexity of the industrial structure, the degree of local ownership (foreign ownership reduces the need for local research and development) and exposure to international competition (more protected economies tend to do less research and development) (table VIII.4).

Research-and-development expenditures as a proportion of GDP in developing Asia is highest in the Republic of Korea, which spends 2.3 per cent of GDP on research and development. This figure is only slightly below that of the main technological leaders in developed countries; more impressively, over 80 per cent of the Republic of Korea's research and development originates in firms rather than from the Government, one of the highest ratios in the world. By 1993, the Republic of Korea had nearly 100,000 researchers, a sharp increase from 41,000 in 1985 and a mere 10,000 in 1975; the number of corporate research-and-development units had risen from 12 in 1975 to 183 in 1985 and 1690 in 1993 (Kim, forthcoming). This was the result of Government policies to promote heavy industry, encourage the growth of the *chaebol* and force them to enter export markets and to import technology at arm's length rather than in the internalized form of FDI (Lall, 1995). This intense research-and-development effort is also the engine behind the technological dynamism of Korean TNCs: there are few other developing country enterprises that can match them in sheer research-and-development "muscle". For instance, in 1994 one of the leading *chaebol*, Hyundai, employed nearly 4,000 researchers only in its automobile division (Kim, forthcoming). The *chaebol* account for an overwhelming proportion of Korean research and development, and they also account for the bulk of its FDI. This means that Korean TNCs resemble developed country TNCs, with a strong technological base, differentiated products and a presence in developed markets, unlike traditional low-technology developing country TNCs. This gives them a distinct edge over firms from other Asian developing economies in investing in Europe.

Taiwan Province of China has the next highest research and development spending as a proportion of GDP of the Asian developing country group, in terms of dollars per capita, even slightly ahead of the Republic of Korea. However, more than half of this comes from public sources: since the industrial structure is dominated by small and medium-sized enterprises, the bulk of private firms is unable to undertake expensive and risky research. Public authorities compensate by providing an extensive infrastructure of public research-and-development institutes and technical services that conduct contract design, development and productivity enhancement for small and medium-sized TNCs. Taiwan Province of China has one of the most effective systems of industrial technology support in the developing world, and this enables small and medium-sized enterprises to grow in world markets. However, most of these enterprises can only undertake FDI in relatively less-advanced economies, mainly the low wage economies of South-East Asia. The relatively small number of large, high-technology enterprises that lead Taiwan Province of China's outward FDI surge are very much like the *chaebols*, but lack the latter's technological "muscle".

Private industrial research and development is weak in other Asian countries. Singapore has increased such research and development in recent years, but much of it is in foreign affiliates and universities and does not feed into the capabilities of local firms (though there are some dynamic firms like Creative Labs and Aztech which are world leaders in their field, in this case computer-sound equipment). Hong Kong lacks a significant research-and-development base altogether, though it is trying to promote one by setting up subsidised science parks and technical universities. There are pockets of technological development in large

Table VIII.4. Asian research and development

(Per cent of GDP)

Economy	Year	Total	By enterprises	Per capita R&D (Dollars)
China	1992	0.5	..	2.4
India	1992	1.0	0.22	3.1
Indonesia	1993	0.2	0.04	1.5
Malaysia	1992	0.4	0.17	11.2
Thailand	1991	0.2	0.04	3.1
Philippines	1984	0.1	-	0.7
Singapore	1992	1.0	0.6	153.6
Hong Kong	1995	0.1	..	19.8
Taiwan Province of China	1993	1.7	0.8	179.6
Republic of Korea	1993	2.3	1.98	176.2
Japan	1992	3.0	1.9	762.9

Sources: UNESCO, *Statistical Yearbook,* and national sources.

economies like China, India, Thailand and Indonesia; some of these are quite advanced, such as space and defence technology in China, and some may in turn lead to technology-based FDI. While most such advantages are likely to be exploited in other developing countries rather than in advanced industrial countries, there will be technological niches that these economies exploit by FDI in Europe.

Looking at research-and-development manpower in Asia (table VIII.5), Taiwan Province of China has the highest number of research and development scientists and engineers per million population in developing Asia, followed by Singapore, Republic of Korea and China.[1] The lowest is Philippines. India, Indonesia and Thailand are somewhat more advanced and all at roughly the same level. The differences between the research-and-development expenditures and manpower reflect different intensities of activity per researcher involved (and perhaps in the definitions of research and development and scientists and engineers between countries).

C. Government support

The governments of the Asian countries have played different roles in creating competitive advantages for their firms and encouraging their overseas exploitation by FDI. Some governments, as in the Republic of Korea and Taiwan Province of China, have been very interventionist in trade, investment and factor markets; their support for indigenous technology development underlies the growth of their competitiveness and the forms that it has taken. Others, like Singapore, have also been very interventionist, but more to target and upgrade inward FDI and gear their human resources to industrial policy aims rather than promote indigenous technological capabilities. Hong Kong is unique in having left all resource allocations to market forces. The new NIEs have adopted strategies that are mixtures of those of the NIEs, with generally a greater reliance on inward FDI than the larger NIEs, but not to the extent of Singapore. Apart from helping develop underlying competitive advantages, Asian governments have helped FDI abroad by their firms through a number of measures (as discussed earlier).

Table VIII.5. Scientists, engineers and technicians in research and development

Economy	Year	R&D scientists and engineers per million population	R&D technicians per million population
China	1992	1129	428
Hong Kong	1990	..	..
India	1990	151	114
Indonesia	1988	181	..
Japan	1992	5677	869
Republic of Korea	1992	1190	349
Malaysia	1988	326	69
Philippines	1984	90	35
Singapore	1987	1284	583
Taiwan Province of China	1991	1673	573
Thailand	1991	174	51
Belgium	1990	1856	2041
Denmark	1991	3241	2663
France	1991	2267	2972
Germany	1989	10701	5115
Greece	1986	53	49
Ireland	1988	1801	366
Italy	1990	1366	742
Netherlands	1991	2656	1777
Portugal	1990	599	381
Spain	1990	956	299
United Kingdom	1991	..	..
Czech Republic	1991	3248	1298
Hungary	1992	1200	697
Poland	1992	1083	1380

Sources: UNESCO, 1995; Taiwan Province of China, Council for Economic Planning and Development, 1995.

CONCLUSIONS TO PART TWO

It is always difficult to predict the precise scale and nature of such a dynamic phenomenon as FDI; it is even more difficult to predict this for such rapidly growing and evolving economies as those in Asia. However, the evidence does allow some broad generalizations to emerge.

The growth of Asian FDI in Europe is bound to increase as exports from Asia to Europe grow and Asian capabilities deepen and become more diversified. As far as manufacturing FDI is concerned, this will be mainly driven by the attractions of the large market, the desire to overcome potential protectionism and the need to be nearer to customers. However, other factors will become increasingly important as Asian economies move into more complex industrial technologies and higher value-added services. These will include the need to access new technologies and learn new skills, the growth of global production strategies by their leading enterprises, and the need for firms to diversify their locational portfolios. At this more advanced stage, FDI in Europe will be considered necessary to maintain competitiveness, and enter into strategic alliances with European counterparts and participate in the liberalized environment for infrastructure and services provision in Europe.

Within Europe, Asian investors can be expected to target locations according to their differing needs for levels of skill, access to suppliers or proximity to customers. Central and Eastern Europe can benefit from Asian investments that seek lower wages and relatively advanced industrial skills, but more high cost sites will also receive FDI that need advanced technology and supplier clusters to operate efficiently.

As far as services-related FDI is concerned, firms from all Asian countries can enter into Europe in a range of activities. The more high-technology end of services—telecommunications, investment banking, media, infrastructure—is likely to be served by TNCs from the new NIEs and the new NIEs that have accumulated sufficient expertise and experience by operating in locations within Asia. For the foreseeable future, this set of activities is likely to be dominated by Hong Kong and Singapore. Major exporters from Asia are likely to invest in downstream marketing-support activities in the main European markets. The lower technology services industries can be entered by firms from almost any Asian economy, since the competitive advantages required are easily acquired.

In sum, four distinct groups of investment patterns are likely to emerge:

- Investment from the technologically advanced NIEs, with advanced skill and research bases and large indigenous firms capable of setting up state-of-the-art facilities in complex industrial activities and undertaking global production. These investors would focus on large-scale manufacturing and trading, and originate largely from the Republic of Korea and, to a lesser extent, from Taiwan Province of China. Over time, other investments in the services sector are also likely to emerge as banks, insurance companies, construction firms and infrastructure providers develop the necessary capabilities.

- Investment from the smaller NIEs (Singapore and Hong Kong), with capabilities in high value-added services and some manufacturing niches (advanced ones for Singapore and simpler ones for Hong Kong). Their investments in services would range from trade and finance to tourism.

- Investment from the new NIEs, Indonesia, Malaysia, the Philippines and Thailand, that are developing indigenous specialized capabilities in industries like components, resource-based activities like food, wood, rubber and petrochemicals and also in some more labour-intensive activities like textiles. Investment from these countries may also develop in some service activities.

- Investment from the large economies of China and India, which have large and diversified industrial bases but need to upgrade their technologies in several major industries. These economies may catch up in a range of industries to the level of undertaking FDI in Europe, in both labour and skill-intensive industries. However, they are unlikely to become major investors in Europe in the foreseeable future rather, they can be expected to concentrate on other developing countries for some time to come.

Notes

[1] According to UNESCO data, China has 1.3 million scientists and engineers in research and development, a higher absolute number than for the United States (under 1 million) (UNESCO, 1995).

Statistical appendix to Part Two

Table A1. Manufactured exports by technological categories, all Asia

(Millions of dollars)

SITC number and product	1980 World	1980 EU	1980 CEE	1985 World	1985 EU	1985 CEE	1994 World	1994 EU	1994 CEE
Resource-based									
12 Tobacco and manufactures	464.7	112.6	2.0	446.3	67.0	14.8	2339.8	108.0	5.7
61 Leather, dressed fur, etc.	581.5	145.4	34.0	390.2	58.1	5.7	4664.4	385.6	1.7
63 Wood, cork, manufactures	2000.7	377.2	0.1	2298.0	284.1	2.2	8771.3	1157.2	2.5
64 Paper, paperboard and manufactures	385.2	29.3	0.1	651.4	30.5	1.8	4155.0	189.0	8.7
66 Non-metal mineral manufactures	1979.0	295.8	1.2	1815.7	137.9	13.1	7509.0	1130.1	4.4
82 Furniture	596.1	54.8	-	1227.4	48.3	0.4	6285.9	821.4	8.5
Sub-total	6007.2	1015.1	37.4	6829.0	625.9	38.0	33725.4	3791.3	31.5
Labour-intensive									
65 Textile yarn, fabric, etc.	7047.7	847.8	48.1	10341.7	777.0	85.3	41596.4	3134.9	241.5
69 Metal manufactures	2559.2	294.8	3.5	4147.2	268.7	13.1	14390.0	2353.4	27.0
83 Travel goods, handbags	1262.3	243.0	0.2	1619.7	209.1	-	4294.9	773.2	15.7
84 Clothing	11854.0	2375.0	59.7	17669.0	1895.4	157.8	54731.6	9755.8	871.7
85 Footwear	2619.4	387.0	0.6	4323.5	390.4	22.9	11884.8	2135.5	246.8
89 Miscellaneous manufactured goods	6111.1	997.0	4.1	9669.8	1061.4	34.1	35001.3	5402.9	115.4
Sub-total	31453.7	5144.6	116.2	47770.9	4602.0	313.2	161899.0	23555.7	1518.1
Scale-intensive									
5 Chemicals	2638.3	115.8	2.3	5016.9	374.1	63.2	28173.5	2780.1	58.0
62 Rubber manufactures	846.5	90.5	1.3	895.4	89.9	19.2	3540.0	716.5	15.2
67 Iron and steel	2419.4	109.0	0.5	2975.7	56.1	0.9	10132.2	304.4	3.6
78 Road vehicles	1353.8	69.2	0.7	2236.8	89.4	2.9	15255.0	2456.6	112.4
79 Other transport equipment	1669.5	166.3	1.1	6518.6	999.0	3.8	10062.3	1330.8	39.9
Sub-total	8927.5	550.8	5.9	17643.4	1608.5	90.0	67163.0	7588.4	229.1
Differentiated									
71 Power generating machinery	606.0	34.5	0.1	885.9	64.7	5.1	5379.2	530.7	23.7
72 Machinery specific industry	924.6	37.5	0.3	1496.6	63.4	7.5	8338.5	462.4	16.5
73 Metal working machinery	323.0	21.1	1.1	423.9	27.6	4.0	2327.1	198.0	1.3
74 General industrial machinery	899.5	48.3	1.3	1550.6	78.7	0.3	12419.8	886.7	13.6
76 Telecom. recording machinery	5663.5	834.1	6.2	7399.0	821.7	3.7	49848.3	8397.8	301.7
77 Electrical machinery and appliances	6501.8	535.7	1.2	11077.6	1090.8	10.4	77128.2	10649.9	92.2
81 Plumbing, heating and lighting equipment	227.2	28.0	-	388.2	27.0	0.6	2063.8	276.3	3.7
Sub-total	15145.6	1539.2	10.2	23221.8	2173.9	31.6	157504.9	21401.8	452.7
Science-based									
75 Office and ADP equipment	884.4	89.9	0.1	4195.4	617.4	2.3	52372.8	11728.2	153.5
87 Professional, scientifc instruments	287.2	35.8	0.1	561.1	48.6	3.9	4283.3	790.2	9.2
88 Photographic aparatus	2393.6	420.6	0.7	2479.8	292.2	1.9	9146.2	1310.1	18.2
Sub-total	3565.2	546.3	0.9	7236.3	958.2	8.1	65802.3	13828.5	180.9
TOTAL	65099.2	8796	170.6	102701.4	9968.5	480.9	486094.6	70165.7	2412.3

Source: UNCTAD, trade database.

Table A2. Manufactured exports by technological categories, four newly industrializing economies[a]

(Millions of dollars)

SITC number and product	1980			1985			1994		
	World	EU	CEE	World	EU	CEE	World	EU	CEE
Resource-based									
12 Tobacco and manufactures	136.3	37.2	-	276.7	38.3	-	1371.3	4.5	1.2
61 Leather, dressed fur, etc.	156.2	20.0	-	283.6	26.2	-	3318.6	96.8	0.6
63 Wood, cork, manufactures	1440.6	259.6	-	989.4	120.5	-	1061.1	177.7	0.4
64 Paper, paperboard and manufactures	353.8	29.1	-	450.1	25.9	-	2458.6	75.7	2.5
66 Nonmetal mineral manufactures	1041.8	121.0	-	1198.9	81.8	-	2382.1	246.7	1.5
82 furniture	463.7	35.7	-	989.7	20.7	-	2289.3	188.9	3.5
Sub-total	3592.4	502.6	-	4188.4	313.4	-	12881.0	790.3	9.7
Labour-intensive									
65 Textile yarn, fabric, etc.	5276.6	478.6	12.0	6402.8	375.0	5.2	24403.6	992.2	174.9
69 Metal manufacturers	2220.2	246.7	1.1	3641.2	228.7	0.1	9369.6	1427.9	19.4
83 Travel goods, handbags	1220.8	233.5	-	1513.7	196.6	-	1323.8	143.5	2.2
84 Clothing	10470.3	1976.9	49.1	14224.9	1527.6	32.6	20125.1	4362.6	38.1
85 Footwear	2447.7	342.6	0.1	3927.3	310.4	-	2551.3	419.9	26.5
89 Miscellaneous manufactured goods	5574.5	887.5	1.2	8308.1	881.2	1.8	16821.5	2371.6	63.0
Sub-total	27210.1	4165.8	63.5	38018.0	3519.5	39.7	74594.9	9717.7	324.1
Scale-intensive									
5 Chimical	2027.1	55.6	0.9	3102.5	134.5	1.7	17907.2	1137.3	12.5
62 Rubber manufactures	744.1	76.3	-	746.1	74.1	0.1	2266.2	449.6	9.8
67 Iron and steel	2200.6	99.7	0.5	2666.7	37.1	-	7200.4	86.1	0.2
78 Road vehicles	1085.5	51.7	-	2123.3	85.2	-	11730.3	2029.0	104.9
79 Other transport equipment	1536.8	144.1	-	6106.0	971.5	0.3	6753.4	988.7	1.8
Sub-total	7594.1	427.4	1.4	14744.6	1302.4	2.1	45857.5	4690.7	129.2
Differentiated									
71 Power generating machinery	499.0	21.7	-	779.9	41.4	-	3410.8	288.9	22.4
72 Machinery, specific industry	812.5	34.6	-	1216.2	60.2	0.4	7029.5	399.8	10.5
73 Metal working machinery	287.8	18.1	-	385.7	26.3	0.2	1854.2	142.6	1.0
74 General industrial machinery	759.5	44.0	-	1317.0	70.6	0.1	8453.1	571.8	11.7
76 Telecom., recording machinery	5520.2	803.9	5.3	6900.0	746.8	3.4	28201.9	4930.6	255.5
77 Electrical machinery and appliances	4735.6	434.0	0.7	8164.3	772.2	4.0	51495.7	6931.8	72.1
81 Plumbing, heating, lighting equipment	212.7	27.8	-	341.4	26.4	-	1028.6	119.9	2.2
Sub-total	12827.3	1384.1	6.0	19104.5	1743.9	8.1	101473.8	13385.4	375.4
Science-based									
75 Office and ADP machinery	876.3	89.6	0.1	4105.2	614.3	2.0	40003.5	9818.7	139.4
87 Professional, scientific instruments	250.6	23.8	-	444.8	38.0	0.4	2958.4	496.3	5.7
88 Photographic apparatus	2263.8	414.8	0.7	2325.4	279.8	0.9	5346.7	855.9	12.5
Sub-total	3390.7	528.2	0.8	6875.4	932.1	3.3	48308.6	11170.9	157.6
TOTAL	54614.6	7008.1	71.7	82930.9	7811.3	53.2	283115.8	39755.0	996.0

Source: UNCTAD, trade database.

[a]   Hong Kong, Republic of Korea, Singapore and Taiwan Province of China.

Table A3: Manufactured exports by technological categories, non-newly industrializing economies

(Millions of dollars)

SITC number and product	1980 World	EU	CEE	1985 World	EU	CEE	1994 World	EU	CEE
Resource-based									
60 Tobacco and manufactures	328.4	75.4	2.0	169.6	28.7	14.8	968.5	103.5	4.5
61 Leather, dressed fur etc.	425.3	125.4	34.0	106.6	31.9	5.7	1345.8	288.8	1.1
63 Wood, cork, manufactures	560.1	117.6	0.1	1308.6	163.6	2.2	7710.2	979.5	2.1
64 Paper, paperboard and manufactures	31.4	0.2	0.1	201.3	4.6	1.8	1696.4	113.3	6.2
66 Nonmetal mineral manufactures	937.2	174.8	1.2	616.8	56.1	13.1	5126.9	883.4	2.9
82 Furniture	132.4	19.1	0.0	237.7	27.6	0.4	3996.6	632w.5	5.0
Sub-total	2414.8	512.5	37.4	2640.6	312.5	38.0	20844.4	3001.0	21.8
Labour-intensive									
65 Textile yarn, fabric, etc.	1771.1	369.2	36.1	3938.9	402.0	80.1	17192.8	2142.7	66.6
69 Metal manufactures	339.0	48.1	2.4	506.0	40.0	13.0	5020.4	925.5	7.6
83 Travel goods, handbags	41.5	9.5	0.2	106.0	12.5	-	2971.1	629.7	13.5
84 Clothing	1383.7	398.1	10.6	3444.1	367.8	125.2	34606.5	5393.2	833.6
85 Footwear	171.7	44.4	0.5	396.2	80.0	22.9	9333.5	1715.6	220.3
89 Miscellaneous manufactured goods	536.6	109.5	2.9	1361.7	180.2	32.3	18179.8	3031.3	52.4
Sub-total	4243.6	978.8	52.7	9752.9	1082.5	273.5	87304.1	13838.0	1194.0
Scale-intensive									
5 Chemicals	611.2	60.2	1.4	1914.4	239.6	61.5	10266.3	1642.8	45.5
62 Rubber manufactures	102.4	14.2	1.3	149.3	15.8	19.1	1273.8	266.9	5.4
67 Iron and steel	218.8	9.3	-	309.0	19.0	0.9	2931.8	218.3	3.4
78 Road vehicles	268.3	17.5	0.7	113.5	4.2	2.9	3524.7	427.6	7.5
79 Other transport equipment	132.7	22.2	1.1	412.6	27.5	3.5	3308.9	342.1	38.1
Sub-total	1333.4	123.4	4.5	2898.8	306.1	87.9	21305.5	2897.7	99.9
Differentiated									
71 Power generating machinery	107.0	12.8	0.1	106.0	23.3	5.1	1968.4	241.8	1.3
72 Machinery, specific industry	112.1	2.9	0.3	280.4	3.2	7.1	1309.0	62.6	6.0
73 Metal working machinery	35.2	3.0	1.1	38.2	1.3	3.8	472.9	55.4	0.3
74 General industrial machinery	140.0	4.3	1.3	233.6	8.1	0.2	3966.7	314.9	1.9
76 Telecom., recording machinery	143.3	30.2	0.9	499.0	74.9	0.3	21646.4	3467.2	46.2
77 Electrical machinery and appliances	1766.2	101.7	0.5	2913.3	318.6	6.4	25632.5	3718.1	20.1
81 Plumbing, heating and lighting equipment	14.5	0.2	-	46.8	0.6	0.6	1035.2	156.4	1.5
Sub-total	2318.3	155.1	4.2	4117.3	430.0	23.5	56031.1	8016.4	77.3
Science-based									
75 Office and ADP machinery	8.1	0.3	0.0	90.2	3.1	0.3	12369.3	1909.5	14.1
87 Professional, scientific instruments	36.6	12.0	0.1	116.3	10.6	3.5	1324.9	293.9	3.5
88 Photographic apparatus	129.8	5.8	-	154.4	12.4	1.0	3799.5	454.2	5.7
Sub-total	174.5	18.1	0.1	360.9	26.1	4.8	17493.7	2657.6	23.3
TOTAL	10484.6	1787.9	98.9	19770.5	2157.2	427.7	202978.8	30410.7	1416.3

Source: UNCTAD, trade database.

PART THREE

POLICY IMPLICATIONS: BUILDING ON
THE EXISTING PARTNERSHIPS

Chapter IX

ACTION BY ASIAN GOVERNMENTS AND FIRMS

Prior to discussing measures that can be taken by Asian economies to encourage FDI in the European Union, three factors need to be underlined. First, the Asian economies differ widely in terms of their development, national objectives and structure of international investment and trade. In consequence, it is important to recognize that it is necessary for each economy to formulate policies towards outward FDI that are particular to its conditions and objectives, albeit in cooperation with other Asian economies where mutually beneficial. Secondly, Asian TNCs vary widely in terms of their investment motivations, characteristics and FDI capability, and Asian policies need to take this into account. Finally, few Asian economies have a well articulated plan or policy regarding FDI in Europe (some, indeed, have no specific or well-articulated policy for outward FDI at all); the formulation of such policy should precede the formulation of further measures. In so doing, governments could consider drawing on input from their firms, many of which may well welcome a commitment to support investment into Europe.

A. Maintaining the momentum of investment liberalization

In recent years, more and more Asian governments have begun to turn their attention to the liberalization of outward FDI — the precondition for FDI to occur, be it in Europe, the region or elsewhere in the world. This trend is unlikely to be reversed in the near future since outward FDI is now increasingly seen as a strategic option needed to establish a presence in foreign markets, access foreign resources and increase the competitiveness of national firms.

Balancing the development strategy of the economy (e.g., increasing investment and utilizing domestic resources more fully while balancing external payments) and the competitive requirements of maintaining — if not improving — the international competitiveness of national companies (which may require the option to invest abroad) is a dilemma faced by many Asian economies. Nevertheless, such internationalization, in the form of FDI, can be ultimately beneficial to the country, for example by assisting in capturing additional overseas markets or the acquisition of technological assets. As chapter V showed, Asian companies with the necessary capabilities can gain considerable advantages by locating in Europe, and constraining them could not only result in a loss of these benefits, but, broader, it could reduce their international competitiveness. This suggests that governments should continue with the liberalization of their policies related to outward FDI — of course, within the framework of national development objectives. There are various ways to liberalize outward FDI policies ranging from permitting exceptions to promoting outward FDI actively. Experience suggests that the liberalization process should be undertaken carefully as it entails a number of risks.[1]

1. Approval approaches

For countries that have not yet begun to liberalize their outward FDI regime, one option is to liberalize all outward FDI at once. A second, more typical option is to phase liberalization (see figure IX.1 for the example of Taiwan Province of China), and this usually involves the construction of a mechanism to approve desired outward FDI. Such an approval process enables governments to control directly the purposes, nature and dimensions of outward FDI projects, while reducing the extent and restrictiveness of general controls. An important step is to publish the evaluation criteria against which proposed projects are measured, with a specified timetable for final decisions. Similar to inward FDI screening procedures, this process increases transparency and limits administrative discretion, thereby permitting better business planning while minimizing potential bureaucratic manipulation.

There are various modalities for evaluating and approving outward FDI proposals among which governments can choose to enable them to meet their particular objectives and concerns. For example:

- A minimal procedure would only examine, basically, whether the applicant is in good standing in respect of its domestic financial obligations. A somewhat different but related approach would be to test the financial soundness of the prospective outward investor, requiring at least a minimum period without bankruptcy or, more positively, a certain level of profitability over a number of years as a measure of management s ability and the probable success of the new venture.

- Another approach would be to organize the approval or licensing process on the basis of the size of the prospective investment, similar to the graduated evaluation procedure established by the Republic of Korea that requires a full assessment only for the largest projects. This approach would lessen the inhibiting effects of regulatory restrictions, especially for small investors, while saving administrative time and expense. On the other hand, the cumulative impact of numerous small investments could still negatively affect a country s balance of payments. Automatic authorizations of small investments might also be abused by investors who could arrange to link multiple small investments together at some point, thereby evading the regulatory scrutiny normally given to larger projects.

- A third approach could be to evaluate all proposed outward FDI projects against a list of benefits desired for the country. The specific benefit criteria may vary from country to country, but would generally aim at obtaining benefits from access to resources and markets, as well as economic restructuring. Measurements for the criteria could include increased exports, inward technology transfers, raw material imports and repatriated earnings. Particular business sectors are often closely associated with certain types of benefits so that criteria may be specified in terms of qualifying industries rather than specific benefits.

- An industry approach would be more appropriate if the opposite, "negative list" approach were chosen, requiring review and licensing only for specified industries in

Figure IX.1. The evolution of the outward FDI regime of Taiwan Province of China

	1962	1979	1984	1987
Financial requirements	• Minimum paid in capital NT $100 million • Debt/equity ratio lower than 200 per cent • Maximum total capital contribution 30 per cent of parent firm's capital • Average net profits to paid-in capital (3 years) higher than 10 per cent • Average net profits in sales (3 years) over 5 per cent • Current assets/current debt ratio lower than 100 per cent	• Minimum paid-in capital NT $50 million • Debt/equity ratio lower than 300 per cent • Maximum total capital contribution 40 per cent of parent firm's capital	• Minimum paid-in capital NT $20 million	• Relaxed exchange controls, lifted maximum capital contribution

Incentives	N o n e	*Incentives*
		• 5 year income tax exemption
		
		type of outward FDI
		to
		• Extractive industries
		• Exploitation of natural resources
			Incentives
			• 5 year income tax exemption
			• Financial assistance
			• Outward investment insurance
			• Government services
			  • Information
			  • Seminars
			  • Business missions
			  • Data bank on business opportunities
			
			type of outward FDI
			to
			• Extractive industries
			• Exploitation of natural resources
			• Production and processing of agricultural products or raw materials for industry
			• Transfer of technology
			• Selected enterprises selling to domestic or foreign markets
				Incentives
				• Reservation for loss in outward investment
				• Financial assistance
				• Outward investment insurance
				• Government support to outward investment to Latin America and the Caribbean
				  • Travel expenses
				  • Preferential loans
				  • Preferential insurance
				• Government services
				  • Overseas Taiwan Investment Centre
				  • Overseas Industrial Estates
				  • Investment missions
				  • Information
				  • Seminars
				  • Data on business opportunities
				  • Negotiating agreements with host countries
				
				type of outward FDI
				to
				• Acquisition of natural resources
				• Expansion of exports/securing markets
				• Acquisition of technology
				• Promotion of exports of technical know-how
				• Promotion of international economic cooperation
				• Helping adjustment of industrial structure
				• Indirect transfer of technology through capital operations

Source: UNCTAD-DTCI, 1995, p. 325.

which outward FDI might involve certain negative impacts for the home economy (e.g., loss of jobs). Such an approach was introduced in the Republic of Korea in 1994.

• Another approach is to review and approve outward FDI applications in terms of country or regional destinations. For example, Malaysia and Singapore encourage outward FDI particularly to neighbouring developing countries.

Each of these options, individually or in combination with each other, would permit Asian economies with restrictive regulations on outward FDI to liberalize their regimes incrementally. The administration of this process could be further facilitated if "one-stop shops" for outward investors would assist in obtaining the required approvals, permits and licences.

2. Dealing with foreign exchange concerns

The feasibility of liberalizing outward FDI policies may be linked to a country s foreign exchange position, and especially its current account balance (box 15). If the underlying philosophy of a country with respect to outward FDI policy is favourable, there are various technical possibilities to deal with any perceived foreign exchange constraint to liberalization:

• Outward FDI could be financed by foreign borrowing. This is, in fact, not an uncommon practice (though not recorded in FDI flow statistics); in the case of Japan, for example, affiliates abroad raised 58 per cent of their funds through the local issuance of corporate bonds and loans from local financial institutions in 1992 (Japan, Ministry of International Trade and Industry, 1994). In the case of a merger or acquisition, the foreign borrowing could be secured by the assets acquired (i.e., they would be pledged to the lender), with the servicing and repayment of the debt being made from profits arising from the new venture (box 16). Where an outward FDI takes the form of a new (greenfield) enterprise, a guarantee could be issued by the parent firm in the home country, with this guarantee to be replaced by the pledging of the assets once these have been established abroad. This guarantee (unless executed) would not appear in the balance of payments of the home country. However, care would have to be taken in the issuance of such "investment guarantees" since they will be taken into account in determining the credit available to the country from abroad for other purposes, such as trade financing, under so-called "country limits" restrictions that determine undue credit exposure to any one country.

• Once an outward greenfield FDI project is approved and a foreign bank has agreed to finance it, the government of the home country could provide a guarantee for the loan required (either by itself or together with, e.g., an international financial institution or a regional development bank). In a variation of this approach, domestic financial institutions could issue the guarantee to obtain the necessary credit from abroad (with the government perhaps giving an implicit guarantee to these institutions). This could be a sort of bridging guarantee, to be replaced by the assets of the foreign affiliate once it becomes established. However, such operations may only be sensible in the case of large projects.

• Foreign-direct-investment venture capital funds could be established by investors permitted to do so and looking for good projects. These funds, in turn, could provide finance to FDI projects, including approved FDI projects by firms in countries that restrict capital outflows on account of foreign exchange difficulties. The Governments of Brunei and Singapore, for example, have jointly established in 1994 a venture capital fund for infrastructure projects in Asia.

• Another possibility would be to allow entities such as insurance companies and pension funds to diversify their investments by investing abroad. Initial permission for such outward portfolio investment could be linked to the funding of approved outward FDI projects from the same country, thereby utilizing the same foreign exchange draw-off for a dual purpose. Such a facility could be of particular interest in the case of mergers and acquisitions, as these provide an immediate collateral.

Box. 15. Liberalizing foreign exchange controls

Liberalized foreign exchange regulations are often a part of broader policy reforms -- including initiatives to attract inward FDI -- that open a country to the world economy. However, there may be various reasons why it is not possible to liberalize controls all at once, and typically outward FDI ranks low on a country s priority list in the use of foreign exchange.

Liberalization of the capital account typically begins with inward investment and explicit conditions governing the repatriation of non-resident capital and interest and dividends. Inward FDI poses less of a potential threat to a host country s foreign exchange position than more volatile flows of liquid capital because the acquired assets are illiquid and, frequently, TNCs will want to reinvest some of their profits into an expansion of their affiliates. Moreover, it is possible, in principle, for the portfolio of inward FDI to be biased towards foreign-exchange saving activities (export-creation and import-substitution) so that inward FDI will cover its own foreign-exchange costs.

The different implications of direct and financial inward investment are also relevant to phasing a possible parallel liberalization of outward FDI. Countries that have sufficient foreign exchange reserves to consider liberalizing restrictions on inward portfolio (financial) investments may have enough of a cushion to consider permitting outward FDI, or at least certain types of it. Hence, a liberalization of the capital account to permit outward FDI does not necessarily need to wait for a fully permissive regime for all inward capital flows to be established.

In this context, it is important to remember that, once liberalization steps are taken, it is costly to reverse them, especially in terms of damaging the country s international financial standing. (For example, reimposing restrictions on outward FDI will underline the weakness of a country s overall reserve position.) Hence, authorities often take a cautious approach to the liberalization of capital controls, to assure that the reforms can be maintained and to allow, in a phased manner, for the economy to adjust gradually to the changes. In other words, phasing allows a government to watch the effects of each step on the economy before taking the next step.

Phasing the liberalization of outward investment policy also affects the relationship between direct and portfolio investment. For example, once outward FDI is derestricted, other external transactions may be made possible through foreign affiliates unless such transactions are regulated and monitored by home country authorities. (A certain level of investment in short-term instruments would constitute a normal business activity to manage cashflow.) Conversely, if a government permitted outward portfolio investments but not outward FDI, potential leakage into FDI-related activities would be even more difficult to monitor or control. This consideration would be relevant, for example, if a country wanted to restrict outward FDI to avoid adverse impacts on domestic employment or for foreign policy purposes; the permitted outward portfolio investment could provide a channel to circumvent such restrictions.

Source: UNCTAD-DTCI, 1995, p. 347.

- In cases where foreign affiliates already exist, a government could permit the free usage of the earnings of these affiliates for (additional) investment abroad, be it for the expansion of an existing venture or the establishment of new ventures. Such "reinvested" earnings involve, for balance-of-payments account purposes, simultaneous and offsetting entries in both the current and capital accounts, i.e., they do not affect the level of foreign reserves.

- Much FDI, particularly by middle income developing countries, involves the establishment of sourcing or marketing affiliates in countries that are less developed than the home country. Such FDI is less likely to be subject to a foreign exchange constraint in terms of convertible currencies. (This is the case in Thailand, as noted earlier.) It is possible that the central bank of the home country has assets denominated in the (non-convertible) currency of the potential host country; in that event, it my be easier to authorize outward FDI.

- The assets used for outward FDI need not always be of a monetary nature. For instance, they can consist of such intangible assets as intellectual property rights (including trademarks and patents), goodwill and brand names or such tangible assets as capital equipment (an approach pursued, for example, by India), or raw materials. Some of these approaches may be particularly suitable for joint ventures. Even where foreign exchange is involved, joint ventures reduce proportionately the contribution to be made by parent firms. China appears to have a preference for this approach.

- Since lasting control over assets abroad -- the defining characteristic of FDI -- can also be established through means other than equity, the use of non-equity forms could be allowed if not encouraged. Management contracts, licensing arrangements and franchising are examples of such non-equity forms that could be used.

Box 16. International financing: a Chinese TNC example

A joint venture between CITIC Canada Inc., a subsidiary established in Canada by the China International Trust and Investment Corporation (CITIC) and Power Corporation of Canada provides an example for raising funds locally for a FDI project. The two companies bought in 1986 the Canadian Celgar Pulpmill which had an annual output of 180,000 tons of bleached long-stable kraft pulp. Each partner holds a 50 per cent share and is committed to provide a half of any required additional investments as well as working capital. The Consolidated Bathurst Inc. (later called Stone Consolidated Inc.) was entrusted with providing expertise for managing the newly purchased factory. As regards the funds required for the acquisition, CITIC Canada Inc. raised the funds locally. It obtained full financing of Canadian $60 million in the form of a syndicated loan through the Royal Bank of Canada, supported by an Equity Equivalent Investment Facility to CITIC Canada and guaranteed by CITIC. The financing was provided on the condition that half of its share in the pulpmill be mortgaged to the bank and a long-term sales contract be signed with its parent company in China. The business was so successful that, in less than three years, CITIC managed not only to pay off its loan with the profits from the pulpmill, but also to reinvest the balance of the profits (together with Swedish and Hong Kong companies) in a sawmill with an annual processing capacity of 310,000 cubic meters of log, at a value of Canadian $40 million. In addition, CITIC Canada Inc. and Stone Consolidated Inc. also succeeded in 1991 in obtaining a loan of Canadian $700 million from the Royal Bank of Canada and the National Westminster Bank of the United Kingdom to expand the production capacity of the pulpmill to 420,000 tons annually, upgrade its technology and improve its pollution control methods.

Source: Zhan, 1995.

In brief, there are a number of ways in which outward FDI can be undertaken without a cost, or with quite limited costs, to the foreign exchange reserves of a country.

Clearly, however, there are situations in which outward FDI requires a capital contribution from the parent firm. In those countries where foreign exchange is still rationed through exchange controls, governments can use the same criteria discussed in the preceding section in the context of alternative approaches to evaluate and appraise outward FDI proposals. As governments become more comfortable with exchange liberalization, the application of such criteria can become less and less necessary.

B. Supporting foreign direct investment in the European Union

Asian firms with a potential for investing abroad would gain considerably from measures to facilitate outward FDI in the European Union, especially since many are relatively inexperienced in FDI activity, and Europe is commonly perceived as a distant, unknown market which is difficult to penetrate. Policies to encourage and support outward FDI consist predominantly of four inter-related activities: education and training; information provision and technical assistance; assisting firms in finding partners; and providing limited financial assistance for firms and investment guarantees. Japan and the newly industrializing economies (NIEs) already have institutions in place conducting all or some of these activities. The following measures supporting FDI in relation to these activities, therefore, apply primarily, though not exclusively, to developing Asian countries that are in the process of building institutions to support outward FDI.

1. *Education, training and orientation*

An important task confronting Asian governments interested in encouraging or facilitating FDI in Europe is the creation of a psychological environment conducive to investment in Europe, especially through collaboration with firms and business associations. There are both psychological and practical elements involved. Psychologically, Europe is far away, is sometimes seen as a "declining" economic region, a "tourist resort" and, besides, many Europeans might object to the acquisition of important European firms by foreign (including Asian) investors (the "Rockefeller Center Syndrome"). These views are, needless to say, generally inaccurate and need to be dispelled. Practically, there are also difficulties, including lack of access to good quality information, little business or managerial experience of Europe (except through trade, which is a beginning), and relatively small numbers of Asian students studying in Europe (especially in business and management areas).

The main tasks of any arrangement for handling education and training are likely to be twofold, reflecting two time-horizons: first, in the short run, efforts may be required regarding the training and preparation of Asian managers and other staff for working in an international environment in general and Europe in particular; secondly, one needs to find ways of creating a long-term pool of Europe-oriented individuals. In both cases, one would have to work in close collaboration with business groups, educational authorities, management schools etc. in order to devise appropriate publications, seminars, training and courses. Some of these activities could be conducted in-house if the arrangement involves a specific agency (e.g., a series of seminars on Europe for business leaders); others might be best left to other institutions. Management schools and other training facilities could be encouraged to establish courses on, for example, European business systems, languages and culture, in anticipation of stronger economic ties with Europe. Programmes or agencies in different countries could support each other, e.g., in the development of materials. Some junior executives could be sponsored to work for a period in European companies, possibly in the context of a joint Asian programme in order to pool resources and costs.

Another task, at least in the early years, would be to dispel myths about Europe. Publications, seminars, public and business education would all help, but ultimately a strong stand by Asian political and business leaders is required. Meetings between Asian and European business organizations, high-profile missions, coverage of Asian success stories in Europe by the media — all this will play a role in re-orienting Asian perspectives on Europe.

2. Information services and technical assistance

The following information- and technical-assistance related activities are among the most important for supporting outward FDI from Asian countries:

- Provision of basic information to businesses and other interested parties. It could consist of general, but fairly detailed, information on Europe, including its culture, history, markets, macroeconomic conditions, prospects and opportunities. The information should normally be free of charge or provided at minimal cost. Overseas commercial offices, consulates and embassies could help to obtain information. For example, Singapore's Economic Development Board has already a programme in place since 1980 aimed at facilitating outward FDI, using overseas offices to establish a database on investment opportunities. Since 1992, the Board's mandate has been to focus its promotional activities particularly on the Asian region; a similar mandate could focus it on the European Union. Among the activities undertaken by the Board that could be reoriented towards Europe is the creation of government-to-government business councils to promote outward FDI. Similarly, in Thailand, the Office of the Board of Investment which facilitates Thai involvement in overseas investment projects in targeted countries (so far, mostly Asian countries) could identify and target European Union countries for its activities. The Office helps identify FDI opportunities, conducts feasibility studies, examines relevant laws and regulations, organizes investment missions and coordinates with agencies in charge of FDI in countries that host Thai FDI.

- Provision of advanced business information and data on, in particular, specific European markets (geographic, industry, product), investment opportunities (and where to look further) and potential partners (listings). An off-shoot of such linkages might be a "cyber" business discussion forum.

- Governments can provide assistance to help their firms prepare to become international investors, including investors in the European Union; management training is particularly important in this respect.

- Technical services on offer could include legal advice (e.g., on drawing up contracts to comply with European Union or member-country company law); advice on standards and similar requirements in the European Union or member countries; financial advice on where to get grants (in Europe and Asia) for feasibility studies and the like, how to fund an investment, which banks to approach, how to establish a tax-efficient affiliate, etc..

3. Partnerships and contacts

A more targeted activity could consist of arranging partnerships between Asian and European businesses, with a view towards encouraging FDI in Europe. This could involve a number of activities, including:

- Identifying partners (partly based on information from other agencies, partly through direct, ongoing contacts with outside sources).
- Establishing a databank of well-researched, reliable partners, with full capability details, for prospective Asian investors.
- Organising investment missions to Europe to meet local businesses, policy makers and civil servants in which Asian firms can participate at relatively low costs and further their knowledge and experience of European opportunities.
- Providing and training interpreters and translators skilled in European languages who could be hired by prospective Asian investors in Europe.

Such a programme could liaise with European investors in Asia who might prove to be a valuable resource, indirectly and directly (perhaps as partners), in furthering Asian FDI in Europe. It could also be worthwhile to work closely with institutions conducting investment missions in the same and opposite direction, including Asian investment agencies in Europe and European investment agencies in Asia. Joint missions of Asian countries in Europe could be organised in association with other national agencies.

4. Financial assistance

A promotion programme would need to raise and manage funds earmarked for promoting outward FDI to Europe. Funding could come from governments, international organisations (such as the Asian Development Bank), commercial banks and business itself. Asian countries might wish to consider the feasibility of extending the mandates of some existing institutions to provide, where appropriate, certain financial support to outward investors. The Export-Import Bank of Japan, for example, has oriented a considerable part of its activities towards supporting outward FDI (UNCTAD-DTCI, 1995, pp. 317-319). The funding could be earmarked, both in terms of the facilities on offer and the type of investment or investor targeted. Eligible investors might include small and medium-sized enterprises, companies in industries deemed suitable for outward FDI, joint ventures with other Asian investors or inexperienced investors. Financial support could also be provided for pre-feasibility and feasibility studies for prospective investors, especially for first-time foreign investors and small and medium-sized enterprises.

The type of facilities offered could include investment guarantees, low interest loans and grants and/or fiscal incentives. Funding (usually part-funding) could be available for a range of activities, including search activities, project feasibility studies, expert/consultancy assistance and technology/product adaptation to European requirements. Applications could go through a formal process which would determine, among other things, the size of the assistance in proportion to a request, the payback period — if relevant — and conditions attached to any assistance.

Examples of financial support and fiscal incentives for outward investors already exist in the Asian region. One example is Thailand. While the Government does not provide fiscal incentives for outward FDI, the Export-Import Bank of Thailand provides enterprises in Thailand (including majority foreign-owned affiliates) with access to the following facilities: (1) investors wishing to export used machinery from Thailand to their foreign affiliates can have access to long-term loans, with interest rates not exceeding LIBOR plus two per cent; the maximum value of a loan is 85 per cent of machinery value; (2) the Bank may participate in certain FDI projects after taking the following factors into account: activities beneficial to the host country's economy; activities that contribute to Thailand's expansion of trade and production; projects that are commercially viable.

Another example is provided by India. The country's Export-Import Bank has added outward FDI promotion to its objectives. An Overseas Investment Finance programme provides equity finance for overseas joint ventures through term export credits serving as bridge finance or by way of refinancing to commercial banks, covering up to 80 per cent of the equity contribution. Indian companies can also obtain equity finance for establishing wholly-owned foreign affiliates or for acquiring foreign companies (Export-Import Bank of India, 1994).

Finally, Singapore's approach to promoting outward FDI attempts to replicate the strategy used for domestic development, combining tax and financial incentives with close government-business coordination. Initial tax incentives in 1988 included a write-off for overseas investment losses and the abolition of some taxes on overseas earnings, dividends and management fees. These measures parallel the type of benefits offered to inward FDI (Capien and Ng, 1990). Specific programmes implemented include the Local Enterprise Finance Scheme Law, 1995. The first of these schemes alone provided $1.2 billion of loans to support local enterprise and their outward investment projects between 1987 and 1993. Fiscal incentives have also played an important role in supporting outward FDI: between 1987 and 1993, these amounted to $326 million. Among the incentives are some that help local firms (including foreign affiliates) to set up regional headquarters in Singapore. New fiscal measures adopted in 1993 include an overseas enterprise incentive allowing a ten-year income tax exemption for firms expanding abroad, a double tax deduction for expenses in developing FDI opportunities, and an overseas investment incentive to facilitate the remittance of foreign income (Sreenivasan, 1994).

These examples suggest that, in many cases, the countries involved have adapted financial techniques from programmes used to promote domestic industrial development and/or incentives provided to inward FDI. Financial support for outward FDI can also evolve from trade-based export promotion programmes, especially where FDI is associated with increased exports.

Finally, outward investment-insurance programmes have not been priority concerns for developing countries because, until recently, there were few potential users of such services. But, as in developed countries, national programmes exist. In the case of the Republic of Korea, the country's Export Insurance Corporation offers outward investors up to 90 per cent coverage against political risk. But perhaps the need to provide such insurance is alleviated by the establishment of MIGA in 1985, which provides insurance for non-commercial risks to firms from member countries undertaking outward FDI.

* * *

The specific promotion package meant to support investment in Europe could be structured in a number of different ways. But it might be useful for each country to dedicate specific agencies for that purpose. This would also assist in the coordination of Europe related investment policies among Asian economies, as well as with their European partners. In any case, the role of outward investment facilitating agencies directed towards Europe should be defined by a specific policy on FDI in Europe, including targeted domestic industries for outward FDI, targeted European markets and opportunities and earmarked funds for particular purposes or special requirements (for instance, assistance for small and medium-sized enterprises).

Most Asian countries that have a well articulated policy on outward FDI explicitly link the liberalization of these policies and their support through promotion programmes to maintaining and enhancing the competitiveness of their firms and, broader, national economic performance. At the same time, there is no clear and consistent pattern. Most Asian economies with outward FDI pursue a mix of objectives as their needs and goals vary over time. It appears, however, that resource-access goals predominate at an early stage of industrialization, followed by broader outward FDI objectives when local firms acquire ownership-specific advantages that can be exploited in overseas locations.

In all these areas, therefore, Asian governments could benefit from an exchange of experiences among themselves.

C. A Europe-Invest Programme

Although the diversity of Asian economies means that it is difficult to have a uniform programme relating to FDI in Europe, it might nevertheless be useful to have an umbrella for the activities described so"Europe-Invest Programme". It could be established by interested countries and could be funded by variable contributions by Asian governments and business.

If such a programme were to be established, it could have offices in each of the participating countries. The brief of each national Europe-Invest office could differ, depending on circumstances and need; and each could link back to national institutions, including export-import banks, and any other agencies involved in outward FDI. They could also usefully be tied into chambers of commerce, business associations, regional secretariats (e.g., the ASEAN Secretariat), regional and international organizations (such as the ADB, UNCTAD and the ITC), partner organizations in participating economies and educational institutions.

Indeed, for Asian economies such as Japan and the Republic of Korea which already possess well-developed outward promotion policies and institutions (or which have given this function to Investment Promotion Agencies that seek to attract inward FDI, thus turning them into inward and outward FDI promotion agencies), a Europe-Invest Agency might act mainly as a gateway, specifically channelling Europe-related corporate requests to the appropriate institutions, making firms aware of the opportunities available, helping promotion institutions adapt their policies so that they can target European countries more effectively, and coordinating Europe-related activities domestically and with Asian partners. On the other hand, for countries newly establishing (or restructuring) their outward FDI support institutions, a Europe-Invest Agency could take on the full range of functions and activities of such an agency. This would effectively make them "one-stop shops". This type of structure may be more viable for developing Asian economies that need to harness their resources efficiently by working very closely with fledgling Asian TNCs. More commonly, such agencies could come somewhere between these extreme forms, supplementing the activities of existing outward FDI promotion institutions in order to target Europe in a manner appropriate to the requirements of domestic business. It would, however, be important to define the division of labour between investment promoting institutions.

D. Action by firms

In the final analysis, it is Asian firms that must spearhead any drive to increase FDI in Europe. They would be the chief beneficiaries of a Europe-Invest Programme, and many can already build on experience acquired from investing in Europe and elsewhere. Asian firms would need to recognize that they, too, benefit from investing in Europe, and they need to adjust their strategies accordingly.

Business associations could work with experienced firms, including European investors in Asia, utilising various means to explain facts related to FDI in Europe and the benefits and problems involved to less knowledgeable firms. They should arrange missions to Europe and meetings with European counterparts, both in cooperation with government agencies and independently. Asian chambers of commerce in Europe would be ideal bodies to utilise in this context, especially if this also led to cooperation between firms from a number of Asian countries. Asian consultancy firms have a golden opportunity to provide other firms with information and services to realise their ambitions in Europe. Investing firms need to train their staff, technically, culturally and linguistically, to operate in the European environment, in alliance with government and educational institutions. Most importantly, they must be willing to help fund long-term measures to increase a Europe-orientated pool of labour through, among other things, scholarships, management exchanges and new management schools. Firms may wish to establish a fund to foster these types of educational activities. In short, actions by firms to foster conditions for successful Asian FDI in Europe can be — and should — be extensive.

Note

1   The following sections draw extensively on UNCTAD-DTCI, 1995.

Chapter X

ACTION BY THE EUROPEAN UNION, ITS MEMBER COUNTRIES AND EUROPEAN FIRMS

In accordance with the stated objective to realise a level playing field for FDI (Commission of the European Communities, 1995), the European Union and its member countries are committed to the full liberalisation of laws and measures pertaining to inward FDI, as well as the elimination of the sort of impediments to investment identified in chapter IV. Although achieving this in practice may take a while, this commitment to liberalisation stems from the recognition that inward investment is a net contributor to the economies of the European Union. Of course European Union liberalisation measures would be non-discriminatory, but may nevertheless particularly benefit Asian TNCs because the latter are young, have relatively less experience and are frequently present in industries that have previously been protected.

A. Liberalization measures

As emphasized earlier, the European Union has one of the most liberal regimes for incoming FDI. Still, chapter IV identified some industries that remain partly restricted to foreign investors in a number of member countries, including telecommunications, construction, banking and insurance, transportation and real estate, as welll as activities related to government procurement. As part of the general process of liberalization, consideration should be given to reducing or eliminating the restrictions to foreign entry that still remain in these industries. This would certainly benefit investors from a number of developing Asian economies since, as seen earlier, Asian FDI in the European Union and Central and Eastern Europe is also undertaken in some of these industries.

In addition, there are a number of impediments facing incoming investors that could be addressed, in particular the following:

- *Reporting requirements* and *foreign exchange regulations,* where still existing, could be streamlined and harmonized across the European Union.

- *Personnel restrictions,* especially nationality and residency requirements pertaining to managing directors or board directors, are among the most significant impediments to foreign investment in a number of countries. Bilateral treaties sometimes relax these restrictions. Smaller, less well-resourced TNCs, such as those from developing countries, are more likely to be affected by such restrictions, and their elimination or amelioration would reduce difficulties for Asian businesses investing in Europe.

- *Visa and residency* requirements exist more generally for employees of Asian companies, or even for Asian business managers travelling around Europe. These should also be examined by European countries with a view towards smoothing out any difficulties. This is, of course, an issue separate from labour movement in general.

- Efforts need to be made to reduce and phase out *performance requirements* such as local content requirements, whether "voluntary" or not. It is worth noting that, under agreed WTO provisions, certain trade-related investment measures (TRIMs) need to be eliminated in any case.

- Certain *investment-related trade measures* (IRTMs) can also influence the flow of investment in a number of ways. For example, countervailing duties, import restraints (often "voluntary") and export requirements all affect inward FDI and a corporation's efficient use of the FDI/trade mix — a fact that in particularly important given that trade and investment are complementary and should be treated as activities that are inextricably intertwined. Such measures should be removed as far as possible.

- A final issue relates to the fact that a number of Asian investments in the Central and Eastern European countries have been made to service primarily the European Union market. The trade-enhancing provisions of the "Europe Agreements" and "Partnership and Cooperation Agreements" signed between the European Union and various Central and Eastern European countries deserve therefore full attention.

This last point deserves emphasis in a broader context. Precisely because FDI and trade are inextricably intertwined and Asian FDI in the European Union is to a considerable extent trade-led, maintaining and improving a liberal trade regime by the European Union is important to ensure that the mix of FDI and trade can be used by firms in the most efficient manner.

B. Promotion measures

Apart from Japanese TNCs, Asian investors are quite new to the region and unfamiliar with many features of the social, legal, political and economic terrain of the European Union. In addition, many Asian firms are small, especially when compared with large European TNCs. Governmnents of member countries and the European Commission can both assist them by providing access, as appropriate, to a number of facilities, including awareness services, market information, data banks, contact brokers, interpretation facilities and financial facilities. Such facilities would mirror, on the inward-side, the support system available for outward investment described earlier. Many of these facilities already exist, but while experienced investors do not need help to find their way around the system, Asian TNCs, especially small and medium-sized enterprises, would need to be given particular assistance in this respect. It is also in the interest of European host countries to assist Asian TNCs after an investment has been made; after-investment support is of particular help to young TNCs (Wint, 1993; Young and Hood, 1994).

Europe's Investment Promotion Agencies (which, after all, seek to attract FDI) (see annex table 7 for a list) could play a useful role in this respect; they should make a special effort to target, attract and help Asian investors. Perhaps most usefully, more European Union member countries could establish branches of their national promotion agencies in Asia. Countries such as Greece, Portugal and Spain, which are less well known to Asian investors, might benefit particularly from this approach. Also, a wider number of Asian economies should be targeted. Japan, the Republic of Korea and Taiwan Province of China are already seen by European agencies as sources of potential investment; but Thailand, Malaysia, China and a number of other countries deserve attention as well.

European Union member countries use a wide range of incentives (see table IV.5) as a way of attracting FDI, even though such incentives typically have only a marginal effect on the location decisions of TNCs (UNCTAD-DTCI, 1996b). Locational incentives need to be set within a comprehensive framework, especially to ensure a full spread of investors throughout Europe (Brewer and Young, 1996). This assists both European Union member countries, which receive FDI from a variety of sources, and Asian firms, for which wider dispersion is a useful learning experience for future expansion in Europe.

C. European Union measures

Since most laws, regulations and administrative procedures governing inward FDI are established by the Union's individual governments, the framework facing a foreign investor wishing to invest somewhere in the European Union is quite complex and sometimes difficult to decipher. A number of European Union directives, e.g., on parent-subsidiary taxation and cross-border mergers, have already led the way in making members' regulations affecting FDI more transparent, but there is scope for a further harmonization of the framework. Such harmonization could be particularly useful if it took the form of a European company law.

The fuller transparency created by such measures would, for instance, make it easier for inward investors to gain access to government procurement and national or European Union-wide research-and-development projects, thereby allaying concerns, especially among less experienced Asian TNCs, that national treatment is not being fully accorded. Another consequence of a harmonized regulatory framework would be that many administrative requirements, for example those related to the establishment of an affiliate, could be handled through "one-stop shops" located anywhere in the European Union.

Following from the above, it has been suggested that perhaps a comprehensive European Union-wide treatment for FDI could be considered, perhaps in the form of a European Union FDI code and a European Commission FDI coordination unit (Brewer and Young, 1995). From the viewpoint of Asian investors, such an approach would be beneficial because it would be comprehensive, increase transparency and reduce transaction costs.

The European Commission could also consider the possibility of extending some existing European schemes devoted to expanding FDI in Asia, in a manner that they can simultaneously promote Asian investment in Europe. This may be relevant for the European Union Business Information Centres (EBICs) in Asia, the European Community Investment Partners scheme (ECIP) and the European Union-ASEAN Junior European Managers Programme (JEM).[1]

Naturally, they would all need to be adapted, for instance, by additional facilities in Asia and Europe and "reverse" activities, but there is considerable scope for joint economies and synergies from such an approach.

Finally, the European Union and its members could take steps to encourage learning about Asia, its languages, cultures and business systems, in schools, universities and training institutions. This is imperative in order to achieve the long-term objective of closer Asian-European investment and trade relations. Resources need to be directed, by business and governments in partnership, for instance, in the form of general educational funds, scholarships and targeted human resource-development programmes.

D. Action by European firms

European firms have to be receptive to inward FDI by Asian business and recognize the opportunities that it creates. For instance, Asian firms have developed alternative methods of production and human resource management which could be of value to European firms in industries ranging from high-technology ones such as electronics to traditional ones such as shipbuilding (European shipbuilders have been less successful than Japanese ones in competing with developing Asia).[2] The Japanese example is well established, but innovations in other Asian firms should not be dismissed. In particular, the sheer diversity of Asian firms, ranging from Korean *chaebol* through overseas Chinese entrepreneurs, to a variety of ASEAN firms means that their investments in Europe could contribute to the local business community through an influx of new ideas and ways of doing things.

A way of benefiting from the experience of Asian TNCs would be by establishing joint ventures and strategic alliances or even merging. European-Asian networks of firms based on complementary technologies and skills could form a viable and competitive basis for a firmer economic link in the Asia-Europe parts of the Triad. Joint projects in nearby countries, especially in Central and Eastern Europe and in south Mediterranean rim economies, could benefit considerably from the pooling of resources. For example, local European knowledge and skills could be effectively married in Central and Eastern European infrastructure projects with Asian firms' recent and successful experience of "building" Asia.

In order to benefit from such arrangements with inward Asian FDI, European firms need to act swiftly and improve their understanding of Asian business and Asian FDI in the European Union. They need to increase their knowledge and awareness of Asian firms, as well as seek out the opportunities available. Action needs to be taken at the level of business associations, national and regional, in both Europe and Asia. Seminars, training, missions and collaborative ventures with governments are all important. European firms currently operating in Asia, because of their links, could be among those most able to benefit from, as well as assist, the entry of Asian firms into the European market. They should be encouraged to share their knowledge with other European companies, especially small and medium-sized enterprises. European firms must be willing to train their staff and help formulate and implement programmes directed at encouraging Asian FDI in the European Union. They should also be willing to channel resources into scholarships, training schemes and other knowledge enhancing activities.

Notes

1   For a description of these programmes, see European Commission and UNCTAD-DTCI, 1996, chapter III.
2   "Europe's yards put value before volume", *Financial Times*, 4 June 1996.

Chapter XI

JOINT ACTION

There are a number of areas in which Asian and European countries can cooperate to their mutual benefit to strengthen their FDI ties. Some of these areas require cooperation by their very nature, especially where the strengthening of the international framework for FDI is concerned; in other areas, practical cooperation would be to the benefit of all countries involved and, therefore, should be considered.

A. Strengthening the international framework

The international framework for FDI consists of various agreements at the multilateral, inter-regional, regional, subregional and bilateral levels which, in one way or another, address FDI issues or aspects thereof (UNCTAD-DTCI, 1996a and 1996c). In order to provide a comprehensive framework for FDI, the proposal has been made (e.g., Brittan, 1995) to establish such a framework in a multilateral body (the WTO); others feel that a further evolution of the current framework is sufficient. (For a review of the arguments of both approaches, see UNCTAD-DTCI, 1996a, Part Three). European Union and Asian countries play a central role in these discussions.

At the interregional-regional level, the most important effort involving countries from both Asia and Europe is taking place in the Organisation for Economic Co-operation and Development (OECD), where member countries decided, in May 1995, to begin negotiations aimed at the conclusion of a Multilateral Agreement on Investment by the time of the OECD ministerial meeting of Spring 1997 (Witherell, 1995). It is intended to provide a comprehensive multilateral framework for international investment, with high standards for the liberalization of investment regimes and the protection of investment, and with effective dispute-settlement procedures. The main aim is to eliminate discrimination between foreign and domestic investors.

It should be noted that, apart from sub-regional links (e.g., between the European Union and ASEAN), there are no Asian-European organizations or structures equivalent to, say, APEC. Furthermore, there are important initiatives underway that will change the investment environment in Asia, with work being undertaken in the context of APEC's "Action Agenda" and the decision by ASEAN in December 1995 to study the establishment of an ASEAN free investment area being particularly important. At the same time, a number of the mechanisms established in the framework of the ASEM dialogue may well become the basis for more structured cooperation.

At the bilateral level, the principal instruments are bilateral agreements on the reciprocal promotion and protection of FDI and double taxation treaties (annex tables 3 to 6).

• While a few Asian countries have bilateral investment treaties with a great number of Europan Union members and Central and Eastern European countries, and this number has increased substantially, especially in recent years (figure XI.1), others have few such treaties. The principal purpose of these treaties is to provide for the protection of investment, an issue that, under current circumstances, is of less saliency as far as the European Union member countries are concerned, although such protection may be more of an issue in some Central European countries; but for these cases, there is also the possibility to ensure investments with the Multilateral Investment Guarantee Agency of the World Bank. On the other hand, the parts of the treaties dealing with investment promotion may deserve more attention and could become the basis of joint efforts in this respect.

• Double-taxation treaties are of immediate relevance to the operations of Asian TNCs, and many Asian countries have concluded such treaties with many European Union members. They become relevant when income and capital of firms operating in more than one tax jurisdiction is considered as taxable income in more than one jurisdiction. In these treaties, the parties agree to observe certain rules for the allocation of tax revenues between the jurisdictions involved and seek to address instances of taxable income that is not taxed in either jurisdiction. Most of these treaties are based on two model conventions, one prepared by the United Nations (which serves as a model for agreements involving developing countries) and one by the OECD (which has generally been used as a model for treaties concluded between developed countries).

There are other areas in which agreements between governments can facilitate the operations of business. The mutual recognition of standards is of particular importance here.

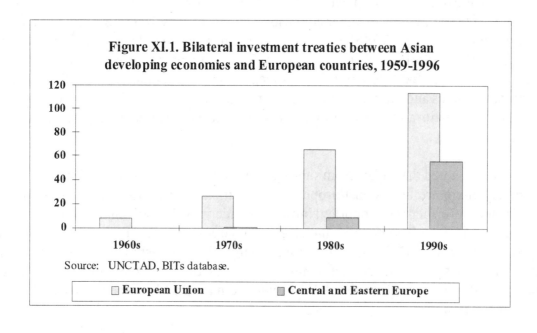

Figure XI.1. Bilateral investment treaties between Asian developing economies and European countries, 1959-1996

Source: UNCTAD, BITs database.

☐ European Union   ▨ Central and Eastern Europe

B. Practical cooperation

The preceding chapters in this Part identify a number of actions that Asian and European Union governments could fruitfully take, each on its own, to increase FDI flows from Asia to Europe. A number of actions have also been proposed elsewhere (European Commission and UNCTAD-DTCI, 1996) for European Union and Asian countries to increase FDI flows from the European Union to Asia; the nucleus for these is the European Commission's Asia-Invest Programme. In each case, the successful implementation of these actions would greatly benefit from—if it does not require—active and practical cooperation between institutions in Europe and Asia, at all levels, and in both the public and private sectors. For example, relevant Asian and European bodies, institutions and associations could work closely to:

- Organize effective missions and services between the regions. Thus, for example, Asian governments could support the establishment of branches of European member country investment promotion agencies within their domain.

- Ensure that existing structures (such as promotion agencies, embassies and business associations) are used as effectively and efficiently as possible. As has been suggested, a number or existing institutions could broaden their mandate so that, for example, the Malaysian Industrial Development Agency could promote Malaysian FDI in Europe, as well as attract European FDI to Malaysia. European and Asian firms and business associations could also consider to what extent they could work together to foster FDI in both directions, e.g., by twinning the activities of European chambers of commerce in Asia with those of Asian chambers of commerce in Europe. Less experienced firms on both sides would thereby be helped considerably because they could work through stronger Asian-European networks.

If a Europe-Invest Programme — or any other mechanism of this sort — were to be established to coordinate and mutually support Asian activities regarding FDI in Europe, the obvious question arises whether it would be appropriate to create a common roof for the Europe-Invest and Asia-Invest Programmes, to coordinate the two Programmes, reduce duplications and enhance synergies. Such an approach could build on existing successful measures and instruments and apply them in either direction. Moreover, some of the objectives of the programmes could be better achieved because policy makers and business people from both areas would be working together in order to facilitate FDI in both directions. And, finally, by having a single programme working in both directions, Asian and European governments and business would have an equal stake in making the process work.

CONCLUSIONS TO PART THREE

The findings of this volume yield significant implications for policy if the expansion of Asian FDI to Europe is to be realized. The pathways for action are most complex for Asian governments and firms, especially because of the diversity of Asian development levels, endowments and institutional frameworks for outward FDI. Nevertheless, a number of developing Asian countries have already built up a momentum in liberalizing their outward FDI policies, with due regard, of course, to foreign exchange and other development concerns. In determining their liberalization strategies, they have often been able to draw upon existing models in Asia and elsewhere, for example in deciding the nature of the FDI approval mechanism utilized. Support for FDI specifically directed at Europe is less evident, and chapter IX discussed the potential benefits of a Europe-Invest programme which could be implemented at a national and regional level. Further liberalization and support for inward FDI in Europe is, in some ways, a more straight forward matter, but the special needs of Asian investors need to be recognized. European firms, in particular, have to reorientate their views of Asian firms and recognize their considerable potential as partners in Europe and elsewhere. This reorientation (also by Asian firms) can be supported by joint actions by Asian and European governments and firms.

References

Agarwal, Jamuna Prasad (1994). "The effects of the single market programme on foreign direct investment into developing countries", *Transnational Corporations*, 3, 2, pp. 29-44.

_____ (1995). "Implications of FDI flows into the European transition economies". Paper presented at the 10th Annual Congress of European Economic Association, Prague.

_____ (1996). "European Union direct investment in ASEAN: present status, future direction and policy implications". Paper presented at the Seminar on Promotion of Foreign Direct Investment in the Context of ASEAN Free Investment Area, 23-24 May 1996, Bangkok, Thailand.

_____, Erich Gundlach, Ulrich Hiemenz, Rolf J. Langhammer, Peter Nunnenkamp (1994). "EC economic integration and its impact on foreign direct investment and developing countries", in Koichi Ohno and Yumiko Okamoto, eds., *Regional Integration and Foreign Direct Investment: Implications for Developing Countries* (Tokyo: Institute of Developing Economies).

Altomonte, Carlo, Richard Bolwijn and H. Peter Gray (1996). "Outward foreign direct investment from Asian industrializing countries" (Geneva: UNCTAD), mimeo.

Asian Development Bank (1994). *Asian Development Report 1994* (Manila: Asian Development Bank).

Brewer, Thomas L. and Stephen Young (1995). "Towards a multilateral framework for foreign direct investment: issues and scenarios", *Transnational Corporations*, 4, 1 (April), pp. 69-83.

_____ (1996). "Global and regional agreements on international investment: implications for investment incentives". Paper presented at the conference on Liberalization and Regionalization, 29-30 May 1996, University Paris-I Pantheon-Sorbonne.

Brittan, Leon (1995). "Investment liberalization: the next great boost to the world economy", *Transnational Corporations*, 4, 1 (April), pp. 1-10.

Chen, Tain-Jy (1992). "Determinants of Taiwan's direct foreign investment: the case of a Newly Industrializing Country", *Journal of Development Economics*, 39, pp. 397-406.

Chen, Edward K.Y.(1996). "Foreign direct investment of Hong Kong in ASEAN: trends, patterns and policy implications. Paper presented at the Seminar on Promotion of Foreign Direct Investment in the Context of ASEAN Investment Area, 23-24 May 1996, Bangkok, Thailand.

Chia Siow Yue (1995). "Foreign direct investment and economic integration in East Asia". Paper presented at the 8th Workshop on Asian Economic Outlook, Asian Development Bank, Manila, Philippines, 23-24 November.

_____ (1996). "Foreign direct investment in Southeast Asia" (Singapore: Singapore University, mimeo.

China Resources (1995). *Almanac of China's Foreign Economic Relations and Trade* (Hong Kong: China Resources).

Cho, Tae-Hyon (1992). "Korea's overseas investment and foreign direct investment: present situation and prospects", Korea Exchange Bank, *Quarterly Review,* 26 (4), pp. 3-17.

Choi, Ki-Chul (1991). "Koreanische Direktinvestitionen in Europa, insbesondere in der Bundesrepublik Deutschland". Dissertation at the University of Göttingen, mimeo.

Choi, Yong Rok (1991). "Foreign direct investment by Korean manufacturing firms". Dissertation at the University of Cincinnati, mimeo.

Deutsch-Koreanische Industrie- und Handelskammer (1990). *Koreanische Auslands-investitionen* (Seoul: Deutsch-Koreanische Industrie- und Handelskammer).

Dunning, John H. (1993). *Multinational Enterprises and the Global Economy* (Wokingham: Eddison-Wesley).

_____ and Rajneesh Narula (1996). "The investment development path revisited. Some emerging issues", in John H. Dunning and Rajneesh Narula, eds., *Foreign Direct Investment and Governments: Catalysts for Economic Restructuring* (London: Routledge), pp. 1-41.

European Commission and UNCTAD, Division on Transnational Corporations and Investment (1996). *Investing in Asia's Dynamism: European Union Direct Investment in Asia* (Luxembourg: Office for Official Publications of the European Communities).

Eurostat (1995). *European Union Direct Investment 1984-93* (Brussels: Statistical Office of the European Communities).

Export-Import Bank of Japan (1995). *Japanese Foreign Direct Investment Outflow by Country and by Industry, Europe* (Tokyo: Research Institute for International Investment and Development, Overseas Investment Division).

_____ (1996). "EXIM Japan questionnaire on foreign direct investment in fiscal 1995", mimeo.

Gundlach, Erich, Peter Nunnenkamp (1995). "Regional trends: development issues and priorities". Background Paper for UNIDO's Global Report 1996, Kiel, mimeo.

Hatem, Fabrice (1996). *International Investment Towards the Year 2000* (Paris: Arthur Andersen).

Hobday, M. (1995). *Innovation in East Asia: The Challenge to Japan* (London: Edward Elgar).

Information Bureau of Fiscal Documentation (1996). *The Taxation of Companies in Europe* (Amsterdam: IBFD).

Japan, Ministry of International Trade and Industry (MITI) (1994). *Dai 5-kai Kaigai Jigyo Katsudo Kihon Chosa: Kaigai Toshi Tokei Soran* (Tokyo: Ministry of Finance Printing Bureau).

_____ (1995). *Dai 24-kai Wagakuni Kigyo no Kaigai Jigyo Katsudo* (Tokyo: Ministry of Finance Printing Bureau).

_____ (1996). "Dai 25-kai kaigai Jigyo katsudo doko chosa gaiyo", mimeo.

Jeon, Yoong-Deok (1992). "The determinants of Korean foreign direct investment in manufacturing industries", *Weltwirtschaftliches Archiv,* 128 (3), pp. 527-542.

Kim, L. (1996). *From Imitation to Innovation: Dynamics of Korea's Technological Learning* (Boston: Harvard Business School Press).

Kögel, Petra and Anton Gälli (1994). "Die 'vier kleinen Drachen': Das Netz ihrer Beziehungen mit Europa wird dichter", *IFO Schnelldienst,* 47 (4), pp. 16-31.

Kojima, Kiyoshi and Terutomo Ozawa (1984). *Japan's General Trading Companies: Merchants of Economic Development* (Paris, OECD Development Centre).

Kumar, Nagesh (1995). "Changing character of foreign direct investment from developing countries: case studies of Asia". UNI/INTECH Discussion Paper, Maastricht, mimeo.

Lall, Sanjayah (1995). "Industrial strategy and foreign direct investment in East Asia", *Transnational Corporations*, 4, 3, pp. 1-26.

_____ (1996). *Learning from the Asian Tigers: Studies in Technology and Industrial Policy* (London: Macmillan).

Lee, Chung H. and Keun Lee (1992). "A transition economy and outward direct foreign investment: the case of South Korea", *Seoul Journal of Economics,* 5 (1), pp. 89-111.

Low, Linda, Eric D. Ramstetter and Henry Wai-Chung Yeung (forthcoming). "Accounting for outward direct investment from Hong Kong and Singapore: who controls what?" (New York: NBER Working Paper), mimeo.

Michalski, Tino (1995). *Japanische Direktinvestitionen in der Europäischen Gemeinschaft* (Wiesbaden: Deutscher Universitätenverlag).

Min, Chung Ki (1991). "Korean direct investment in European Community: strategies for Korean firms", in Chung Ki Min, ed., *The Economic Cooperation between EC and Korea: Problems and Prospects* (Seoul: Korea Institute for International Economic Policy and Friedrich-Ebert-Foundation).

Nunnenkamp, Peter, Erich Gundlach and Jamuna P. Agarwal (1994). "Globalisation of production and markets" (Kiel: Kieler Studien, 262).

Organisation for Economic Co-operation and Development (OECD) (1992). *International Direct Investment. Policies and Trends in the 1980s* (Paris: OECD).

_____ (1994). "Statistics on international direct investment of dynamic non-member economies in Asia and Latin America (Paris: OECD Working Paper), mimeo.

_____ (1994/1995). *International Direct Investment Statistics Yearbook* (Paris: OECD).

_____ (1995). *National Accounts 1991-1993* (Paris: OECD).

Oman, Charles (1994). *Globalisation and Regionalisation: The Challenge for Developing Countries* (Paris: OECD Development Centre).

O'Neil, Kirsty (forthcoming). "Samsung's views on regionalization tendencies in East Asia and elsewhere", in Hafiz Mirza, ed., *Beyond Protectionism: the Strategic Responses of Transnational Firms to the Regionalization of the World Economy* (London: Edward Elgar).

Plan Econ (1996). *Plan Econ Report* (Washington, D.C.: Plan Econ), vol. XII (9-12).

Republic of Korea, Ministry of Finance (1994). *Korea's Outward Direct Investment* (Seoul: Ministry of Finance).

Schultz, Siegfried (1995). *Auslandsinvestitionen ostasiatischer Länder in Europa und in der Bundesrepublik Deutschland* (Berlin: Deutsches Institut für Wirtschaftsforschung, Beiträge zur Strukturforschung, 160).

_____(1996). "Interregional foreign direct investment: the case of APEC and the European Union" (Berlin: Deutsches Institut für Wirtschaftsforschung, discussion paper 133), mimeo.

Singapore, Department of Statistics, various years, *Singapore's Investement Abroad* (Singapore: Ministry of Trade and Industry).

Taiwan Province of China, economic affairs authorities (1993). *Outward Investment from Taiwan Republic of China: A New Source of International Capital* (Taipeh: Industrial Development and Investment Center).

Taiwan Province of China, Investment Commission (1993). *Statistics on Overseas Chinese and Foreign Investment, Technical Cooperation, Outward Investment, Outward Technical Cooperation, Indirect Mainland Investment* (Taipeh: Investment Commission).

_____(1995). *Statistics on Overseas Chinese and Foreign Investment, Technical Cooperation, Outward Investment, Outward Technical Cooperation, Indirect Mainland Investment* (Taipeh: Investment Commission).

_____(various years). *Statistics on Overseas Chinese and Foreign Investment, Technical Cooperation, Outward Investment, Outward Technical Cooperation, Indirect Mainland Investment* (Taipei: Investment Commission).

Taiwan Province of China, Council for Economic Planning and Development (1995). *Taiwan Statistical Data Book 1995* (Taipeh: CEPD).

Tolentino, P. E. E. (1993). *Technological Innovation and Third World Multinationals* (London: Routledge).

Toyo Keizai (1996). *Kaigai Shinshutsu Kigyo Soran, 1996* (Tokyo: Toyo Keizai Shimposha).

United Nations Development Programme (UNDP) (1995). *Human Development Report 1995* (New York: United Nations).

UNESCO (1995). *Statistical Yearbook 1995* (Paris: UNESCO).

United Nations Conference on Trade and Development (UNCTAD) (1994).*Handbook of International Trade and Development Statistics* (New York : United Nations), United Nations publication, Sales No. E/F.95.II.D.24.

United Nations Industrial Development Organisation (UNIDO) (1995). *Industrial Development: Global Report 1995* (Vienna: UNIDO).

United Nations, Transnational Corporations and Management Division (UN-TCMD) (1993).*Transnational Corporations from Developing Countries: Impact on Their Home Countries* (New York: United Nations), United Nations publication. Sales No. E.93.II.A.8.

United Nations Conference on Trade and Development, Division on Transnational Corporations and Investment (UNCTAD-DTCI) (1993). *Small and Medium-sized Transnational Corporations: Role, Impact and Policy Implications*(New York: United Nations), United Nations publication, Sales No.: E.93.II.A15.

_____ (1994). *World Investment Report 1994. Transnational Corporations, Employment and the Workplace* (Geneva: United Nations), United Nations publication, Sales No.: E.94.II.A. 14.

_____ (1995). *World Investment Report 1995. Transnational Corporations and Competitiveness* (Geneva: United Nations), United Nations publication, Sales No.: E.94.II.A.9.

_____ (1996a). *World Investment Report 1996. Investment, Trade and International Policy Arrangements* (Geneva: United Nations), United Nations publication, Sales No.: E.96.II.A.14.

_____ (1996b). *Incentives and Foreign Direct Investment* (Geneva: United Nations), United Nations publication, Sales No.: E.96.II.A.6.

_____ (1996c). *International Investment Instruments: A Compendium,* (Geneva: United Nations), United Nations publication, Sales No.: E.96.IIA.12.

United Nations Economic Commission for Europe (UNECE) (various issues). *East-West Investment News* (Geneva: United Nations publication).

Vernon, Raymond (1966). "International investment and international trade in the product cycle", *Quarterly Journal of Economics,* 80, pp. 190-207.

Wallraf, Wolfram (1996). "Wirtschaftliche Integration im asiatischem Raum, ASIEN - deutsche Zeitschrift für Politik", *Wirtschaft und Kultur,* 59, pp. 7-33.

Wint, Alvin G. (1993). "Promoting transnational investment: organizing to service approved investors," *Transnational Corporations,* 2, 1, pp. 71-90.

Witherell, William H. (1995). "The OECD multilateral agreement on investment", *Transnational Corporations,* 4, 2, pp. 1-14.

World Trade Organisation (WTO) (1996). *GATT Activities 1994-95* (Geneva: WTO).

World Bank (various years). *World Development Report* (New York: Oxford University Pres).

World Bank (1994). *World Debt Tables 1994* (Washington, D.C.: World Bank).

Young, Steven and Neil Hood (1994). "Designing developmental after-care programmes for foreign direct investors in the European Union," *Transnational Corporations*, 3, 2, pp. 45-72.

Zhan, James (1995). "Transnationalization and outward investment: the case of Chinese firms", *Transnational Corporations*, 4, 3, December 1995.

Zhang, Hai-Yan and Danny Van Den Bulcke (1996). "China: rapid changes in the investment development path", in John H. Dunning and Rajneesh Narula, eds.,*Foreign Direct Investment and Governments: Catalysts for Economic Restructuring* (London: Routledge), pp. 381-422.

ANNEX

Annex table 1. Recent changes in the regulatory and policy framework for inward FDI in European Union countries, 1992-1995

Country	Relevant legislation	Changes
France	Decree N° 92-134, of 11 February 1992	Eases rules governing foreign investment in France by extending the free EC investment regime to the vast majority of FDI; requires prior notification instead of authorization regime for investments of less than FF 50 million affecting French companies with turnover of up to FF 500 million.
	Act N° 93-923 of 19 July 1993 on privatization.	Limits acquisitions by non-EU investors in privatized companies to 20 per cent of share capital in each company at the time of privatization; allows unlimited subsequent non-EU holdings once the initial placement is completed; allows for an exception where there is an existing financial, commercial or industrial agreement between a EU or a non-EU investor and a company directly controlled by the State, in which case there will be no restriction on investment in that company.
	Law N° 95-115 on Regional Development. Entered into force on 4 February 1995 with Decree N° 95-149 of 6 February 1995.	Grants new regional incentives for investment in rural areas in difficulty and urban areas with high unemployment rates. Specific research-and-development incentives are available for foreign investors locating their investment in said regions. Modifies the eligibility criteria for the "Prime d'Amenagement du Territoire", a regional grant available to national and foreign companies.
Greece	Residential Decree N° 96 of 23 March 1993. Bank of Greece Governor's Decisions N° 2199 and 2200 of 7 May 1993 and N° 2227 of 30 June 1993.	Eliminates requirements of Government review and authorization for all foreign investment in Greece; replaces this with requirements of a posteriori review by the Bank of Greece; delegates to commercial banks the task of assessing authenticity and legality of projects; liberalizes all forms of long-term and most of the short-term capital movements with respect to EU member countries; removes restrictions on repatriation of capital invested before 1980 by investors from the non-EU countries.
	Presidential Decree 104/94 and Bank of Greece Governor's Decision N° 2302 and 2303 of 16 May 1994. Together with Law 2234/94 of 1994 amending Law 1892/90.	Lifts all residual restrictions or derogations of the exchange controls system. Contains two basic alternative incentives to investment: cash grants and subsidized loans or tax deductions, with a ceiling on grant aid up to 3 billion Drachma. These incentives are available for both domestic and foreign investment without restriction.
	Law N° 2324/95 of July 1995 amends Law N°1892/90 and completes Law N° 2234/94. Entered into force retroactively on 1 January 1995.	Provides for grants or tax exemptions for high technology products, environmental protection and quality standardization as well as high-quality tourism projects in regions defined by Law N°. 1892/90. Amends application procedure for incentives under the laws. Provides two alternative incentives: cash grants and interest rate subsidies or tax allowances. Restores the provisions for accelerated depreciation rates in both cases.
Ireland	Lapse of Exchange Control legislation of 31 December 1992. Coming into force on 1 January 1993.	Expiration of all remaining exchange controls, removing all restrictions and reporting requirements for FDI in Ireland.
	Industrial Development Bill of 6 July 1993. Coming into force on 1 January 1994.	Converts the existing Industrial Development Authority and the existing Science and Technology Agency into three new agencies, among which the Industrial Development of Ireland (IDA Ireland) is responsible for the promotion of FDI (except for the natural resource-based industries).

(Annex table 1, cont'd)

Country	Relevant legislation	Changes
Italy	Law N° 537/93.	Abolishes the requirement for prior approval from the Interministerial Committee for the Coordination of Industrial Policy for major industrial investments, whether domestic of foreign.
Netherlands	Patent Law of March 1995 replaces Rijksoctrooiwet dated 1910, as amended in 1964 and 1991. Entered into force on 1 April 1995.	Introduces a " registration system" for patent applications and abolished the previous "examination as to substance system". Proposes two types of patents: a six-year patent and a twenty-year patent.
Portugal	Banking Law, implemented on 1 January 1993.	Harmonizes procedures for opening a new bank or a Portuguese branch of an existing EU bank, in line with EU Directives; still requires non-EU banks to apply to the Government for permission to open a new bank or branch.
	Decree Law N° 298/93 of 27 May 1993.	Eliminates the requirement that a foreign investor seeking to establish a travel agency in Portugal can do so only by incorporating in Portugal; applies to EU investors only.
	Regulatory Decree N° 17/93 of 1 June 1993.	Introduces a special contractual regime for large foreign investment projects, especially those involving high technology or the establishment, expansion, restructuring or modernization of economic units; such projects may benefit from tax, financial and other incentives.
	Decree Law N° 379/93 of 5 November 1993.	Opens up the water production and distribution and basic sanitation services sectors to private participation; allows foreign and Portuguese private investors to hold up to 45 per cent of the equity of companies engaged in providing these services.
	Decree Law N° 380/93 on privatization of 15 November 1993.	Eliminates the power of the council of Ministers to set discretionary thresholds for foreign participation in companies to be privatized; Requires any individual investor or company, resident or non-resident, that wants to purchase more than 10 per cent of a privatized company's shares to obtain prior authorization from the Minister of Finance.
	Decree-Law 37/95 of 14 February 1995. Entered into force on 19 February 1995.	Introduces a Controlled Foreign Corporations (CFC) legislation as authorized by Law 75/93 of 20 December 1993. Applies to the banking, financial and insurance sector, and technology transfer and technical assistance only. Does not apply to the industrial and agricultural sector: Introduces a requirement to prove that payments made to companies located in low-tax jurisdictions relate to actual transactions and that the amount of said payment is not abnormally high. A part of the profits of the non-resident company, regardless of its distribution, will be attributed to the Portuguese resident partner.
Spain	Royal Decree N° 303 of February 1993.	Completes the new Special Zones to promote domestic and foreign investments under the Regional Incentives scheme of Law N° 50/85.

(Annex table 1, cont'd)

Country	Relevant legislation	Changes
	Budget Act for 1994 of December 1993.	Gives a more flexible basis for 20 per cent withholdings of corporate income tax to Spanish and foreign companies; raises tax rebates for investments abroad from 20 to 25 per cent and establishes a 95 per cent tax exemption for small and medium-sized enterprises incorporated in Spain during 1994.
	Law 19/1994 of 7 July 1994. Entered into force on 1 January 1995.	Sets forth measures to promote investment in the Canary Islands by amending the tax regime and creates the Canary Island Special Zone. Companies registered in the Register of the Canary Island Special Zone are subject to corporate income tax at a rate of 1 per cent and are exempt from all indirect taxes. Income and capital gains derived from movable property in the Canary Island Special Zone by foreign investors are exempt from tax. Companies registered in the Register of the Canary Island Special Zone are considered as non-residents as far as exchange control and investment regulations are concerned.
	Law 2/1995 of 23 March 1995. "Law on Limited Liability Companies" entered into force on 1 June 1995.	Sets out new conditions for the creation of a *sociedad de responsibilidad limitada (srl).* Authorizes Srls with a single owner. Sets out a new legal minimum of 500.000 Pesetas for the capital. Requires specification of the nominal share value and number of shares into which the capital is divided.
Sweden	Law on Right for Foreigners to Transact Business in Sweden of 1 July 1992, repealing existing law.	Eliminates authorisation requirements for foreign citizens and corporations seeking to transact business in Sweden; requires only registration procedure for FDI.
	Amendment of Swedish Companies Act, Swedish Banking Companies Act and Swedish Insurance Business Act, of December 1992. Effective 1 January 1993.	Eliminates authorization requirements for FDI in Sweden, including for the banks, finance and insurance sector.
	Bill 1994/95-204 approved on 23 March 1995 amending the Controlled Foreign Company legislation. Entered into force on 1 July 1995.	Removes Cyprus, Malta and Spain (Canary Islands) from the list of treaty partner countries whose residents are not subject to CFC rules.
	Government Decision of 1 July 1995.	Establishes a new agency to promote foreign investment in Sweden, the Invest in Sweden Agency (ISA), to provide information and assistance to foreign investors.

Source: Compiled by the UNCTAD Secretariat.

Annex table 2. Liberalization of national policies on outward FDI in developing Asia

Economy	Outward FDI policies
China	Following the "Provisional regulation for approval procedures and administration of non-trade related outward FDI" of 1985 and the "Administration of foreign exchange for outward investment" of 1989, the Government issued the "Approval procedures and administration of overseas investment" in 1993 in a direction of liberalization, which still regulates all outward exchange remittances, and limits capital export, all borrowing from foreign services is subject to approval. Profits earned by Chinese enterprises must be sold to the Bank of China except for a portion that may be retained locally as a working balance.
India	By amending the Foreign Exchange Regulation Act of 1973, in 1993, the Government lifted restrictions for non-resident Indians, Indian companies and residents on the opening of foreign currency accounts in India and the export and transfer of securities, lifted certain restrictions on the holding of immovable property outside India, and lifted restrictions on residents in India associating themselves with or participating in business concerns outside India. Prior approval conditions for outward FDI have been substantially relaxed and automatic approval within 30 days is provided for many outward FDI projects.
Korea, Republic of	As part of an overall economic liberalization plan, the Government relaxed regulatory controls on outward (and inward) FDI. Small projects (under $300,000) need only obtain validation from foreign exchange banks , while outward FDI valued at up to $10 million requires notification only. In 1994, the Government adopted a "negative list" system, permitting outward FDI in all but a few business areas specifically listed by the Government. Both the Export-Import Bank of Korea and the Overseas Investment Information Center provide information and support for outward investment, including loans and FDI credits.
Malaysia	The Government started relaxing exchange controls and capital export controls. On 1 December 1994, the Controller of Foreign Exchange implemented measures allowing residents to obtain loans denominated in foreign currencies and to guarantee the obligations of non-residents. On 22 June 1995, the Ministry of Finance announced measures to liberalize the Malaysian capital market and relax monetary restrictions: Malysian companies acquiring foreign assets need only to inform the central bank, Bank Negar, for amounts not exceeding $10 million.
Singapore	In 1986, the Government issued a policy document titled " The Singapore economy: new directions", supporting outward FDI. In 1992, the Economic Development Board received a clear mandate to promote outward FDI and set up the programme Regionalization 2000, which encourages and supports local firms wanting to invest abroad. The Business Development Scheme Law, 1995 proposes tax incentives and measures to promote outward FDI.
Taiwan Province of China	The authorities relaxed its foreign exchange controls in 1987 and announced an extensive plan to encourage outward FDI. It relaxed the 1962 " R e g u l a t i o n s governing the screening and handling of outward investment and outward technical cooperation projects". Approved projects are required to meet one of conditions considered to meet national interest criteria. In June 1995, the authorities took additional measures concerning outward investment loss reserve: a domestic company which owns at least 20 per cent of the stock of a foreign company in which it has made an investment, may deduct 20 per cent of the outward investment cost, as a reserve for outward investment loss, in the first year of the investment.
Thailand	In 1991, the Boad of Investment issued poliy guidelines to encourage outward FDI. Its Overseas Investment Unit facilitatesThai involvement in overseas investment projects. In February 1994, the Government lifted the approval requirement for outward FDI of more than $5 million and maintained it for outward investment exceeding $10 million regardless of industry. Residents are permitted to use foreign exchange that originates from abroad to service external obligations without surrendering or depositing it in domestic bank accounts. In 1996, Thailand established the Thailand Overseas Investment Promotion Board, chaired by the Prime Minister. The board includes representatives from the private sector, as well as government agencies, and is involved in all aspects of outward investment.

Source: Compiled by the UNCTAD Secretariat.

Annex table 3. Bilateral investment treaties between Asian developing economies and European Union member states, July 1996

Asian developing economy	Austria	Belgium and Luxembourg	Denmark	Finland	France	Germany	Greece	Ireland	Italy	Netherlands	Portugal	Spain	Sweden	United Kingdom	Total
Afghanistan															-
Bangladesh		X			X	X			X	X				X	6
Brunei Darussalam															-
Cambodia															-
China	X	X	X	X	X	X	X		X	X	X	X	X	X	13
Hong Kong			X		X	X			X	X			X		6
India			X			X			X	X				X	5
Indonesia		X	X	X	X	X			X	X		X	X	X	10
Korea, Democratic People's Republic															-
Korea, Republic of	X	X	X	X	X	X	X		X	X	X	X	X	X	13
Lao Democratic People's Republic					X									X	2
Macau															-
Malaysia	X	X	X	X	X	X			X	X		X	X	X	11
Maldives															-
Mongolia		X	X		X	X			X	X				X	7
Myanmar															-
Nepal					X	X				X					3
Pakistan					X	X			X	X		X	X		6
Philippines		X			X					X		X		X	5
Singapore		X			X	X				X				X	5
Sri Lanka		X	X	X	X	X			X	X			X	X	9
Thailand		X		X		X				X				X	5
Viet Nam		X	X	X	X				X	X			X	X	8
Total	3	10	9	7	14	14	2	-	11	14	2	6	8	14	115
Memorandum:															
Japan															-

Source: UNCTAD, BITs database.

Annex table 4. Bilateral investment treaties between Asian developing economies and Central and Eastern European countries, July 1996

Asian developing economy	Albania	Belarus	Bulgaria	Croatia	Czech Republic	Estonia	Hungary	Latvia	Lithuania	Former Yugoslav Republic of Macedonia	Moldova	Poland	Romania	Russian Federation	Slovakia	Slovenia	Ukraine	Total
Afghanistan																		-
Bangladesh													X					1
Brunei Darussalam																		-
Cambodia																		-
China	X	X	X	X	X	X	X		X		X	X	X	X	X	X	X	15
Hong Kong														X				1
India							X					X			X			3
Indonesia																		-
Korea, Democratic People's Republic																		-
Korea, Republic of					X		X		X			X	X	X	X			7
Lao Democratic People's Republic																		-
Macau																		-
Malaysia	X			X			X					X	X					5
Maldives																		-
Mongolia							X						X	X			X	4
Myanmar																		-
Nepal																		-
Pakistan													X					1
Philippines					X								X					2
Singapore					X							X						2
Sri Lanka													X					1
Thailand					X		X					X	X	X	X			6
Viet Nam		X					X					X	X	X				5
Total	2	2	1	2	5	1	7	-	2	-	1	7	10	6	4	1	2	53
Memorandum:																		
Japan																		-

Source: UNCTAD, BITs database.

Annex table 5. Double taxation treaties between Asian developing economies and European Union member states, July 1995

Economy	Austria	Belgium & Luxembourg	Denmark	Finland	France	Germany	Greece	Ireland	Italy	Netherlands	Portugal	Spain	Sweden	United Kingdom	Total
Afghanistan															-
Bangladesh					X	X				X			X	X	5
Brunei Darussalam														X	1
Cambodia															-
China	X	X	X	X	X	X			X	X		X	X	X	11
Hong Kong							X								-
India	X	X(a)	X	X	X	X	X		X	X		X	X	X	12
Indonesia	X	X	X	X	X	X				X			X	X	9
Korea, Democratic People's Republic															-
Korea, Republic of	X	X	X	X	X	X		X	X	X		X	X	X	12
Lao Democratic People's Republic															-
Macau														-	-
Malaysia	X	X(a)	X	X	X	X			X	X			X	X	10
Maldives															-
Mongolia															-
Myanmar															-
Nepal															-
Pakistan	X	X(a)	X		X	X		X	X	X			X	X	10
Philippines	X	X(a)	X	X	X	X			X	X		X	X	X	11
Singapore			X	X	X	X			X	X			X	X	8
Sri Lanka		X(a)	X	X	X	X				X			X	X	8
Thailand	X	X(a)	X	X	X	X			X	X			X	X	10
Viet Nam					X								X	X	3
TOTAL	8	9	10	9	12	11	1	2	8	11	-	4	12	13	110
Memorandum															
Japan	X	X	X	X	X	X		X	X	X		X	X	X	12

Source: Information Bureau of Fiscal Documentation, 1996.

(a)   Only Belgium has concluded a treaty with India, Malaysia, Pakistan, Philippines, Sri Lanka and Thailand.

Annex table 6.   Double taxation treaties between Asian developing economies and Central and Eastern European countries, July 1995

Economy	Albania	Belarus	Bulgaria	Croatia	*Czech* Republic	Estonia	Hungary	Latvia	Lithuania	Former Yugoslav Republic of Macedonia	Moldova	Poland	Romania	Russian Federation	Slovakia	Slovenia	Ukraine	Total
Afghanistan																		-
Bangladesh													X					1
Brunei Darussalam																		-
Cambodia																		
China			X				X					X	X		X	X		6
Hong Kong																		-
India			X				X					X	X		X			5
Indonesia			X				X					X						3
Korea, Democratic People's Republic																		
Korea, Republic of			X				X					X	X					4
Lao Democratic People's Republic																		-
Macau																		
Malaysia	X	X					X					X	X					5
Maldives																		
Mongolia		X																1
Myanmar																		-
Nepal																		
Pakistan							X					X	X					3
Philippines												X						1
Singapore												X						1
Sri Lanka												X	X		X			3
Thailand							X					X						2
Viet Nam												X						1
Total	1	2	4	-	-	-	7	-	-		-	11	7	-	3	1	-	36
Memorandum:																		
Japan		X					X					X		X	X			5

Sources: UNCTAD-DTCI, 1995 and International Bureau of Fiscal Documentation, 1996.

Annex table 7. Investment Promotion Agencies in the European Union

Austria
Abteilung für Aussenhandel
Wirtschaftsministerium
Stübenring 1
A-1011 Vienna
tel: (431) 71100
fax: (431) 714 2723

Belgium
Société Regionale d'Investissement
32 Rue de Stassart
1050 Bruxelles
tel: (322) 548 22 11
fax: (322) 511 90 74

Denmark
Investment Promotion Agency
Ministry of Business and Industry
10 Slotsholmsgade
1216 Copenhagen
tel: (4533) 923350
fax: (4533) 123778

Finland
Invest in Finland Bureau
Arkadiankatu 2
00100 Helsinki
tel: (3580) 695 92 85
fax: (3580) 694 79 34

France
Ministère de Economie,
Direction du Trésor
Bureau D3
139 Rue de Bercy
75572 Paris Cedex 12
tel: (331) 4004 0404
fax: (331) 4004 2971

Germany
Abteilung II, Wirtschaftsfördernde Strukturpolitik,
Senatsverwaltung für Wirtschaft und Technologie
Martin Luther Str. 105
D-10820 Berlin
tel: (4930) 783 83 00
fax: (4930) 783 35 68

Greece
Department for International Investors
Ministry of National Economy
Nikis Street 5/7
10563 Athens
tel: (301) 333 2312
fax: (301) 333 2326

Ireland
International Development Ireland
Wilton Park House, Wilton Place
Dublin 2
tel: (3531) 668 75 55
fax: (3531) 660 17 33

Italy
Instituto per la Promozione Industriale
Viale Pilsudski 124
00197 Rome
tel: (396) 80 97 23 45
fax: (396) 80 97 23 38

Luxembourg
Ministère des Affaires Etrangères
Hotel Saint Augustin
6 Rue de la Congregation
L-1352 Luxembourg
tel: (352) 478 23 50
fax: (352) 22 20 48

Netherlands
Netherlands Foreign Investment Agency
Postbus 20101
2500 EC Den Haag
tel: (3170) 379 88 18
fax: (3170) 379 63 22

Portugal
Investimentos, Comercio e Turismo de Portugal
Avenida 5 de Outubro 101
1050 Lisboa
tel: (3511) 793 01 03
fax: (3511) 797 01 86

Spain
Ministry of Trade and Tourism
Paseo de la Castellana 162-13a
28071 Madrid
tel: (341) 349 3622
fax: (341) 349 35 62

Sweden
Ministry of Finance
Drottninggetan 21
10333 Stockholm
tel: (468) 763 14 75
fax: (468) 21 43 37

United Kingdom
Securities and Investment Board
2-14 Bunhill Road
EC1Y8RA London
tel: (44171) 638 12 40
fax: (44171) 382 59 00

Selected UNCTAD publications on transnational corporations and foreign direct investment

A. Individual studies

World Investment Report 1996: Investment, Trade and International Policy Arrangements. 332 p. Sales No. E.96.II.A.14. $45.

World Investment Report 1996: Investment, Trade and International Policy Arrangements. Overview. 22 p. Free-of-charge.

International Investment Instruments: A Compendium. 1, 337 p. Sales No. E.96.IIA.12 (the set).

Foreign Direct Investment, Trade, Aid and Migration. 100 p. Sales No. E.96.II.A.8.

Incentives and Foreign Direct Investment. 98 p. Sales No. E.96.II.A.6.

World Investment Report 1995: Transnational Corporations and Competitiveness. 491 p. Sales No. E.95.II.A.9. $45.

World Investment Report 1995: Transnational Corporations and Competitiveness. Overview. 51 p. Free-of-charge.

Small and Medium-sized Transnational Corporations: Executive Summary and Report on the Osaka Conference. p. 60. UNCTAD/DTCI/6. Free-of-charge.

World Investment Report 1994: Transnational Corporations, Employment and the Workplace. 482 p. Sales No. E.94.II.A.14. $45.

World Investment Report 1994: Transnational Corporations, Employment and the Workplace. An Executive Summary. 34 p. Free-of-charge.

World Investment Directory. Volume IV: Latin America and the Caribbean. 478 p. Sales No. E.94.II.A.10. $65.

Liberalizing International Transactions in Services: A Handbook. 182 p. Sales No. E.94.II.A.11. $45. (Joint publication with the World Bank.)

Accounting, Valuation and Privatization. 190 p. Sales No. E.94.II.A.3. $25.

Environmental Management in Transnational Corporations: Report on the Benchmark Corporate Environment Suvey. 278 p. Sales No. E.94.II.A.2. $29.95.

Management Consulting: A Survey of the Industry and Its Largest Firms. 100 p. Sales No. E.93.II.A.17. $25.

Transnational Corporations: A Selective Bibliography, 1991-1992. 736 p. Sales No. E.93.II.A.16. $75. (English/French.)

Small and Medium-sized Transnational Corporations: Role, Impact and Policy Implications. 242 p. Sales No. E.93.II.A.15. $35.

World Investment Report 1993: Transnational Corporations and Integrated International Production. 290 p. Sales No. E.93.II.A.14. $45.

World Investment Report 1993: Transnational Corporations and Integrated International Production. An Executive Summary. 31 p. ST/CTC/159. Free-of-charge.

Foreign Investment and Trade Linkages in Developing Countries. 108 p. Sales No. E.93.II.A.12. $18.

World Investment Directory 1992. Volume III: Developed Countries. 532 p. Sales No. E.93.II.A.9. $75.

Transnational Corporations from Developing Countries: Impact on Their Home Countries. 116 p. Sales No. E.93.II.A.8. $15.

Debt-Equity Swaps and Development. 150 p. Sales No. E.93.II.A.7. $35.

From the Common Market to EC 92: Regional Economic Integration in the European Community and Transnational Corporations. 134 p. Sales No. E.93.II.A.2. $25.

World Investment Directory 1992. Volume II: Central and Eastern Europe. 432 p. Sales No. E.93.II.A.1. $65. (Joint publication with ECE.)

World Investment Report 1992: Transnational Corporations as Engines of Growth: An Executive Summary. 30 p. Sales No. E.92.II.A.24.

World Investment Report 1992: Transnational Corporations as Engines of Growth. 356 p. Sales No. E.92.II.A.19. $45.

World Investment Directory 1992. Volume I: Asia and the Pacific. 356 p. Sales No. E.92.II.A.11. $65.

B. Serial publications

Current Studies, Series A

No. 28. *Foreign Direct Investment in Africa*. 119 p. Sales No. E.95.II.A.6. $25

No. 27. *The Tradability of Banking Services: Impact and Implications*. 195 p. Sales No. E.94.II.A.12. $50.

No. 26. *Explaining and Forecasting Regional Flows of Foreign Direct Investment*. 58 p. Sales No. E.94.II.A.5. $25.

No. 25. *International Tradability in Insurance Services*. 54 p. Sales No. E.93.II.A.11. $20.

No. 24. *Intellectual Property Rights and Foreign Direct Investment*. 108 p. Sales No. E.93.II.A.10. $20.

No. 23. *The Transnationalization of Service Industries: An Empirical Analysis of the Determinants of Foreign Direct Investment by Transnational Service Corporations*. 62 p. Sales No. E.93.II.A.3. $15.00.

No. 22. *Transnational Banks and the External Indebtedness of Developing Countries: Impact of Regulatory Changes*. 48 p. Sales No. E.92.II.A.10. $12.

No. 20. *Foreign Direct Investment, Debt and Home Country Policies*. 50 p. Sales No. E.90.II.A.16. $12.

No. 19. *New Issues in the Uruguay Round of Multilateral Trade Negotiations*. 52 p. Sales No. E.90.II.A.15. $12.50.

No. 18. *Foreign Direct Investment and Industrial Restructuring in Mexico*. 114 p. Sales No. E.92.II.A.9. $12.

The United Nations Library on Transnational Corporations. (Published by Routledge on behalf of the United Nations.)

      Set A (Boxed set of 4 volumes. ISBN 0-415-08554-3. £350):

Volume One: *The Theory of Transnational Corporations*. 464 p.

Volume Two: *Transnational Corporations: A Historical Perspective*. 464 p.

Volume Three: *Transnational Corporations and Economic Development*. 448 p.

Volume Four: *Transnational Corporations and Business Strategy*. 416 p.

Set B (Boxed set of 4 volumes. ISBN 0-415-08555-1. £350):

Volume Five: *International Financial Management*. 400 p.

Volume Six: *Organization of Transnational Corporations*. 400 p.

Volume Seven: *Governments and Transnational Corporations*. 352 p.

Volume Eight: *Transnational Corporations and International Trade and Payments*. 320 p.

Set C (Boxed set of 4 volumes. ISBN 0-415-08556-X. £350):

Volume Nine: *Transnational Corporations and Regional Economic Integration*. 331 p.

Volume Ten: *Transnational Corporations and the Exploitation of Natural Resources*. 397 p.

Volume Eleven: *Transnational Corporations and Industrialization*. 425 p.

Volume Twelve: *Transnational Corporations in Services*. 437 p.

Set D (Boxed set of 4 volumes. ISBN 0-415-08557-8. £350):

Volume Thirteen: *Cooperative Forms of Transnational Corporation Activity*. 419 p.

Volume Fourteen: *Transnational Corporations: Transfer Pricing and Taxation*. 330 p.

Volume Fifteen: *Transnational Corporations: Market Structure and Industrial Performance*. 383 p.

Volume Sixteen: *Transnational Corporations and Human Resources*. 429 p.

Set E (Boxed set of 4 volumes. ISBN 0-415-08558-6. £350):

Volume Seventeen: *Transnational Corporations and Innovatory Activities*. 447 p.

Volume Eighteen: *Transnational Corporations and Technology Transfer to Developing Countries*. 486 p.

Volume Nineteen: *Transnational Corporations and National Law*. 322 p.

Volume Twenty: *Transnational Corporations: The International Legal Framework*. 545 p.

Transnational Corporations (formerly *The CTC Reporter*).

Published three times a year. Annual subscription price: $35; individual issues $15.

Transnationals, a quarterly newsletter, is available free of charge.

United Nations publications may be obtained from bookstores and distributors throughout the world. Please consult your bookstore or write to:

United Nations Publications

Sales Section   OR   Sales Section
Room DC2-0853   United Nations Office at Geneva
United Nations Secretariat   Palais des Nations
New York, N.Y. 10017   CH-1211 Geneva 10
U.S.A.   Switzerland
Tel: (1-212) 963-8302 or (800) 253-9646   Tel: (41-22) 917-1234
Fax: (1-212) 963-3489   Fax: (41-22) 917-0123

All prices are quoted in United States dollars.

For further information on the work of UNCTAD Division on Investment, Technology and Enterprise Development, please address inquiries to:

United Nations Conference on Trade and Development
Division on Investment, Technology and Enterprise Development
Palais des Nations, Room E-8006
CH-1211 Geneva 10
Switzerland

Telephone: (41-22) 907-5707
Telefax: (41-22) 907-0194

QUESTIONNAIRE

Sharing Asia's Dynamism:
Asian Direct Investment in the European Union

In order to improve the quality and relevance of the work of the UNCTAD Division on Investment, Technology and Enterprise Development, it would be useful to receive the views of readers on this and other similar publications. It would therefore be greatly appreciated if you could complete the following questionnaire and return to:

Readership Survey
UNCTAD Division on Investment, Technology and Enterprise Development
United Nations Office in Geneva
Palais des Nations
Room E-8006
CH-1211 Geneva 10
Switzerland

1. Name and address of respondent (optional):

_____
_____
_____
_____

2. Which of the following best describes your area of work?

Government	☐	Public enterprise	☐
Private enterprise institution	☐	Academic or research	☐
International organization	☐	Media	☐
Not-profit organization	☐	Other (specify) _____	

3. In which country do you work? _____

4. What is your assessment of the contents of this publication?

Excellent	☐	Adequate	☐
Good	☐	Poor	☐

5. How useful is this publication to your work?

Very useful ☐ Of some use ☐ Irrelevant ☐

6. Please indicate the three things you liked best about this publication:

_____

_____

_____

7. Please indicate the three things you liked least about this publication:

_____

_____

_____

8. If you have read more than the present publication of the UNCTAD Division on Investment, Technology and Enterprise Development, what is your overall assessment of them?

Consistently good ☐ Usually good, but with some exceptions ☐

Generally mediocre ☐ Poor ☐

9. On the average, how useful are these publications to you in your work?

Very useful ☐ Of some use ☐ Irrelevant ☐

10. Are you a regular recipient of *Transnational Corporations* (formerly *The CTC Reporter*), the Division's tri-annual refereed journal?

Yes ☐ No ☐

If not, please check here if you would like to receive a sample
copy sent to the name and address you have given above ☐

كيفية الحصول على منشورات الامم المتحدة

يمكن الحصول على منشورات الامم المتحدة من المكتبات ودور التوزيع في جميع انحاء العالم · استعلم عنها من المكتبة التي تتعامل معها
أو اكتب الى : الامم المتحدة ،قسم البيع في نيويورك او في جنيف ·

如何购取联合国出版物

联合国出版物在全世界各地的书店和经售处均有发售。请向书店询问或写信到纽约或日内瓦的联合国销售组。

HOW TO OBTAIN UNITED NATIONS PUBLICATIONS

United Nations publications may be obtained from bookstores and distributors
throughout the world. Consult your bookstore or write to: United Nations, Sales
Section, New York or Geneva.

COMMENT SE PROCURER LES PUBLICATIONS DES NATIONS UNIES

Les publications des Nations Unies sont en vente dans les librairies et les agences
dépositaires du monde entier. Informez-vous auprès de votre libraire ou adressez-vous
à : Nations Unies, Section des ventes, New York ou Genève.

КАК ПОЛУЧИТЬ ИЗДАНИЯ ОРГАНИЗАЦИИ ОБЪЕДИНЕННЫХ НАЦИЙ

Издания Организации Объединенных Наций можно купить в книжных мага-
зинах и агентствах во всех районах мира. Наводите справки об изданиях в
вашем книжном магазине или пишите по адресу: Организация Объединенных
Наций, Секция по продаже изданий, Нью-Йорк или Женева.

COMO CONSEGUIR PUBLICACIONES DE LAS NACIONES UNIDAS

Las publicaciones de las Naciones Unidas están en venta en librerías y casas distri-
buidoras en todas partes del mundo. Consulte a su librero o diríjase a: Naciones
Unidas, Sección de Ventas, Nueva York o Ginebra.

Printed in Switzerland
GE.96-52281–December 1996–4,655

UNCTAD/ITE/IIT/1

United Nations publication
Sales No. E.97.II.D.1

ISBN 92-1-112405-0